DOLLARS THROUGH
THE DOORS

DOLLARS THROUGH
THE DOORS

A Pre-1930 History of
Bank Marketing in America

Richard N. Germain

Contributions in Economics and Economic History
Number 174

GREENWOOD PRESS
Westport, Connecticut • London

Library of Congress Cataloging-in-Publication Data

Germain, Richard.
    Dollars through the doors : a pre-1930 history of bank marketing
in America / Richard N. Germain.
        p.   cm. — (Contributions in economics and economic history.
    ISSN 0084–9235 ; no. 174)
    Includes bibliographical references and index.
    ISBN 0–313–29921–8 (alk. paper)
    1. Bank marketing—United States—History. I. Title.
    II. Series.
    HG1616.M3G467   1996
    332.1′068′8—dc20   95–48368

British Library Cataloguing in Publication Data is available.

Library of Congress Catalog Card Number: 95–48368
ISBN: 0–313–29921–8
ISSN: 0084–9235

First published in 1996

Greenwood Press, 88 Post Road West, Westport, CT 06881
An imprint of Greenwood Publishing Group, Inc.

Printed in the United States of America

The paper used in this book complies with the
Permanent Paper Standard issued by the National
Information Standards Organization (Z39.48–1984).

10 9 8 7 6 5 4 3 2 1

To Gilles and Zoria

Contents

Tables and Figure

Table

Figure

Acknowledgments

This project would have been impossible without the help of many people. I am indebted to the following, who provided access to or material from corporate archives: Robert Becton, formerly with Albert Frank–Guenther Law advertising agency; David Boucher, corporate archivist, Royal Bank; Ann Gibson, formerly with the Chase Manhattan National Bank; Mary Jane Mekeland, executive secretary, The First National Bank of Chicago; Jane Nokes corporate archivist, Bank of Nova Scotia; Millie Pulleyblank, corporate archivist, Toronto Dominion Bank; Gord Rabchuk, corporate archivist, Royal Bank; Frank Scorny, formerly with Albert Frank–Guenther Law advertising agency; Dr. Joan Silverman, Citibank historian; Jill ten Cate, assistant archivist, Canadian Imperial Bank of Commerce; Paul C. Wise, executive vice president and cashier, Stillwater National Bank; and Donald D. Yokel, Office of Corporate Clearance & Editorial Review, Eastman Kodak Company.

I am deeply indebted to Robert Sandmeyer, past dean of the College of Business Administration at Oklahoma State University, and to Lee Manzer and Stephen Miller, Marketing Department heads at the same institution, for their support, patience, and encouragement.

The support staff at Oklahoma State University was of immense help throughout the project. Joan Kirkendall, Jennifer Thompson, Linda Stone, and Danielle Banister are thanked for their help. I am especially appreciative of the work done by Beverlee Dunham. Without her assistance in preparing the manuscript, the project would not have been completed.

I thank Ronald Fullerton, who commented on a draft of the manuscript. I save my greatest appreciation for last. Without Stanley C. Hollander, this project would have been impossible. My natural predilection for history was piqued in a marketing history seminar taught by Stan. Since then, he has knowingly and in many cases unknowingly provided the guidance and inspiration that made this project possible.

Source Abbreviations

A number of sources are frequently cited. They are identified by the following abbreviations.

Journals and Newspapers

ABAJ	*American Bankers Association Journal*
AR	*Architectural Record*
BMa	*The Bankers' Magazine*
BMo	*The Bankers' Monthly*
JABA	*Journal of the American Bankers Association*
NYT	*New York Times*
PI	*Printers' Ink*
TC	*Trust Companies*

Institutions

AFGL	Albert Frank–Guenther Law, New York
BNS	Bank of Nova Scotia, Toronto
CB	Citibank, New York
CIBC	Canadian Imperial Bank of Commerce, Toronto
CM	Chase Manhattan, New York
FNBC	The First National Bank of Chicago
RB	Royal Bank, Montreal
TD	Toronto Dominion Bank, Toronto

1

Introduction

An important trait of banking in the United States is the aggressive search for business. This orientation is characterized by reliance on advertising and promotion, development of new product services, a service marketing orientation, and segmentation and positioning strategies. Despite the current prevalence of aggressive bank marketing, there has been little effort to understand and document how bank marketing developed and evolved. The thesis of this book is that the roots of the transformation of banks from passive business accepters into aggressive business seekers can be traced as far back as banking in America, and that the transformation was complete by 1930. Similar transformations have been seen in other industries. For example, the insurance industry transformed itself between 1840 and 1930 through the adoption of the agency (i.e., personal selling) method. In retailing, department stores revolutionized American shopping habits. In the production of goods where significant economies of scale or scope were present—such as in the automobile, tobacco, and beverage industries—or where transaction assets were specialized—such as in the oil industry—vertical integration and national marketing went hand in hand, a phenomenon well under way by the start of the twentieth century.

The evidence supporting the thesis of the transformation of American banking by 1930 is presented in three parts on service, segmentation, and staff. In the first part, the behavior and thoughts of bankers in relation to service are examined. I demonstrate that many service marketing concepts are much older than one would believe from a review of the current literature. Chapter 2 reveals that bankers increasingly paid attention to what are currently called "service quality determinants" between 1870 and 1930. Material is presented on how bankers (1) created confidence through promotions and architecture; (2) improved transaction velocity through adoption of technological and administrative innovations; (3) increased accessibility by improving hours of operation, staff availability, and location; (4) fostered a more courteous staff; (5) enhanced security; and (6) increased accuracy of operations. In Chapter 3 it is shown that between 1900 and 1930, bankers discussed the distinction between functional service (the service being performed) and how the service was performed, gap theory, and service traits such as intangibility and heterogeneity. Moreover, during the 1920s a debate developed on the difference between product and service marketing.[1]

The second part of the book deals with segmentation, which may be defined as the act of splitting a heterogeneous market into homogeneous groups and then targeting one or more of those groups with a specialized mix of price, product (or service), place, and promotion. This part, which consists of Chapters 4 through 9, demonstrates that by 1930, bankers were aggressively segmenting the market. After 1870, specialized marketing mixes were increasingly developed for specific demographic groups identifiable by age (such as children), gender (women in particular), and ethnic group (such as German or Asian). I trace the evolution of user status segmentation—that is, splitting the market into potential, current, and past customers—and show that by 1930, banks had developed specific, and in many instances formalized, policies based on customer consumption status. Geographic segmentation, or bank by mail, became popular during the very late nineteenth century. Finally, I demonstrate how socio-economics and end use in the credit market have long been used by banks to ferret out specific segments to serve.

The three-phase production economies periodization discussed by Richard Tedlow provides a useful backdrop against which to compare bank segmentation efforts. During the first phase, fragmentation (which ended about 1880), the economy consisted mostly of small, regional suppliers who sold goods on a low-volume, high-margin basis. Underdeveloped transportation and communication infrastructures restricted suppliers to meeting local market needs. This was followed by the unification phase, which lasted from 1880 to 1920, depending on the industry. Suppliers distributed standardized, branded goods on a national basis. They tended to sell a single product suitable for the entire market on a high-volume, low-margin basis. Coca-Cola and the Ford Model T are examples. Suppliers concurrently took advantage of scale economies, and falling prices enlarged demand. The final phase, segmentation, is a post-1920 phenomenon (again, depending on the industry). The market became large enough to support the production of specialized goods for specific demographic and psychographic segments. Continued infrastructure and production economy improvements allowed organizations to service specific segments at low cost. General Motors during the 1920s and Pepsi Cola during the 1960s displaced rivals by using a phase three segmentation strategy. They still sold on a high-volume basis, but used value-based rather than cost-based pricing. As seen in the automobile and soft drink cases described by Tedlow, not all industries experienced the three phases of segmentation simultaneously.[2]

Little effort, however, has been devoted to determining whether a service industry such as banking progressed through a similar developmental pattern. A secondary goal of the book is to examine the "fit" of the bank segmentation evidence to a historical periodization of segmentation that has been applied to manufacturing industries almost exclusively.

The third part of the book concerns staff and addresses two issues unresolved by an examination of service and segmentation: (1) that the transformation of banking into an aggressive, market-oriented industry would not be complete without a transformation of employee attitudes; and (2) appropriate organizational structures for managing promotional, service, segmentation, and staff-related efforts. Chapter 10 demonstrates that banks avidly sought to create an esprit de corps among staff to foster better service to customers. I demonstrate that this was accomplished through various mechanisms including publishing of employee magazines, formalizing rules, providing benefits such as dining facilities and financial benefits (e.g., pension plans), and creating a sociable work environment through corporate-sponsored employee clubs. Chapter 11 demonstrates how marketing developed in banks from one-person, part-time advertising endeavors to full-time staffed, aggressive "new business departments" that controlled, designed, and coordinated bank marketing efforts.

Before presenting evidence in support of the thesis that by 1930, banks had transformed themselves into aggressive institutions, it is necessary to elaborate on the context of the study. This is accomplished by discussing the focus of bank marketing efforts, the regulatory environment in which banks operated, and two additional themes interwoven into the book.

THE FOCUS OF PRE-1930 BANK MARKETING EFFORTS

Table 1.1 presents historical statistics on bank assets, loans, and deposits. Column (1) provides GNP percentage growth estimates. Columns (2) through (5) provide growth estimates in bank assets, deposits, loans, and the number of banks, while columns (6) through (8) provide estimates of changes in bank assets, deposits, and loans relative to GNP growth. Column (9) shows growth in deposits relative to loans.

In Table 1.1, three broad phases of American banking are observed. The first extends from the mid-nineteenth century to 1929. Excluding World War I, during the entire 1869–1928 period, bank assets, deposits, and loans grew faster than GNP. There were banking and economic crises during the period, but the banking industry enjoyed a relatively long period of prosperity and sustained growth. Bank assets grew significantly during World War I, though not when discounting for high, wartime inflation. Excluding the World War I period, during which the decline in loans was greater than the decline in deposits, bank deposits grew at a rate faster than loans during the entire 1834–1928 period. The growth period was also one of capital shortage, and as a consequence American bankers were more concerned with attracting depositors than borrowers. The most remarkable feature of the period is the stunning growth of bank assets

Table 1.1
U.S. Banking Statistics

Period	(1)	(2)	(3)	(4)	(5)	(6)	(7)	(8)	(9)
Post–World War II (1946–1970)	3.55	2.38	1.89	7.45	-0.14	0.67	0.53	2.10	0.25
World War II (1939–1945)	9.21	8.19	9.25	-0.83	-0.61	0.89	1.00	-0.09	-11.14
Depression (1929–1938)	-0.62	0.85	-5.91	-3.96	-5.46	-1.37	9.53	6.39	0.67
Interwar growth (1919–1928)	2.99	5.99	6.28	6.72	-1.32	2.00	2.10	2.25	1.07
World War I (1914–1918)	4.85	-2.14	-1.76	-2.60	-1.42	-0.44	-0.36	-0.54	1.48
Turn of the century (1886–1913)	4.59	5.12	5.60	5.06	4.89	1.12	1.22	1.10	1.11
Late 19th century (1889–1895)	4.13	6.48	6.55	5.74	5.20	1.57	1.59	1.39	1.14
Mid-19th century II (1869–1888)	6.98	7.50	10.58	8.58	6.88	1.07	1.52	1.22	1.23
Mid-19th century I (1834–1868)	–	–	–	–	4.06	–	–	–	3.69

Source: Historical Statistics of the United States: Colonial Times to 1970 (Washington, D.C.: U.S. Government Printing Office, 1975), series F-5, col. 3, p. 224; series X 580–87, cols. 581, 585, and 582, pp. 1019–20; series X 580–87, col. 580, pp. 1019–20.

Notes: Column headings are as follows: (1) percentage growth in GNP; (2) percentage growth in bank assets; (3) percentage growth in bank deposits; (4) percentage growth in bank loans; (5) percentage growth in the number of banks; (6) rate of change of bank assets relative to GNP (column 2 ÷ column 1); (7) rate of change of bank deposits relative to GNP (column 3 ÷ column 1); (8) rate of change of bank loans relative to GNP (column 4 ÷ column 1); and (9) rate of change of bank deposits relative to bank loans (column 3 ÷ column 4).

Percentage growth rates were calculated as the compound annual rate of increase, using 1958 current dollars for the relevant time period.

Post-1913 periods correspond to social and economic eras.

Pre-1914 periods reflect data availability and shifting measurement bases.

In 1896, the method of estimating the number of banks, bank assets, deposits, and loans was changed, and ten-year GNP and price index averages are available for 1869–1878 and 1879–1888. GNP and price indices are unavailable prior to 1869.

relative to GNP between 1919 and 1928: during this period, bank assets grew twice as fast as GNP.

The second phase begins with the onset of the Depression and ends with the cessation of World War II. As can be seen in column (5), the decline in the number of banks in America that began during the early 1920s accelerated during the Depression. While the economy was contracting, bank assets grew at an annual rate of 0.85 percent between 1929 and 1938. Despite this growth, loans declined more than six times faster than GNP, and deposits more than nine times faster. Because of the contraction in demand for commercial credit, banks turned to government securities as a source of income, and the decline in interest paid on them during the 1930s resulted in banks' discouraging deposits. If anything, the Depression was characterized by demarketing as banks aggressively sought to purge their books of deposit customers or paid no interest on large deposits. The bankers' world changed abruptly between 1939 and 1945. Government demand for credit was enormous, and the American banking industry participated in the war effort. Deposits once again were encouraged, but it was the government that required massive amounts of capital. During World War II, deposits increased more than eleven times faster than the decrease in loans.[3]

The last period extends from 1946 to the current time (though data is presented only until 1970). During this period, the American banking industry is almost the mirror of its pre-1929 self. Whereas before 1929 when the industry generally grew faster than the economy (in terms of both assets and number of banks) and deposits grew faster than loans, after 1946 the industry grew more slowly than the economy (in both assets and number of banks) and deposits grew more slowly than loans. Whereas the period before 1929 was one of capital shortage, the one after 1946 is one of capital excess. Whereas before 1929, banks concentrated on stimulating thrift among the masses (to feed corporate credit demand), banks since 1946 have concentrated more on stimulating immediate credit-driven consumption (to invest excess deposits).

The shift from stimulating thrift to stimulating credit-based consumption did not occur entirely during the Depression. Early in the twentieth century, manufacturers of mass-produced goods were aware of the need to stimulate and finance consumption to ensure plant throughput, and thereby assure continued economy-of-scale advantage. Some department stores provided charge accounts by 1900, especially to upper-income customers. In finance, loan sharks first, and nonbank finance companies second, provided consumer credit, some as early as the 1870s. Some banks and philanthropic institutions were organized around 1900 expressly to provide consumer credit on fair lending bases, and commercial banks entered the consumer credit field during the 1920s.

A transition from selling thrift to selling credit is entirely different from a transition in orientation from passive to aggressive. It is with the latter phenomenon and the century-long transition that led to growth of bank assets at twice the rate of GNP during the 1920s that this book is concerned. It is not concerned per se with the transition from a thrift-based consumer orientation to a consumption-based one.

THE REGULATORY ENVIRONMENT

Three elements of the regulatory environment are mentioned. First, certain industries suffered from restrictive laws curbing their ability to trade freely across states or within a state. For example, in 1810, Pennsylvania prohibited out-of-state firms from selling life insurance in the state. During the mid-nineteenth century, some states protected local interests from emerging vertically integrated manufacturers. They forbade drummers (or salesmen) from one state to sell goods in another or enacted onerous licensing regulations for out-of-state sellers. Supreme Court decisions between 1875 and 1900 on the Commerce Clause ended protectionism of this sort and were as important in creating a unified national market as were technological improvements in transportation and communication infrastructures. Few regulatory barriers were enacted against the department store industry, which did not undertake interstate operations until the 1940s. Perhaps no other industry faced as many regulatory barriers as banking. During the entire period under investigation, interstate banking was prohibited. In 1929 only nine states allowed statewide branch banking (up from none in 1910) and 22 states prohibited branch banking (up from nine in 1910). Some states allowed limited branching if metropolitan branches were viewed by regulators as extra tellers' windows. The transformation of banks into aggressive institutions and the growth between 1919 and 1928 occurred despite barriers to trade.

Second, in 1903 the comptroller of the currency ruled that the National Bank Act of 1863 did not specifically forbid national banks to accept savings deposits, and the request by The First National Bank of Chicago to accept savings deposits was officially granted. That The First National Bank was required to establish a subsidiary, locked in perpetuity to the parent, for accepting savings deposits does not diminish the significance of the ruling. Other national banks were quick to follow suit, competitiveness increased markedly for consumers' savings, and commercial banks were thus able increasingly to adopt a "department store of finance" orientation.

Finally, the Banking Act of 1933 created the Federal Deposit Insurance Corporation to insure a portion of time and savings deposits against loss, reducing overnight the importance of conservative, sound management as a unique selling point.[4]

ADDITIONAL THEMES

Two additional themes are interwoven with the thesis that by 1930 banks had transformed themselves into assertive marketing organizations. The first theme recognizes that developments in one industry are not independent of those in another. Two major service industries are discussed throughout the book—insurance and retail department stores—and the parallels in evolution between them and in banking.

The second theme recognizes that developments in one location are dependent on those in other locations. Particular attention is paid to the

Canadian banking industry, which contrasts with the American one in three important ways: (1) Canadian chartered banks could operate on a coast-to-coast basis (i.e., they were more dispersed geographically and more concentrated economically); (2) the Canadian banking industry was more reliant on European and English banking philosophy as a guide than was the American industry (i.e., it was more conservative); and (3) Canadian banks, from their inception, were allowed to accept both savings and demand deposits. It will be shown that for the most part, Canadian banks lagged their American counterparts in adopting an aggressive orientation.

SUMMARY

The purpose of this book is to confirm the thesis that the transformation of American banks from a passive to an aggressive marketing orientation was complete by 1930. The transformation was accomplished, as will be demonstrated, through attention to service, segmentation, and staff. The main focus of these efforts was directed toward savings (i.e., thrift) and not credit (i.e., consumption). I show that the transformation was complete by 1930, despite restrictive banking laws, and how the transformation was connected to banking developments in other geographic regions and other industries.

NOTES

1. See, e.g., Philip Kotler and Sidney J. Levy, "Broadening the Concept of Marketing," *Journal of Marketing*, 33 (January 1969): 10–5; G. Lynn Shostack, "Breaking Free from Product Marketing," *Journal of Marketing*, 41 (April 1977): 73–80; Philip Kotler, forward to *Service Management and Marketing–Managing the Moments of Truth in Service Competition*, Christian Gronroos, ed. (Lexington, MA: Lexington Books, 1990); Leonard Berry, Jeffery S. Conant, and A. Parasuraman, "A Framework for Conducting a Services Marketing Audit," *Journal of the Academy of Marketing Science*, 19 (Summer 1991): 255–68; Valerie Zeithaml, Leonard L. Berry, and A. Parasuraman, "Communication and Control Processes in the Delivery of Service Quality," *Journal of Marketing*, 52 (April 1988): 35–48.

2. Richard A. Tedlow, *New and Improved: The Story of Mass Marketing in America* (New York: Basic Books, 1990), 4–12.

3. American Bankers Association, *Response to Change* (Washington, D.C.: American Bankers Association, 1965), 41–61.

4. Owen J. Stalson, *Marketing Life Insurance Life: Its History in America* (Cambridge, MA: Harvard University Press, 1942), 49–50; John M. Chapman and Ray B. Westerfield, *Branch Banking* (New York: Harper & Brothers, 1942), 3–5; American Bankers Association, *Response to Change*, 133–42; Stanley C. Hollander, "Nineteenth Century Anti-Drummer Legislation in the United States," *Business History Review*, 38 (Winter 1964): 479–500; Charles W. McCurdy, "American Law and the Marketing Structure of the Large Corporation," *Journal of Economic History*, 38 (September 1978): 631–49.

I

Service

2

Service Quality

CONFIDENCE

In the context of service quality as it relates to banking, "confidence" refers to the faith that individuals have in the continuing existence of an institution. When a department store fails, customers lose assortment, but they infrequently suffer directly from the loss. Thus, confidence in continued existence, while important, is not paramount. In banking and mutual insurance, failure results in direct loss to customers. Creating and maintaining confidence among the public in these industries was thus incalculably important. Confidence was inspired by architecture, by using tangibles in promotions, by confidence themes in promotions and slogans, and by how the bank handled runs. This part of the chapter discusses each of these mechanisms.

Physical Structures

Confidence inspired by the physical structure was more important to bankers than to insurance or department store operators. In insurance, many customers never visited the office because agents were well equipped to handle transactions on the road or at branch offices. Insurance organizations erected impressive edifices, but these balanced functionalism and symbolism equally. Prudential's "Rock of Gilbralter" campaign, begun during the late nineteenth century, was more important than its head office in inspiring confidence. In the department store industry, the physical structure was important, but for an entirely different reason: its purpose was to showcase merchandise, and promote opulence and a culture of consumption. In banking, the physical structure was a symbol of the financial strength of the bank. The two sections that follow discuss the development of bank architecture and what was called the "standing advertisement effect."

Bank Architecture

The development of bank architecture can be periodized into two overlapping phases. The first phase was between 1780 and 1820, when the Federal style dominated American bank architecture. Adopted initially by merchants along the eastern seaboard, the three-floor blockish buildings failed to stand out from residences or portray an image other than that of a general business establishment. Thomas Jefferson had a great impact on bank architectural style. His design of the Virginia State Capitol, completed in 1789, was the first application of the Roman temple style to a public building in modern times. Designers of the earliest banks in America followed Jefferson's lead in erecting democratic, open structures that inspired feelings of longevity and permanence. The First Bank of the United States, designed by Samuel Blodget, Jr., and completed in 1797, was a Grecian temple and signals the onset of the second phase. Benjamin Henry Latrobe—architect of the U.S. Capitol between 1803 and 1817—designed the Bank of Pennsylvania. The 1800 structure embodied classical Greek and Roman lines: six columns fronted a circular, domed banking hall. The Second Bank of the United States, designed by William Strickland, a pupil of Latrobe, was completed in 1824. His design "sought as close a copy of an ancient Greek Temple as was practicable." So ingrained was the temple design that during the twentieth century, some architects fronted the first several floors of a skyscraper with Greek columns (e.g., Continental & Commercial National Bank of Chicago).

Despite the dominance of the temple design, bank architectural style varied more than a brief review would indicate. In small towns during the latter half of the nineteenth and the early twentieth centuries, banks, except for exterior signage, often looked like any other business establishment. There were exceptions, though. Louis H. Sullivan designed a string of Midwest banks, the most notable being the National Farmers' Bank of Owatonna (Minnesota), erected during the 1900s. As late as the 1920s a few banks used a colonial style to foster an impression of age and, hence, permanence. The interior of the State Street Trust Company (Boston) resembled a New England merchant's counting-house of the late eighteenth century, complete with furnishings from the period.[1]

Canadian bank architectural styles differed somewhat. The Bank of Montreal, established in 1817, by 1819 was housed in a Republican structure devoted exclusively to banking. Some of the next bank buildings constructed in Canada mixed Georgian and Republican features (e.g., the Bank of Upper Canada, completed in 1827; the Commercial Bank of the Midland District [Toronto], completed in 1845). But the temple design was eventually adopted. The Bank of Montreal's new 1847 structure, fronted by six Corinthian columns, was the first application of the Greek temple design to a bank in Canada.

Standing Advertisement Effect

The standing advertisement effect was mentioned as early as the 1860s when the *New York Times* said that banks "deem the erection of attractive buildings in leading thoroughfares a profitable standing advertisement." By the 1920s the concept had often been commented upon. For bankers, the effect centered on choosing between two types of buildings. The first, which took advantage of the standing advertisement effect, was dedicated solely to the needs of the bank. Such dedicated structures were standard in small towns and cities, and in less central parts of major American cities. In the second type, the bank shared the building with other establishments. Shared buildings were often skyscrapers; only the largest banks in the nation were able to occupy an entire skyscraper in the financial districts of America's larger cities. Some small- to medium-sized banks operated dedicated buildings in New York City's financial district during the early part of the twentieth century, however. But banks such as the Liberty National Bank (New York) required innovative designs as adjoining skyscrapers blocked out light. In other instances, such as that of the National Park Bank (New York), adjacent property was purchased to prevent skyscrapers from being erected too near. The choice of skyscraper versus dedicated structure in large cities was not clear because of the difficulty of ascribing a financial return to the standing advertisement effect.[2]

During the 1910s, some bank managers made the standing advertisement effect an around-the-clock proposition by illuminating structures with floodlights until midnight or later (e.g., First National Bank [Cleveland], Industrial Bank & Finance Company [New Britain, Connecticut], Fletcher Savings Bank & Trust Company [Indianapolis]). The Second National Bank (Toledo, Ohio) placed a lit dome atop its building that was visible from miles away and was referred to as the "Second National Light."[3]

Creating Confidence by Promoting Tangibles

Physical structures were also used in promotional material. Prior to 1890, financial newspaper advertisements and related promotions resembled classified advertisements; it was only after that date that banks commenced blending images of tangibles into promotions. These may be classified into two general types: new building campaigns and tangibles in emblems, logos, and advertising.

New Building Campaigns

Bankers must have learned much from observing the department store industry's elaborate campaigns promoting new store openings or renovations. John Wanamaker epitomized the approach with his "New Kind of Store" in 1876. On opening day, the count of customers was proclaimed a world's record, President Ulysses Grant visited the store, employees provided guided tours, booklets and brochures were handed out, and efforts were made to ensure favorable press coverage.[4]

The public excitement aroused by new bank campaigns never equaled that of department stores because, to varying extents, banks sold service (and not goods), the product offered was not sought after by the masses, and the average bank scale was dwarfed by the average department store scale. But bankers did attempt to create interest. The Lenawee County Savings Bank (Adrian, Michigan), established in 1869, celebrated the groundbreaking for a new facility in 1906 and its opening one year later. An open house, orchestra music, flowers, and distribution of booklets, photographs of the bank, pencils, and other premiums marked the latter. In 1915 the Security Trust Company (Lynn, Massachusetts) campaigned on its new building. Projecting strength, advertisements said that "fire, water, wear, tear, sun or storm will waste their strength on the powerful, massive Security Trust Building," and "every detail that would make this building fireproof throughout, every convenience that would give greater comforts and better service must, of a necessity, be found in this finest office building in Essex county." Other copy emphasized elevator speed, efficient janitorial service, and clean, well-lit surroundings. The completion of the Commercial Trust Company's (New Britain, Connecticut) 1926 residence was preceded by a four-month radio and newspaper campaign describing cageless counters, natural lighting from vaulted windows, and a spacious main banking hall. Just prior to opening, an eight-page promotion was inserted in local newspapers; engraved invitations were sent to directors, large shareholders, commercial customers, and other "friends of the bank"; and 10,000 invitations were delivered to the town's households in paper "market" bags bearing the bank's logo. On opening day, the building was decked with bunting and balloons, and 10,000 roses were distributed.[5]

Tangibles as Emblems, Logos, or Advertising Images

To battle the intangibility of service, banks relied on a variety of tangibles on stationery and in advertising and related promotions. By 1910, images of bank buildings, eagles, lions, dogs, mountains, vaults, and well-recognized antiquities such as the Tower of Babel were in regular use. In pre-1910 promotional material, dogs were "alert and faithful," the institution was as "permanent as the pyramids" or "as lasting as the Sphinx," and the vault as "tough as a battleship." The symbolic content of these images was clearly understood by bankers. Of a 1908 advertisement showing a lion, *The Bankers' Magazine* said: "The idea conveyed by the lion and the massive chain border of the design is, of course, that of strength, and the design and copy are appropriately tied up by the reference to the institution's stability." The magazine also said: "The Rock of Gibraltar, used as a trade mark by Prudential, connotes strength, of course, and the dog emblems used by some institutions stand for fidelity, and so on." Not all tangibles selected by banks were deemed appropriate. A 1909 advertisement by the Safe Deposit & Trust Company (Pittsburgh) showed a dam and said "Experience is The Dam." *The Bankers' Magazine* criticized it, saying: "We may be mentally obtuse, but we can't just see the point to that damn ad. . . . if experience is the dam that retards the flow of your financial success, the answer seems to be, don't get the experience."[6]

Confidence Promotion Themes

Confidence also was enhanced in promotions. Four distinct yet related confidence themes were used by bankers: growth, director and management integrity, size, and longevity.

First, banks used the growth theme to demonstrate the public's high regard for the institution. A typical example illustrated deposits at various times. For instance, in a promotional folder the Fidelity National Bank of Spokane presented 1904, 1905, and 1906 deposits—which grew from $432,000 to $1,032,000, a nominal growth rate of 55 percent per annum—and a 1911 advertisement by the German-American Trust & Savings Bank (Los Angeles) showed deposits from 1900 through 1911—they grew from $1,234,241 to $14,117,731, a nominal growth rate of 25 percent per annum.[7]

Banks also instilled confidence by stressing director and management quality. Representative of the period are copy from a City Trust Company of Boston 1908 advertisement saying the bank offered the "advantage of a conservative and wise management under Directors who number men at the head of New England's leading enterprises," and a Manufacturers' National Bank of Lynn (Massachusetts) advertisement that read: "Confidence is the chief requisite of a bank. We get it and maintain it because our success rests upon the business success of our board of directors." Similar statements were echoed in booklets with such titles as *Men Ripe of Experience*.[8]

The third confidence theme was size. Simple slogans such as "New England's oldest and largest financial institution" and "St. Louis' Largest Bank" were used.[9]

The final theme, longevity, stressed institutional age. In 1908 *The Bankers' Magazine* observed that "The argument of age is one of the very strongest that any bank can use to prove that it is worthy of the confidence of prospective customers." Longevity was demonstrated in age-based promotions by presenting the date of establishment, and on the basis of geography, by boasting that an institution was the oldest in a region. Operators of the Old National Bank of Spokane, the Old National Bank of Battle Creek, and similarly named institutions, touched a chord among the populace. "First National Bank of . . ." names demonstrated geographically bounded age. Banks marked anniversaries with elaborate promotions, referred to in the trade press as "historical bank advertisements." For example, the Marine National Bank (Buffalo, New York) celebrated 65 years of operation with a full-page advertisement in the August 16, 1915, issue of the *Buffalo Express*. It contained drawings of the bank's 1850, 1880, 1900, and 1915 homes; 1850 and 1915 bank statements; and explanatory text. In 1928 The First National Bank of Chicago simultaneously celebrated its sixty-fifth anniversary and the opening of a new structure. The bank's main lobby housed a four-day historical exhibit connected to the bank's slogan: "Building with Chicago Business since 1863."[10]

Another mechanism that promoted longevity was commemorative retrospectives (many are listed in the bibliography). Corporate retrospectives, of course, are used by all manner of enterprises to promote themselves to customers, employees, shareholders, and the general public, and in this regard bankers were following a well-established practice. Retrospectives were not limited to the United States; banks in Canada, Japan, and Europe also published them. Some bankers denied a promotional dimension to their retrospectives, despite the obvious purpose. The preface to *A History of The State Bank of Chicago from 1879 to 1904* said, "The purpose of this little volume is not to advertise the institution which it describes."[11]

Many banks worked several confidence themes into one advertisement. A 1910 advertisement by the First National Bank (Richmond, Virginia), under the heading "A Clean Record of Forty-five Years," said: "A bank strong in resources, conservative in its management, progressive in its policy, with ample capital, modern equipment, splendid organization, officers of experience and a strong directorate."[12]

Slogans

Another mechanism for promoting confidence was a slogan: "You can convey more in a short snappy slogan about the strength, safety and service of your bank than in a booklet of finely-phrased literature," said Ernest Densch, who collected for publication in *The Bankers' Monthly* the slogans presented in Table 2.1. The slogans in the table specifically stress confidence.

Handling Runs

Prior to the establishment of deposit insurance during the 1930s, the financial panics that swept the nation struck at the heart of bankers' ability to foster institutional confidence. An understanding of mob psychology and an ability to communicate effectively were incalculable assets. Obviously, not all bankers were equally endowed in their capacity to deal with a public irate over the possibility of their deposits being swept away, and not all banks were equally solvent when a crisis struck. One response was to close the bank for a short period of time, an event sometimes announced by banks in paid newspaper advertisements (e.g., during the crisis of 1875, the Farmers & Merchants Bank and the Temple & Workmen's Bank announced in the *Los Angeles Daily Star* the cessation of operations for 30 days). But not all banks in a region closed when a panic struck. The 1893 crisis and the response of two Los Angeles banks is illustrative. The First National Bank utilized the "lunch counter" withdrawal policy. The recent death of the bank's president added to the confusion, and the attitude of the new president, Major George H. Bonebrake, was described at that time as "pay 'em and get rid of 'em." Over $500,000 was withdrawn in a two-day period. A judicious policy would have required ten days to draw that amount; the eight-day difference could have been used to draw funds from other institutions and might have stemmed the run. On the second day of the run, the City Bank and the University Bank (both of Los Angeles) closed, adding to the panic. On the morning of June 21, a line of nervous depositors two blocks long formed outside the First National Bank. Bonebrake stood on the steps of the bank and "harangued the crowd." He said that the bank had survived the two-day run and would pay all depositors in full—a sign was posted later that day, however, telling depositors that only a fixed portion of their deposits could be withdrawn. Bonebrake ordered employees with deposits to see him personally if they needed cash, and threatened to dismiss any who joined the nervous

Table 2.1
Confidence Bank Slogans (1920)

Slogan	Institution	Location
Safety–First of All	Peoples Savings & Dime Bank	Scranton, PA
Safety–First	First National Bank	Davenport, IA
A Financial Stronghold	Florida National Bank	Jacksonville, FL
Adding Strength to Strength	Asbury Park Bank	Asbury Park, NJ
Resources over $9,000,000	Dallas Trust & Savings Co.	Dallas, TX
A Bank of Strength and Character	Kansas National Bank	Wichita, KS
A Guaranteed Bank	Peoples State Bank	Cherryvale, KS
Service and Security	Guaranty Trust Company	Yakima, WA
The Bank of Safety and Service	First National Bank	Medina, PA
Prudence Points the Way	First National Bank	Glens Falls, NY
The Old Reliable	Greensboro National Bank	Greensboro, NC
The U.S. Government Deposits Money in This Bank–Why Don't You?	Commercial National Bank	Madison, WI
Identified with Aurora's Progress Since 1863	First National Bank	Aurora, IL
Oldest Trust Company West of the Mississippi	Iowa Loan & Trust Co.	Des Moines, IA
Fifty-fourth Year	First National Bank	Chattanooga, TN
Organized in 1869 for Service	Citizens Bank	Greenville, MA
Oldest Bank in Memphis	First National Bank	Memphis, TN
Oldest, Strongest, and Largest Bank in the State	First National Bank	Fort Smith, AR
We Have Been in Business Over 72 Years	Western Savings Fund Society	Philadelphia, PA
Oldest State Savings Bank in Iowa	Iowa State Savings Bank	Burlington, IA
Oldest and Largest Bank in the City	Savings Bank	Belleville, IL

Source: Ernest C. Densch, "Every Bank Needs a Slogan," *BMo*, 27 (April 1920): 30–31.

depositors outside. The bank announced in the *Los Angeles Times* on June 22, 1893, that it was ceasing operations for one month. The badly shaken bank survived the run.

In contrast, Isaiis W. Hellman, president of the Farmers & Merchants Bank, just a few doors down the street from the First National Bank, demonstrated an uncanny understanding of mob psychology. When rumor spread that the First National Bank was near to closing its doors, Hellman, whose office was in San Francisco, immediately boarded a train for Los Angeles with $500,000 in gold. The day before the First National Bank temporarily closed, Hellman personally supervised the transfer of the gold into the bank's vault in full view of a crowd of onlookers. When the bank opened the next day—the day on which the First National Bank ceased operations—Hellman had $250,000 in gold placed in large piles behind the tellers' cages. Furthermore, the paying teller purposely worked slowly, "looking up balances and signatures with which he was perfectly familiar." Together these created an atmosphere of stability, orderliness, and control. The Farmers & Merchants Bank never closed its doors during the crisis.[13]

If practical, mollifying a nervous crowd during a crisis with a display of financial reserves was the best policy. A. P. Giannini of the infant Bank of Italy (San Francisco) followed Hellman's policy during the 1907 crisis. The bank had $100,000 in gold on deposit with the Crocker National Bank, far in excess of minimum legal requirements. During the governor-declared bank holiday, many California banks required depositors to provide 10 to 90 days' notice for withdrawals over $100. Other banks handed out clearinghouse scrip. The Bank of Italy, a single-location operation at that time, displayed impressive piles of gold in the bank, enforced no amount or advance-notice withdrawal limitations, and paid withdrawals, if desired, in gold. Deposits at many California banks declined during the two-month crisis, but those at the Bank of Italy increased.

Giannini again followed this policy during a 1921 run on the Santa Rosa branch. No financial crisis existed in 1921, yet the day-and-a-half run siphoned off $500,000 of the branch's $3 million in deposits. Private detectives infiltrated the crowd outside the branch but gained no information; a formal investigation by state bank regulators never revealed what caused a run on a branch of the most successful California bank at that time. Rumormongers told of a customer who waited a day to make a $70,000 withdrawal, and Italian depositors, many unable to read English, may have misunderstood the one-hour closing of the town's three banks several days earlier to honor the recently deceased mayor. The evening of the run, Boss Scatena, Giannini's stepfather and chairman of the board, and two other senior officers drove to Santa Rosa with $1.5 million in gold and currency in the trunk of their car. The display stopped the run.[14]

The public's perception of stability (not necessarily actual stability) was thus critical during a crisis. The difference was well understood by T. M. Richardson, president of the First National Bank (Oklahoma City), who bluffed the crowd that had assembled outside his bank during the 1893 crisis. Richardson paid depositors late into the evening. From the steps of the bank, he finally announced that the bank would close for the night and that all depositors would be paid in full in the morning. Pointing to a pole, he said he would allow himself to be hanged from it if his promise was not kept. At that moment, several men toting heavy, jingling money sacks loudly pushed through the crowd and entered the bank. The next morning, customers waited in line to deposit money, not withdraw it. What the customers did not know was that the vault had been emptied the night before and that the money sacks contained iron washers.[15]

Finally, banks that survived a crisis often used the fact to bolster confidence. For example, the American Trust Company (Boston) in a 1908 leaflet, *Boston After the Crisis*, said: "The test of a financial institution is its ability to take care of its customers in time of stress [crisis]. In other parts of the country, depositors have been refused currency or necessary accommodations by their banks, whereas the American Trust Company has not refused a single depositor cash."[16]

TRANSACTION VELOCITY

Obviously, transaction velocity is critical regardless of the type of business, albeit the locus of effort varies with the particular circumstances. Department stores focused many of their efforts on the selling floor during the early part of the twentieth century. The adoption of specialized fixtures, for instance, did much to increase the productivity of the selling staff. Items as simple as hangers were a great improvement over piled merchandise. Shorter cabinets—five rather than seven feet tall—greatly speeded the process of locating merchandise, especially for female staff. When cash register operations were decentralized, retailers positioned them to serve multiple departments. In banking, service speed, while transparent to customers, occurred much more as a function of unseen activities behind the cages. Machine technology, administrative and systems development, and mail-handling operations were critical to the quick performance of functions. Not only were banks quick to adopt innovations, but managers understood that transaction velocity was a service quality determinant. During the 1910s, W. R. Morehouse, a California banker who wrote extensively on bank marketing, said:

> Although personal attention, courteous treatment, accuracy, and complete equipment appear at first thought to be paramount elements in any service, fully 80 percent of all bank customers consider these secondary to time. To them time is almost everything, and they *determine the quality of the service* upon the length of time it takes for them to transact their business with their bank. [Emphasis added.][17]

The remainder of this section is devoted to transaction velocity in banking. Unit tellers, transaction bulges, filing systems, technological process innovation, and mail operations are discussed.

Unit Tellers

Prior to the start of the twentieth century, large banks had separate paying and receiving tellers. The small-bank, single-teller model that combined both functions was problematic for large banks because of back office operational limitations. But the policy of separate paying and receiving tellers had several limitations. Stoddard Jess, vice president of the First National Bank (Los Angeles) noted in 1907 that (1) customers entered more than one line when conducting multiple transactions; (2) paying tellers were busy in the morning but had "little to do" in the afternoon, while receiving tellers were busy in the afternoon but not the morning; and (3) paying and receiving tellers were handling so many customers that little opportunity existed for them to know the customers personally. These problems were exacerbated in 1905 when the bank's customer base jumped from about 8,000 to 15,000 through the absorption of two Los Angeles banks. Jess solved the problem by designing what was called the "unit teller" system (implemented in 1905). The bank split customers into alphabetical groups and created a "small bank" for each that was capable of performing multiple transactions. Nine customer groups were formed, and each unit teller consisted of a teller, an assistant, and a bookkeeper. Customers lined up before their respective unit teller; time-consuming work was delegated to the assistant if that line became long, resulting in a second, slower-moving line. The benefits, according to Jess, were (1) reduced waiting time; (2) increased teller transaction capability; and (3) increased teller familiarity with customers.[18]

The two unit tellers adopted by the Harris Trust & Savings Bank (Chicago) in 1925 improved service and reduced operating costs. Customers could make club deposits and savings account withdrawals, cash checks, and obtain cashier's checks. Each unit teller consisted of three teller cages, one bookkeeper, two mechanized filing cabinets, and one mechanized bank posting machine, each capable of handling 20,000 active accounts (about half of the bank's savings account customers). The bank posting machine simultaneously entered transactions on passbooks and bank ledgers, increasing accuracy across both. Furthermore, interest was added to customers' passbooks on the first visit after the interest payment date, regardless of whether it had been asked for. By 1930, a number of other banks had adopted unit teller transaction technology.[19]

Banks also advertised their adoption of unit tellers. The National Exchange Bank's (Roanoke, Virginia) 1913 adoption was advertised in newspapers: "Our unit system of tellers and bookkeepers means quick service. Make your deposits, get checks cashed, payroll, your passbook or information about your account—all at the same window. You do not have to go to different windows and probably have to wait your turn at each."[20]

Transaction Bulges

Service suppliers wrestle with the problem of maintaining transaction velocity when demand fluctuates. The standard strategic response is training workers in multiple tasks and assigning them temporarily to departments experiencing demand bulges. This section demonstrates that banks have long relied on the standard strategic response to counter both unexpected and expected variance in demand. In the case of expected variance, unit tellers smoothed fluctuations across paying and receiving functions. During the late 1920s, the Franklin Trust Company (Philadelphia) offered free payroll service to companies maintaining an account of twice the weekly payroll value. Many Franklin employees worked one day a week in the payroll department to handle the increase in traffic. The American Exchange Irving Trust Company (New York) in 1927 advertised its ability to handle seasonal variance in demand through the employment of well-trained, part-time workers.[21]

To counter unexpected departmental flows, in 1904 The First National Bank of Chicago created a "flying squadron, consisting of a dozen to fifteen higher clerks, who are sent all over the bank as the need arises." Squadron positions were highly prized among the bank's clerks. In 1913, W. R. Morehouse recommended that a bank always have a reserve new account teller who could quickly transfer to the new account department to accommodate unusual numbers of new customers. A 1923 booklet on the history of the Chicago-based Continental and Commercial group of banks said that "Trained men and an elastic system by which capacity may be instantly doubled or tripled, are very necessary." Finally, during the late 1920s a bank consultant called training employees to handle transaction bulges the "swinging crew principle" and described it as an attempt to keep all employees busy all the time.[22]

Filing Systems

Advancements in filing systems were a key part of productivity increases in American business between 1870 and 1930, and banks, like other American enterprises, took advantage of them. Sometimes the innovation was simple. For example, at the end of nineteenth century, banks normally entered customer's signatures in a journal chronologically. The system was appropriate for small banks whose employees could mentally track customers, but very inefficient for large, growing banks. An improvement introduced at the end of the nineteenth century was placing signature cards alphabetically in a filing cabinet on wheels. The cabinet was easily moved from department to department. More complex filing systems overcame coordination difficulties arising from size. The Mercantile Trust Company and its affiliate, the Mercantile National Bank (St. Louis), in 1907 centralized the storage of correspondence. Steel filing cabinets with a capacity of 700,000 documents were put under the charge of a single individual, and to enforce orderliness, an "iron-clad" rule required that documentation accompany document removal. The bank's president liked to impress visitors by locating their correspondence with the bank in a matter of seconds. Another example is provided by the American Security & Trust Company (Washington, D.C.) during the 1920s. The number of customer authority documents had grown quickly, and tracking specific ones was time-consuming. The bank collected letters of administration, powers of attorney, authorities to sign, copies of government powers of attorney, indemnity and surety bonds, partnership agreements, and references to documents in other bank files and departments, then centrally filed them alphabetically by customer name in active or inactive files.[23]

Technological Process Innovation

This section examines technological process innovations and how, in a number of instances, banks promoted their adoption as a sign of modernity. Invention of telegraph and telephone technology tremendously reduced communication barriers in America after the Civil War, and helped to create a unified national market necessary for marketing and distributing goods on a national basis. The first telegraph exchange system in America was installed for the benefit of New York City bankers. In 1869 the Gold and Stock Telegraph Company, a subsidiary of Western Union, connected 25 banks to the clearing-house. The initial system was a printing telegraph. Messages were relayed from one bank to another, but delays were incurred because messages had to be retransmitted within the exchange hub. Two years later, Gold and Stock Telegraph replaced the manual exchange with a pin switchboard that directly connected any two banks. The exchange provided rapid communication and allowed banks to clear checks more efficiently. However popular the system, it was easily superseded by a telephone exchange in 1880.[24]

The TelAutograph reproduced handwriting at remote locations. It was perfected in 1893 by Elisha Gray, who is better known for his telephone patent caveat that led to a long battle, which he lost, with Alexander Graham Bell, and for his technical genius in electrical machinery design and production. He helped create Gray & Barton in 1869. That firm became Western Electric Company in 1872 when it was purchased by Western Union. Tellers used TelAutographs to make inquiries to bookkeepers without arousing the customer's suspicion. Other banks used them to communicate between floors. In 1906 the Home Trust Company of New York promoted its adoption of the TelAutograph—among other technologies—in a sixteen-page booklet titled *Old and New Methods of Banking*: "Labor and time-saving inventions used in the Home Trust offices—such as special telephone trunk lines with private switchboard and operator, the commercial phonograph, the adding machine or arithometer, devices for reproducing facsimile letters, and the telautograph."[25]

Another Bell Systems product was telephotography, the electronic transmission of photographs. Bell demonstrated the technology in 1924 by transmitting pictures to New York City from the Republican National Convention in Cleveland and from the Democratic National Convention in Chicago. Publication of the photographs in New York City dailies had a fantastic effect on the subsequent pictorial content of newspapers. One year later, Bell installed regular telephotographic service connecting most of America's metropolitan areas; news network service suppliers were initially the heaviest users. Some banks honored telephotographic checks from their best customers. In 1929 the American Trust Company of New York allowed a businessman to transfer $40,000 to another bank on the basis of a telephotographic check sent from Chicago.[26]

As early as the 1860s, manually powered coin-counting machines were on the market, but many were unreliable. During the very late nineteenth century, electric coin machines became available. The First National Bank of Chicago used an electric Johnson Coin Counter in its silver department in 1902. Able to tally with "absolute accuracy" two to five times faster than by hand, machine capacity was 500 per minute for silver dollars and 1,000 per minute for dimes and pennies. Two examples of banks' promoting adoption of coin-counting machinery follow (1909 and 1912 advertisements, respectively).

> Electric coin-counting machines and the best computing apparatus are used. The credit department has complete records of all of the bank's depositors so that if an application is made for a loan it can be given prompt attention. In transferring money by telegraph or cable, the National Bank of Commerce in St. Louis presents unparalleled advantages for prompt service. . . . Time is money. Save time and money by doing business with this great institution.

> The American National Bank [Hartford, Connecticut] has recently added to its equipment a Batdorf coin-wrapping machine, which automatically counts and wraps all denominations of coin, and will now receive on deposit from its customers coin in bulk instead of requiring that it be rolled into packages and marked with the depositor's name, as has been the custom in the past. This should prove of great convenience to merchants and others who receive a large amount of coin in the course of their business, as it eliminates the slow and laborious process of doing up coin by hand. In installing this machine the bank is maintaining its well-known policy of keeping its facilities abreast of the times and giving its patrons the best of service.

Manual coin technology remained predominant throughout the period for disbursing change from the teller's cage. But even here improvements were observed. Prior to the start of the twentieth century, tellers stacked coins in metal racks, then counted and proofed each transaction. Brandt Cashiers, introduced at the beginning of the century, quickened the process: a teller pressed a set of keys corresponding to the total coinage desired, and the machine deposited the correct value of coins in a receptacle. The First National Bank of Chicago purchased several of the machines in 1904.[27]

Banks used newspapers, booklets, brochures, pamphlets, and window displays to promote their adoption of technology. In the case of the latter, the National City Bank of Chicago in 1919 placed a Rand Company sorter in its window display, accompanied by the following: "Sorting can be done in a very small space with greater accuracy and rapidity than the old method of sorting on a desk." A Cummins perforator, Brandt Cashier, and Safeguard check writer were also displayed, each with a message of improved service in relation to speed, safety, or accuracy.[28]

Banks were influenced in their technology adoption decisions by the selling efforts of bank machine suppliers. A tremendous number of firms promoted machine technologies in *The Bankers' Magazine* and *The Banker's Monthly*, especially during the 1920s. Furthermore, just as typewriter suppliers during the late nineteenth century organized speed typing contests, so Burroughs organized "check listing contests." As early as 1911 the company offered standardized sets of 100, 200, 225, and 500 checks for contests. They were pleased to announce that all 1911 world record holders accomplished their feats on Burroughs adding machines.[29]

Canadian banks required means to coordinate far-flung branches, and telegraph technology filled that need. In 1924 the Canadian Bank of Commerce arranged private telegraph wires to connect its Toronto head office to its agency in New York and to a branch in Havana, and by 1934 to its major North America branches. The same was true to varying extents for the other large Canadian banks. "Private telegraph wire" technology at that time was page-printer-based or an early version of the Teletype. Disconnected machine technology developments in Europe and America between the 1840s and 1900 eventually led to practical page-printing telegraphs. The year 1915 marked the introduction of Bell System's private-line, page-printer service. Initial heavy users were news network service suppliers, but demand was substantial and the innovation was adopted by banks. Banks used Teletype technology to speed the sale and purchase of stocks and bonds, the transmission of head office currency exchange-rate reports, and the clearance of large commercial loans. Canadian banks promoted their adoption of private-wire technology. The Bank of Montreal, in 1930 New York City newspaper advertisements, said: "When Saving Time Means Saving Money" and "Private wires connect the leading offices of the Bank of Montreal in Canada with those it maintains in the United States. . . . Prompt economical action is thus assured."[30]

The Mail

How banks handled correspondence reveals a great deal of concern with service quality. A 1905 article in *The Review*, The First National Bank of Chicago employee magazine, demonstrates management attitude toward mail operations. "A neatly written and well copied letter, folded evenly and put in a plainly addressed envelope, sealed with care and correctly stamped, is worthy of the biggest bank in the west, and it is this standard that the management of this department [the out-mail department] is constantly trying to maintain." The in-mail and out-mail departments of The First National Bank of Chicago in 1905 required about 100 employees. Shifts were staggered, and employees moved between departments as the need arose. By 1909 the bank mailed over one million items per year. Two Thexton envelope sealers were used: small, electric machines that sealed pregummed, prefolded envelopes. The Thexton envelope sealer was improved upon during the twentieth century. In 1917 the Mailometer Sales Company marketed a machine that both sealed and stamped envelopes. It had a capacity of 250 documents per minute, and loss and theft of stamps were reduced because responsibility for stamp coils was centralized with a single individual. "The National," a competing machine of similar capacity, was marketed at the same time by the National Automatic Machine Company.[31]

During the early 1920s, the Guaranty Trust Company of New York employed 40 individuals to process the 4.5 million pieces of correspondence that passed through the bank annually. The staff arrived at midnight, 1 A.M., 6 A.M., and 1 P.M. Mechanical devices were used to open as well as seal and stamp correspondence. Outgoing letters were checked to verify that the address on the envelope matched that of the correspondence and that stated enclosures were present. Knowledge of train and boat schedules was used to deliver mail to the post office to meet various deadlines.[32]

Banks' advertisments that their superior mail-handling operations provided customers with an advantage are suggestive of time-based competition. For instance, the Union Trust Company (Cleveland), in an effort to attract commercial customers during the 1920s, ran full-page advertisements in *The Bankers' Magazine* stressing service speed. One said that the bank had special pouches on incoming mail trains that bypassed the post office and were delivered directly to the bank. Under a heading "All night and the Union Trust," another said that "a full day is saved in presenting checks for payment" due to the bank's night workforce. A third said "A day and night force of 120 people are constantly working at high speed to get your collections turned into interest bearing cash. In many cases, you save one to two days interest." At the same time, the Equitable Trust Company of New York promoted service speed in *The Bankers' Magazine* with a full-page advertisement that said, "When a letter or a package must be delivered without a moment's delay, The Equitable sends it by air mail." Concerned with safety, the bank noted that duplicates were sent by surface mail.[33]

ACCESSIBILITY

Accessibility may be defined as the ability to enter, approach, or communicate with, and is here discussed as it relates to hours of operation, staff accessibility, and location. Operating on a skeleton staff during the late night hours and offering only the essential services of check cashing, deposits, and withdrawals, one can imagine a bank being open around the clock. As well, one can also imagine newly started savings banks being open just a few evening hours each week. In the case of the former, the service would be welcomed, especially in large cities, and in the case of the latter, the hours would match consumer availability. Other service industries would find one or both alternatives difficult or unnecessary to implement. In insurance, purchasing a policy or making a claim can often wait one day without undue hardship. In the department store industry, operating an outlet 24 hours a day would be prohibitively expensive. As a compromise, around World War I some New York City department stores began operating telephone order-taking services between closing hours and midnight.[34]

At the begining of the twentieth century, a number of bankers in America prided themselves on their open door policy. Openness came from the desire to demonstrate a democratic ideal. The approach was less necessary in the department store, and to a lesser extent in the insurance industry, where public and regulatory acceptance of products was more forthcoming. After considering personal accessibility, the connection between location and accessibility is discussed.

Hours of Operation

Savings Banks

The operating hours of savings banks reflected their traditional role of serving individual consumers and were consistent with daily work hours. Table 2.2 presents a sample of the operating hours of savings banks; many, but by no means all, have been cognizant since their inception of the need for operating hours tailored to consumers' needs. For example, the Albany Savings Bank, the Beneficial Savings Fund Society, and the Knickerbocker Savings Bank were open after 6 P.M. at least one evening a week. These were the norm rather than the exception, and included both part-time and full-time institutions. Adjustments in operating hours in some instances may have had more to do with the desires of operators than of customers. The Albany Savings Bank shifted evening hours from Saturday to Monday in 1874, only to shift them back to Saturday two years later. The bank's policy of reserving Wednesdays for female customers was a matter of gender segmentation and is covered in another chapter.

Three mechanisms were used by banks to inform the public of their operating hour policy: passbooks, pamphlets, and newspapers. The Philadelphia Saving Fund Society, the first savings bank in America (1816), used all three very early in its history. Passbooks were used to convey many messages, especially ones centering on thrift and security. In addition to providing operating hours, the bank's passbook showed a strongbox, and said "to save is to earn" and "economy secures independence." Prior to 1880, classified-type advertisements were used regularly by banks, and these often mentioned operating hours. The 1855 opening of the Dollar Savings Bank was advertised in nine Pittsburgh dailies. Copy detailed operating hours and a special guaranty bond by bank trustees that provided security against defalcation. The initial passbook had a beehive and operating hours on the cover. Bees as symbols of thrift had long been used by banks: the Bank for Savings in New York City adopted the beehive logo on its passbooks as early as the 1830s; thus the Dollar Savings Bank capitalized on an established symbol. The operating hours of savings banks remained relatively stable for the rest of the nineteenth and the early twentieth centuries. Banks continued to promote operating hours, though such promotions echoed new societal concerns and a less shameful selling approach. For example, a Peoples Bank & Trust Company (Pittsburgh) 1908 newspaper advertisement presented information on recent robberies and said that Saturday night bank hours were "for the convenience of our depositors and merchants who have large sums of money."

Banks adjusted operating hours if local conditions warranted it. Miners in Bisbee, Arizona, at the turn of the century were paid in cash on Friday evening. The Bank of Bisbee, organized in 1900, closed before the miners were paid and did not reopen until Monday morning. This afforded the saloon keepers and other entertainment proprietors an entire weekend to relieve the miners of their

Table 2.2
Savings Bank Operating Hours

Institution	Location	Year and Operating Hours
Philadelphia Saving Fund Society	Philadelphia	1816*: 9 A.M.–11 A.M., Monday, for deposits, and same hours on Thursday, for withdrawals. Mid-19th century: 4 P.M.–7 P.M., Monday and Thursday, for deposits and withdrawals.
Albany Savings Bank	Albany, NY	1820*: 6 P.M.–9 P.M. Saturday for deposits only; withdrawals on four specified days of the year. 1874: Saturday evening hours replaced with Monday evening hours. 1876: pre-1874 policy reinstated. 1884: 6 P.M.–9 P.M. Saturday; 4 P.M.–5 P.M. Wednesday, for females only. 1890s: 10 A.M.–2 P.M. Monday through Friday
The Savings Bank	New Haven, CT	1820*: 10 A.M.–12 noon on first and third Mondays of each month
New Haven Savings Bank	New Haven, CT	1838*: 11 A.M.–1 P.M. weekdays; 2 P.M.–6 P.M. Saturday
Broadway Savings Bank	New York City	1851*: 5 P.M.–6 P.M. Monday, Wednesday, and Saturday
Knickerbocker Savings Bank	New York City	1852: 4 P.M.–8 P.M. Monday, Thursday, and Saturday
Irving Savings Institution	New York City	1852: 4 P.M.–7 P.M. six days a week. 1854: 11 A.M.–1 P.M., 4 P.M.–7 P.M. six days a week
Beneficial Savings Fund Society	Philadelphia	1853*: 9 A.M.–1 P.M. and 3 P.M.–8 P.M. five or six days a week. 1856: 9 A.M.–6 P.M. except on Monday and Thursday, when open until 8 P.M.
Mariners Savings Institute	New York City	1854: 10 A.M.–3 P.M. six days a week

Table 2.2 (Continued)

Emigrant Savings Institute	New York City	1854: 11 A.M.–1 P.M., 5 P.M.–7 P.M. several days per week
Erie County Savings Bank	Buffalo, NY	1854*: 9 A.M.–3 P.M., 6 P.M.–7:30 P.M. several days per week
Dollar Savings Bank	Pittsburgh, PA	1855*: 9 A.M.–2 P.M. weekdays, 7 P.M.–9 P.M. Saturday
Third-Avenue Savings Bank	New York City	1862: 10 A.M.–3 P.M. six days a week; 6 P.M.–8 P.M. Monday, Wednesday, and Saturday
Union Dime Savings Bank	New York City	1862: 5 P.M.–7 P.M. six days a week
Rose Hill Savings Bank	New York City	1862: 1 P.M.–5 P.M.; Wednesday and Saturday until 7 P.M.

*First year of bank operation.

Sources: Albany Savings Bank, *Albany Savings Bank: 1820–1899* (Albany, NY: Albany Savings Bank, 1899), 3–17; "Banking Publicity," *BMa*, 73 (December 1906): 1005; Erie County Savings Bank, *An Historical Sketch of the Erie County Savings Bank: 1854–1909* (Buffalo, NY: Erie County Savings Bank, 1909), 32; William F. Haas, *A History of Banking in New Haven* (New Haven, CT: privately published, 1946), 17, 30; John T. Holdsworth, *Financing an Empire: History of Banking in Pennsylvania* (Chicago: S. J. Clarke, 1928), 689, 704–5; Charles E. Knowles, *A History of the Bank for Savings in the City of New York: 1829–1929* (New York: Bank for Savings, 1929), 44; William T. Shoyer, *A Century of Saving Dollars: 1855–1955* (Pittsburgh: Dollar Savings Bank, 1955), 10–13. Also see advertisements in *NYT*, 18 September 1851; 1 January 1852; 2 January 1854; 7 June 1862.

pay before the bank had a turn at fostering thrift. The bank decided to remain open until 8 P.M., a policy that resulted in 53 new accounts within three days. Similarly, the Lafayette-South Side Bank in St. Louis opened during evening hours in 1926 after a number of factories began operating nearby.[35]

Commercial Banks

Because commercial banks primarily serve business customers, their operating hours were more restricted than those of savings banks. Table 2.3 presents a sample of commercial bank operating hours. As a rule, prior to the twentieth century, commercial banks were open five or six days a week. Some closed for one or two hours in the early afternoon to allow bank officers to visit customers and markets, although this was less common after the mid-nineteenth century among banks located in major metropolitan areas. Limited commercial banks hours naturally led to the term "bankers' hours." In addition, since the volume of note discounting was quite small and fraught with risk, early commercial banks in both America and Canada set aside specific days for receiving bank notes for discounting.

Bankers sometimes colluded to restrict commercial bank operating hours. In October 1850, advertisements appeared in San Francisco dailies proclaiming that "banking hours will be on and after the 21st of November from 9 A.M. to 4 P.M." They were signed by the leading private banking houses of the city: Argenti & Company; Page, Bacon & Company; Wells & Company; Burgoyne & Company; and Tallanty & Company. The leading commercial banks of the city thus signaled one month in advance their intent to eliminate competition in operating hours. But the proclamation was probably ineffective because of a lack of enforceability and it probably did not apply to indirect competitors, such as savings banks, that targeted consumers. Clearinghouses were somewhat better at enforcing operating hours because of their power (i.e., they could bar entry and evict rule breakers). An admission requirement to the Chicago Clearing House Association when it was organized in 1865 was keeping bankers' hours. The First National Bank of Chicago and the Union National Bank, two of Chicago's largest banks, had for some time been open from 9 A.M. to 4 P.M., but both curtailed their operating hours to gain admittance. Later in 1865, the Third National Bank was expelled after violating the edict, but was readmitted in 1866 after capitulating to the Clearing House Association rule. Organizers of the Denver Clearing House, established in 1885, sanctioned interest and exchange rates and operating hours of 10 A.M. to 3 P.M. on weekdays and 10 A.M. to noon on Saturday. Thomas Noel, who wrote extensively on the Colorado National Bank, said, "So powerful were the clearing house banks that smaller banks regarded their policies as unofficial laws."[36]

Note can be made of the operating hours of commercial banks in other nations. Prior to 1745, the Royal Bank of Scotland was open twice a day: in the morning and the afternoon. Yet such hours were not always sufficient. In 1837 the "inspector of branches" of the Royal Bank of Scotland reported unfavorably to the head office regarding the operating hours of the Dalkeith

Table 2.3
Commercial Bank Operating Hours

Institution	Location	Year and Operating Hours
The Bank of New York	New York City	1784*: 9 A.M.–1 P.M., 3 P.M.–5 P.M.; notes discounted Thursday had to be left at the bank on Wednesday morning
New Haven Bank	New Haven CT	1795*: 10 A.M.–1 P.M., 3 P.M.–4 P.M. weekdays; 10 A.M.–1 P.M. Saturday 1802: with the exception of a director, an assistant, and a customs collector, no employees were allowed to deal with customers outside of banking hours
Trenton Banking Co.	Trenton, NJ	1805*: 10 A.M.–3 P.M. weekdays
Hagerstown Bank	Hagerstown, MD	1807*: 9 A.M.–2 P.M. six days a week
Gettysburg National Bank	Gettysburg, PA	1814*: Tuesday was day of note discounting
Farmers National Bank of Bucks County	Bristol, PA	1814*: Tuesday and Friday were days of note discounting
Merchants National Bank	New Bedford, MA	1825*: Saturday was day of note discounting
Farmers Fire Insurance & Loan Co. (Farmers Loan & Trust Company)	New York City	1822*: 9 A.M.–sunset weekdays. 1822: curtailed hours during yellow fever outbreak—10 A.M.–1 P.M., 3 P.M.–5 P.M. 1840: 9 A.M.–3 P.M. Board stipulated that when called for, operations would resume at 5 P.M. and "continue during the afternoon"

agent. The agent (as branch managers were called) defended himself by writing that the operation of a country branch "requires us to be as accommodating as possible. I have had experience of a landed proprietor in this county calling upon me at 4 A.M. for money, and almost daily waited upon before and after Bank hours both to give and receive money." By the start of the twentieth century, the standard operating hours of Scottish commercial banks were 9 A.M. to 3 P.M. and 5 P.M. to 7 P.M. In Canada the first advertisement of the Bank of Montreal was placed in two Montreal newspapers, the *Herald* and the *Canadian Courant*, on October 23, 1817. The hours of operation were 10 A.M. to 3 P.M., and discount days were Tuesdays and Fridays. The 1885 *Rules and Regulations* manual of the Merchants' Bank of Halifax (now the Royal Bank, Montreal) stated that operating hours were 10 A.M. to 3 P.M. on weekdays and 10 A.M. to 1 P.M. on Saturday.[37]

Extended Banking Hours

Early in the twentieth century in America, some innovative banks, both commercial and savings, extended operating hours beyond traditional norms. The first and most innovative was the Night & Day Bank (New York), which began operations in 1906. It operated on three shifts and was open 24 hours a day, six days a week (not including legal holidays). The bank's site was carefully chosen:

> The location of the Night and Day Bank, on Fifth avenue and Forty-fourth street, was no chance selection. It was purposely made central to as diversified interests as probably ever were gathered into one banking institution. And, besides this, it was put within easy reach of the hundred thousand commuters who daily travel in and out of Grand Central Station.

In an effort to attract diamond and gem merchants, the bank had a naturally lit safety deposit inspection area. Having 24-hour access to the vault, more than a dozen such merchants were housed in the building's upper floors by 1907. An officer was always on hand to deal with loan and other inquiries. Securities sales made over dinner could be finalized that evening in the bank, saving out-of-town customers an overnight stay in New York City. Dated checks could be cashed one second into the calendar day, and bills were not overdue until one second after the calendar day. Time zone differences allowed some customers to save 24 hours or more on international remittances. The bank operated a women's department from 9 A.M. to 6 P.M., but serviced women's accounts 24 hours a day by keeping two sets of signature cards. The Night & Day Bank posted $3 million in deposits and over 7,000 customers by the end of its first year. An employee of the bank said that 24-hour banking was infeasible across the nation. New York City was able to support the service because it was large, the financial capital of the nation, and a 24-hour-a-day city.[38]

The Night & Day Bank was innovative in another manner. It was the first bank in the city to offer armored automobile service (in 1906). Between 3 P.M. and 5 P.M., the car served retailers, followed by a 9 P.M. to 10 P.M. theater, and a midnight to 1 A.M. restaurant, run. Earlier in the day, and between scheduled night runs, the "wagon," as it was called by bank employees, made cash deliveries to customers who requested them by telephone. Armored car service was quickly offered by other banks. By 1911, the Old Colony Trust Company, the First National Bank, and the National Shawmut Bank (all in Boston); the Cleveland Trust Company; and the Lincoln Safe Deposit Company (New York City) offered similar service. Unlike the Night & Day Bank limousine that blended with everyday traffic, many armored vehicles of the 1910s were electric, vividly emblazoned with the bank's name, and of unmistakable color (such as canary yellow).[39]

Extended operating hours spread quickly across the nation; some banks opted for midnight hours owing to local demand. By the 1920s, the term "night and day bank" was widely used to describe any bank that adopted midnight or all-night operating hours.

In Oklahoma City, the Night & Day Bank, chartered in 1908, ceased operations in 1933, presumably because of the Depression. A 1910 advertisement in the *Daily Oklahoman* used the growth confidence theme by showing total deposits at various intervals in increasingly large type. Part of the copy said "Open day and night"—we are uncertain whether it was open all night or just until midnight—and "Your money when you want it." A major selling point was that the bank had 4,000 depositors. This, the bank assured the reading public, led to financial stability since it would be highly unlikely for all 4,000 customers to simultaneously withdraw their deposits. In 1908, a group of investors headed by a former president of the Central National Bank subscribed to an all-night bank in St. Louis. It was to be located near the city's Union Station and, among other services, was to rent safety deposit boxes on a daily basis. Beginning in 1909, the Franklin Trust Company's (Philadelphia) main office, but not branches, was open until midnight on a daily basis. The policy, which was continued through the 1920s, "contributed greatly to the growth of the bank." Local banks such as the Peoples Bank & Trust Company responded with similar hours by the 1920s. In 1910 the Greenwich Bank's branch off Times Square, in direct response to the Night & Day Bank, adopted midnight operating hours. At that time, they were the only two New York City banks open until midnight or later. The *New York Times* in 1912 reported that a group of investors had obtained a premises in Picadilly for London's first 24-hour bank, with the anticipated name of Day & Night Bank. Early in the 1910s, the German National Bank (Little Rock, Arkansas) supplemented normal daytime hours with a 6 P.M.-to-midnight shift. The "night department" limited its services to deposits, withdrawals, and check cashing.[40]

In Los Angeles, the All Night & Day Bank commenced operations in 1908. It was open until midnight six days a week, the first in the area to keep such hours. Its operating hours contravened a Los Angeles Clearing House rule, and the resulting denial of membership in the association may have contributed to a minor run that was weathered. The bank was closed by the state superintendent of banks in 1910, but reopened four days later under new management. In 1913 it was absorbed by the Hellman Commercial, Trust & Savings Bank (previously the Merchants Bank & Trust Company of Los Angeles), and sometime between the merger and 1916, Hellman adopted a 24-hour operating policy. In 1916 the bank advertised in newspapers that it was "Open All Night and All Day," and differentiated itself from the competition by boasting that "The Hellman Bank is the only Los Angeles institution maintaining 24-hour service." By the end of the decade, about three-fifths of the bank's savings business was conducted between 4 P.M. and midnight. The bank was not shy about playing on fear: "if you should lose your purse at night," "if your husband dies," and "if you get a telegram late at night that requires hasty preparation and the catching of an early morning train, will you have the funds available immediately?" were copy material in a 1919 advertising series. Not all bank services were offered late at night (e.g., safety deposit vaults closed at 10 P.M.). Other Los Angeles banks that met the challenge and responded with midnight operating hours were the International Savings & Exchange Bank, the Citizens Trust & Savings Bank, and the American Savings Bank. Midnight operating hours spread to San Francisco sometime during the 1910s (e.g., the Liberty Saving Bank of San Francisco).[41]

When Joshua Green gained controlling interest in Peoples Bank (Seattle, Washington), he assiduously set about increasing deposits. Part of his efforts materialized in a 1926 letter to William Timson of the Alaska Packers Association (San Francisco). In it he said:

> I understand the Liberty Bank in San Francisco keeps open until midnight. We are seriously considering keeping our little bank open until midnight. It is the heart of the night life of the city, theaters, restaurants, etc., and there is an insistent call for a place to make deposits after regular banking hours. . . . Would you be good enough to ask some of your friends there whether they think the Liberty Bank is making the headway on account of keeping open at night and whether they think it is actually accommodating their customers? . . . I want to be the first Seattle Bank to start this innovation, so if you could make some inquiries, old man, I would certainly appreciate it.

Green never introduced night operating hours to the Seattle region.[42]

Even more accessible than the 24-hour-a-day banks was the S. C. Osborn & Co. safety deposit company (Seattle, Washington). Starting in 1910, it was open 24 hours a day, 365 days a year. It was the first all-night vault company in the Pacific Northwest. In 1910 *The Bankers' Magazine* said: "Mr. Osborn decided to throw his vault open, not only day and night, but Sundays and holidays also, and, as he states, cater to the people instead of having the people cater to the owners of the vault."[43]

Some banks shortened operating hours after introducing night depositories (e.g., National City Bank of New York did so with its Flatbush branch in 1927). The first banking "drive through" facility in America was installed in 1929 by the Central National Bank of Oakland. The "curbside" depository was constructed of concrete and steel, and had "Day & Night" brightly printed on it.[44]

No reference was found to extended operating hours among Canadian, Scottish, or English banks. Although I am unable to speak for the remainder of the globe, 24-hour banking would seem to be a testament to the ingenuity of American bankers.

Personal Accessibility

Another dimension of accessibility is the extent to which officers of the institution are accessible or at least visible to the public. Two of the best-known writers on bank marketing commented upon the necessity of officer accessibility:

> If National City Bank of New York, the largest bank in the country, has its officers' quarters out in plain sight from the lobby and makes its easy for anybody to see them who has any legitimate business to do so, we think any other bank can profitably do so. (T. D. MacGregor, 1914)

> Officers should be accessible during banking hours for consultation and advice, should customers desire this service. The service of the bank is not efficient if the officers are either screened away from the public, or if, upon meeting the public, they consider themselves in an "I am It" manner. Any service which conveys the impression of exclusiveness or superiority is inefficient especially . . . from the standpoint of the customer. (W. R. Morehouse, 1918)

The philosophy was put into practice. Very early in the twentieth century the desks of the president, secretary, and treasurer of the Erie County Savings Bank (Buffalo, New York) were "readily accessible to all who have business with them," and J. P. Morgan's desk was clearly visible from the private bank's main entrance. A. P. Giannini of the Bank of Italy maintained an office in the open, beside the main entrance of the San Francisco head office. He traveled frequently to track branch operations, but his accessibility to the public made the bank a success. Often reluctant to discuss business while at his desk, he was far more interested in who in the old neighborhood had married, died, and had children. John G. Lonsdale, president of the National Bank of Commerce (St. Louis) had a similar policy toward personal accessibility during the late 1910s.

> [He] is so accessible to the public that his friends often wonder how he attends to the many tasks for which other men require silence and seclusion. His desk is right near the front door with only a low counter separating him from the public and there is always a line of people waiting to talk to him.

Accessibility was a promotional selling point. A 1907 advertisement by the National Exchange Bank (Baltimore) said: "The officers are always accessible and will be pleased to confer with you relative to your banking needs." Direct mail material of the Mechanics Bank (New Haven, Connecticut) in 1913 stressed personal accessibility and other service quality determinants. The following was one of several letters signed by bank president William M. Douglas:

> Are you receiving the proper service and assistance from your bank? Is every detail of your banking business being handled in a way that is perfectly satisfactory to you? The Mechanics Bank has every facility for attending to your wants properly and promptly. Our splendid building and central location offers you every convenience. You may always feel free to consult with our officers at any time about any financial problem. Between our depositors and

ourselves exists an intimate, personal bond of confidence and co-operation. Many of our customers have told us that this individual service has played an important part in their business success. We aim to be genuinely helpful—even beyond the mere routine of banking courtesy. This service we place at your disposal. Backed by the ample security and complete facilities of the Mechanics Bank, it is worth your careful consideration. If you are thinking of changing or enlarging your banking connections, Mr. Frisbie or I would be very glad indeed to talk it over with you.

In the same year, the bank ran a series of newspaper advertisements. One said, "If you were a banker would you sit in a secluded office where it was difficult for your depositors to see and talk with you. . . . the officers of The Mechanics Bank believe in the 'open office policy.'"[45]

The accessibility policy of American bankers was not without shortcomings. Although democratic from the customer's perspective, the policy played havoc with scheduling. In Europe and Canada through the 1920s, clients and bank officers arranged appointments by mail or phone. In America, "If an American must write or phone for an appointment with one whom he wishes to see, he considers the latter is giving himself airs . . . [and] . . . will go elsewhere to seek a more democratic environment." During the late 1920s an Englishman visiting New York City complained about lengthy delays in meeting bank officers. *The Bankers' Magazine* confirmed the legitimacy of the complaint, but saw little that could rectify the situation. The Englishman R. M. Mottram in 1930 implicitly acknowledged the American–English cultural difference: "One is agreeably impressed by the openness of their [London offices of American banks] banking halls and the accessibility of their personnel."[46]

Location

Despite branch banking obstacles, banks incorporated location into promotional material primarily because of its importance in consumer decision-making processes. Table 2.4 lists banks that stressed location convenience in their advertisements. All the banks are in larger metropolitan areas and, with the exception of Security Trust & Savings Bank, they had few, if any, branches. A city map with an arrow pointing out the "convenient" location was often the centerpiece of the advertisement. The geographically dispersed Security Trust & Savings Bank stressed location over a broad region (southern California), much as Canadian banks did (e.g., the Eastern Townships Bank [Sherbrooke, Quebec] distributed a folder in 1908 showing the location of its many branches on a map of the region). Some banks stressed location convenience in a slogan. Table 2.5 presents several of them.[47]

Canadian Prefabricated Banks

The expansion of Canadian banks into the western territories illustrates how banking laws indirectly affected marketing. This section describes Canada's use of prefabricated structures early in the twentieth century. One can only speculate on whether the clever use of prefabricated facilities would also have occurred in America if banks had been allowed to operate on a national basis. The

Table 2.4
Convenient Location Advertising

Institution	Location	Year
Seaboard National Bank	New York City	1907
New Netherland Bank of New York	New York City	1907
Third National Bank	Springfield, MA	1908
First Trust & Savings Bank (of The First National Bank of Chicago)	Chicago, IL	1909
Astor Trust Company	New York City	1913
Title Guarantee & Trust Company	New York City	1913
Home Savings Bank	New York City	1914
Brooklyn Trust Company	Brooklyn, NY	1915
Citizens Trust & Savings Bank	New York City	1916
The Importers & Traders National Bank	New York City	1922
The Coal & Iron National Bank	New York City	1924
Blair & Co.	New York City	1926
Security Trust & Savings Bank	Los Angeles, CA	1926
National Newark & Essex Bank Co.	Newark, NJ	1927

Note: Year refers to year during which the advertisement appeared.

Sources: Advertisements reprinted in *BMa*, 75 (August 1907): 256; *BMa*, 75 (September 1907): 410; *BMa*, 76 (April 1908): 583; *BMa*, 78 (January 1909): 107; *BMa*, 86 (January 1913): 62; *BMa*, 89 (December 1914): 675; *BMa*, 91 (August 1915): 234; *BMa*, 92 (April 1916): 520; *PI*, 118 (January 19, 1922): 153; *BMa*, 108 (February 1924): 232; *BMa*, 113 (July 1926): 106; *BMa*, 114 (February 1927): 295.

technology was clearly available to Americans. In 1867 the Union Pacific Railroad transcontinental route bypassed Colorado in favor of Wyoming. Cheyenne spring up overnight as the railroad off-loaded prefabricated stores and boardinghouses, and within a year its population exceeded that of Denver. In Canada, prefabricated structures were erected on Baffin Island in 1578 and in Halifax in 1750 (the latter was the city's first church, St. Paul's, and was shipped from Boston). But the prefabrication industry of Canada lagged that of America by the later settlement of the Canadian West.

An early leader in the Canadian prefabrication industry was the British Columbia Mill Timber and Trading Company. In 1904 models were displayed at trade fairs in Manitoba and British Columbia. To handle long, cold winters, Canadian prefabricated buildings were more sturdy and airtight than their American predecessors. The company marketed structures ranging from a $100, 12-foot × 12-foot, single-room structure to a $785, 2-story, 4-bedroom permanent house. Rail shipping charges were offset by the shortage of timber and skilled tradesmen on the prairies. By 1910, the company's structures had been adapted for schools, churches, telephone companies, railroads, and banks (the latter being the supplier's best commercial customers).

Table 2.5
Location Bank Slogans (1920)

Slogan	Institution	Location
The Bank on Fourth Street	Peoples Savings Bank	Zanesville, OH
Sixty-three Years on South Main Street	First National Bank	Carbondale, PA
In the Heart of Flatbush	Irving Trust Company	Brooklyn, NY
The Bank Next to the Post Office	Old Commercial National Bank	Oshkosh, WI
In the Heart of Everything	City Bank	Raleigh, NC
The Bank on the Corner	Citizens Savings & Trust Co	Wabash, IN
The Bank in the Middle of the Block	Citizens Commercial & Savings Bank	Flint, MI
The Most Conveniently Located Bank in the City	Central State Bank	Dallas, TX
In the "Big Building"	National Bank	Kalamazoo, MI
The Convenient Corner	First National Bank	Duluth, MN
The Bank with the Big Chimes Clock	National Bank	Lockport, NY
The Bank with the Clock	City Savings Bank	Kalamazoo, MI

Source: Ernest C. Densch, "Every Bank Needs a Slogan," *BMo*, 27 (April 1920): 30–31.

The Bank of Montreal and the Winnipeg-based Northern Bank purchased town houses as branch buildings or as managers' residences for use in British Columbia. But it was the Canadian Bank of Commerce that most assiduously utilized B.C. Mill Timber and Trading Company products. The first prefabricated structures purchased by the bank were "off the shelf" models, and one of the earliest was shipped by rail to Cobalt (Ontario) in 1905 to replace the bank's canvas tent branch. Yet the desire for prefabricated structures went beyond a "least-cost solution." Banks wanted a "first mover" advantage in new towns, but uncertainty existed over which towns would flourish. Prefabricated structures lessened the risk, since they could be knocked down and moved to another location. At the same time, banks wanted their prefabricated structures to look like banks. The Canadian Bank of Commerce retained the well-known architectural firm of Darling and Pearson, which had designed many of its stone-and-mortar buildings, to design a unique prefabricated structure. The result was three designs, two of which were different-sized neoclassical styles with hipped roofs and multicolumned verandas. The Canadian Bank of Commerce had the B.C. Mill Timber and Trading Company keep two prefabricated banks in reserve for emergencies, a policy that proved valuable. They were sent to San Francisco in 1906 to replace the bank's permanent structure destroyed by the earthquake and fire. Between 1906 and 1910, about 70 of the prefabricated banks were erected in the Canadian west. In many small, muddy towns, the most elegant and striking building was the Canadian Bank of Commerce prefabricated bank.[48]

Other Means of Increasing Accessibility

A number of other means were used by banks to increase accessibility. During the 1910s and 1920s, teller nameplates created a more personable environment, bank lobby signs directed customers to departments, staggered employee lunch hours improved staff availability, and windows connecting the lobby to back offices increased customers' access to bookkeepers. An information desk also improved accessibility. During the 1920s, the Rhode Island Hospital Trust Company desk was said to convey a "spirit of friendly business."

> Here the information clerk, Stanley C. Johnson, is *accessible* to all, and is the first representative of the company with whom hundreds of new customers are coming into contact, and to whom, it may be added, many old customers are learning to turn for quickly available information. [Emphasis added.]

Aside from directing customers to specific departments, Johnson opened new savings and checking accounts and distributed tax lists, times-tables, and other bank publications. In 1913 the National Copper Bank (Salt Lake City) employed an information clerk who was promoted in the following manner: "We wish you to feel free to come into the bank at any time, whether you are a regular customer or not, to ask his help in looking up a forgotten address, a want ad, or any other information you may need at the moment."[49]

COURTESY

The discrepancy between the social class of customers and of employees perplexed many service organizations. The problem was particularly acute for central city department stores during the late nineteenth and early twentieth centuries: the majority of customers were middle- and upper-class women, but the majority of direct workers were lower-class women lacking education and refinement. Employees assuming an air of equality to customers led to resentment on the part of patrons, and between 1910 and 1940 retailers developed a range of sales training programs to remedy the situation and increase overall sales force effectiveness.[50]

The social standing of bank tellers was much higher relative to department store floor workers, a situation attributable to greater skill and training, better pay, and a greater likelihood of advancement. Bank teller positions, unlike those of retail direct workers, were not entry-level jobs. In banking, the traditional entry-level job was messenger or page boy. Despite their high standing relative to other service employees who had contact with customers, tellers, especially those in commercial banks, were socially equal or inferior to customers to varying extents, especially prior to the 1870s and 1880s. When bank markets became more inclusive between 1870 and 1930, the social position of bank employees relative to customers changed. New customers included small savers or those of lesser means, women, children, and immigrants. As the social position of tellers rose relative to those of customers, airs of superiority became more common. It was in this context, early in the 1870–1930 expansion of bank markets, that courtesy was first mentioned in the trade press. One of the first was an 1885 article, written by "An Old Cashier," that appeared in *The Bankers' Magazine* under the title "Advice to Bank Clerks." The cashier said: "I would earnestly urge, then, that true courtesy, which has no taint of servility, be cultivated by every one connected with a bank, and as a first step toward reaching so desirable a point, that every thought of superiority be dismissed from the mind." A New York City employee of the Canadian Bank of Commerce wrote in 1893:

> Courtesy, civility and attention are his [the teller's] chief requisites. He should always do his best to please the bank's customers, never taking self into consideration while they are waiting his attention. It often happens that a customer will come in just as the teller is in the middle of a long line of additions, and while it is sometimes annoying and aggravating to be interrupted, the ideal teller will at once drop his calculations and serve the customer. Prompt attention to the wants of customers is certain to enlist and hold their good-will.

Between 1895 and 1930, an explosion of articles on courtesy occurred. Tellers, cashiers, loan officers, security guards, telephone operators, presidents, and janitors were the target of courtesy messages.[51]

Banks spread the word on courtesy internally in employee magazines. David R. Forgan, vice president of The First National Bank of Chicago and brother of president James B. Forgan, in a 1905 issue of *The Review*, after introductory comments on the "fierceness of competition," said:

> There are various ways in which different employees may share in this work, but there is one in which all can help—courtesy of manner toward the public. There is some temptation in our size and leading position for us to assume an air of indifference, especially toward people who do not represent a large business. This should be carefully avoided. . . . Courtesy is more a matter of manners than words. It is easy enough to be courteous when you can do just what the customer wants you to do. It is when you say "no" that the true test comes. . . . In my opinion nothing can make our present customers more ready to recommend us to others, nothing can attract the casual caller and convert him into a permanent customer more than the practice on our part of courtesy, combined with firmness and self respect.[52]

Between 1900 and 1920 banks began stressing courtesy in advertising, and the connection to "gap theory" was made: the bank "should breathe courtesy through every letter and advertisement issued, and such public promises should be backed up by performance." Banks also benchmarked their performance. One bank president who hired a detective to open accounts in leading banks in his city was surprised when the detective reported that the president's bank offered the most discourteous service.[53]

CLEAN MONEY

A dimension of service quality unique to banking was handing out clean money. Banks were especially eager to provide clean money to female patrons. An 1895 24-page booklet celebrating the completion of the First New Haven National Bank's new building described the women's department and said that "new bank-bills will always be given to ladies in payment of their checks." The policy continued into the next century; a 1903 advertisement said that "new bills are always given ladies in payment of their checks." During the 1910s, a few large banks began operating currency washing machines expressly for the purpose of providing clean bills to female customers. The 3 × 14-foot machine used by The First National Bank of Chicago in 1914, with a capacity of between 2,000 and 5,000 notes per hour, required two operators to feed and stack bills.[54]

NOISE

Because a bank's factory is in the main banking hall and because open interiors were desired—to demonstrate accessibility and democratic ideals—noise and echo were a problem. This can be contrasted with department stores, where nonselling functions were normally separated physically from the selling floor. Throughout the nineteenth and well into the twentieth century, many bankers instructed staff to speak in whispered tones to ensure confidentiality and inspire a "hallowed halls" atmosphere. The sentiment that "noise of any kind is outrageous" was common. But mechanical innovations, such as typewriters, adopted during the latter part of the nineteenth century caused problems, especially in older, reverberating structures. Between 1900 and 1920, banks began draping over walls or attaching to ceilings sound-absorbing felt covered by a "decorative membrane." Bankers also found appealing the porous metal-, sand-, and stone-based materials that absorbed 75 percent of the noise striking them that were developed during the 1920s. Mellon National Bank (Pittsburgh), the Seamen's Bank for Savings (New York City), and The First National Bank of Chicago installed these types of materials.[55]

Banks designed after the introduction of mechanical banking devices set aside special areas for machinery. The Oakland Bank's (California) 1924 structure was carefully designed: "Arrangement of the main banking floor is such as to give the maximum service with the greatest efficiency." Italian marble counters, mahogany furniture, travertine marble pillars, and a doorway built to control wind gusts and cold air, "permitting an even, comfortable, working temperature to be maintained throughout the entire main banking rooms," marked the design. The bookkeeping machinery was placed in a special sound-absorbing room.[56]

Typewriter suppliers were aware of the problem facing bankers. In 1929 Remington Rand marketed the "Remington Noiseless Typewriter." Advertisements in *The Bankers' Magazine* said, "With one of these machines, your secretary can type your letters within whispering distance of your desk and you will scarcely be conscious of her presence." The influence of Remington and other service and product suppliers on bank managers cannot be overlooked.

Suppliers of architectural services, flooring and soundproofing materials, and lighting fixtures bombarded banks with promotional messages in the trade press. For instance, Hoggson Brothers, a leading designer of banks, promoted its one-stop architectural, engineering, decoration, construction, and equipment procurement service in *The Bankers' Magazine* during the 1910s. At the same time, New York Belting & Packing promoted interlocking rubber tiles as "the most satisfactory flooring for banks. It is odorless, noiseless, sanitary and non-slippery."[57]

CHECK SECURITY

A unique problem long faced by banks concerned how to mark checks to show that they had been paid or canceled. Stamping checks with the word "paid," tearing a piece of the check, or stamping a hole in it could be overcome by fraud. A late-nineteenth-century innovation was stamping many miniature holes in a check to form the word "paid" and a date, but some checks became illegible and difficult to handle because of the number of holes. At the start of the twentieth century, words and dates stamped by machines on checks were replaced with codes. The Cryptographic Perforating Machine adopted by The First National Bank of Chicago just before 1910 stamped a date and the name of the clearing bank on a check in code. Another security problem for banks concerned the alteration of their own checks. By 1910, The First National Bank of Chicago had purchased several Protectograph machines manufactured by G. W. Todd & Co. (Rochester, New York). The machine embossed the amount of a check in a special colored ink, most often red. Other innovations in checks served customers' interests. In 1919 the J. C. Hall Company (Providence, Rhode Island) introduced a check that served as both bill and receipt. The payer wrote one check to cover multiple bills from the same source and recorded the separate bills in a space on the check. This saved time, bank handling charges, and postage.[58]

The invention of the microfilm machine by George L. McCarthy during the 1920s had a great impact on bank security. There were earlier applications of photography in banking, however. During the 1880s, French banks photographed unsavory-appearing check cashers as a security measure, and during the mid-1920s the Northern Trust Company (Chicago) photographed trust documents, such as tax returns and wills, thus eliminating the need for customers to leave important documents at the bank or bring along on visits.[59]

McCarthy, a banker for more than 25 years, realized that returning canceled checks to depositors resulted in the bank's inability to verify whether the issuer had written the check. Fraud was difficult to detect. Intrigued by a slow-motion movie during the mid-1920s, he designed the Check-O-Graph, part of which was a 16-millimeter Kodak camera. His efforts to sell his invention to bankers failed, but in 1926 George Eastman, himself a former bank employee, heard of McCarthy's invention. In 1928, Eastman Kodak Company created a subsidiary, the Recordak Corporation, with $1 million in capital. McCarthy was appointed chief executive officer of the subsidiary, which by 1930 was granted numerous patents on the machine. The company's first customer was McCarthy's previous employer, the Empire Trust Company (New York City).

The machine consisted of three components: (1) the Recordak, a photo-graphic machine equipped with two lenses enabling dual production; (2) a projector; and (3) a screen. Recordak could operate alone or in conjunction with most adding machines. A numbering system allowed operators to easily locate a check on developed film, and any particular copied check could be enlarged and printed on paper.

The Recordak Corporation distributed and serviced the machines that were manufactured by Kodak and managed and operated overnight film development facilities. By October 1928, the Chase National Bank, the National City Bank of New York, American Trust Company, Bankers Trust Company, Manufacturers Trust Company, and Federal Reserve Bank of New York had bought the machine, and more than 100 machines had been rented to banks in the first year of operation. By 1930, the technology quickly spread to Canada: six out of the seven banks with head offices in Toronto purchased one within one week of its introduction.

Promotional brochures of the 1920s stressed the technology's advantages. One was the retention by the bank of indisputable proof that a check had been written (i.e., claims of fraudulent withdrawal or bank error could be verified). A second advantage was the labor savings realized by bank transit departments, in some cases up to 60 percent of a clerk's time. Third, departments speeded up check clearings by a day, making funds available earlier. Fourth, lost checks could be replaced by copying them on paper. The Recordak brochure also stressed that film storage was inexpensive because of limited space requirements. Early 1930s brochures continued to stress fraud detection by reprinting newspaper accounts of actual instances. Banker testimonials touted the effectiveness of the machine in fraud detection, cost, and velocity.[60]

ACCURACY

Accuracy was a critical determinant of service quality across a spectrum of industries, and banking was no exception. During the 1910s an employee of the Market & Fulton National Bank (New York) said that "The motto should be accuracy first as well as safety first," and in 1922 an employee of the Anglo-American Trust Company (San Francisco), in an article titled "What Is This Thing Called 'Service'?" wrote that "One of the most important elements of service is accuracy—accuracy in bookkeeping, accuracy in checking signatures, accuracy in every phase of the bank's relations with its clients." This section discusses accuracy and technology and accuracy promotion.[61]

Technology Adoption

The term "bookkeeping by machinery" came into use about 1910 as productivity- and accuracy-improving machines increasingly displaced the manually maintained "Boston ledger" system. An Elliot-Fisher machine available during the early 1910s simultaneously marked the depositor's statement, posted the ledger, and made debit and credit journal entries. Adoption by the County Trust Company (White Plains, New York) led to the release of one bookkeeper and the reassignment of two others. *The Bankers' Magazine* gushed over the cost and accuracy implications of the machine: "Perhaps there is a third equation justifying the use of machines in banks, and this is service to depositors" in the form of "protection and security to depositors in increased accuracy." [62]

Another machine introduced during the early 1910s was the Remington Adding Subtracting Typewriter, which found use in transit departments for writing remittance letters. Prior to its introduction, two or more machines were required to complete the task. Since the operation was completed on one machine, fewer errors were reported in aligning columns of figures; and when errors were made, they could easily be subtracted from or added to the total. In 1912 the Continental & Commercial National Bank of Chicago used 18 of the machines in its transit department and 43 in total. Banks also began using the machines to track daily balances on demand deposit accounts, thereby gaining valuable information on individual account profitability.[63]

During World War I, the St. Louis Union Bank (St. Louis) confronted labor problems due to the loss of a portion of its male workforce. The bank adopted various technologies, apparently to cope with the influx of untrained females. Three additional ledger units were added and the workload per unit was decreased, in the belief that women were incapable of producing the same volume of work as men. Since women were thought to be inaccurate and not mathematical, the bank purchased a comptometer. The machine cut month-end interest calculation time by half, eliminated month-end overtime wages, and reduced errors substantially. The old manual system lacked checks and balances, such as the daily totals provided by the comptometer, and errors easily passed through the system. Arguments with customers occurred all too frequently. In spite of the implied chauvinism, the lesson of technology adoption was not lost on one of the bank's auditors.

> It is probably true that machinery represents an initial expense which justifies careful consideration but in the long run it will almost always be found that the machines in skillful hands take a heavy load off the accounting department, improves the *quality* of the service to customers, keeps the working force contented and cuts the cost of doing business. [Emphasis added.][64]

Another example of machine technology adoption in part spurred by the turnover in staff accompanying World War I is provided by the Security National Bank (Minneapolis). The transit department, which employed 65 clerks at the start of the war, had 85 personnel changes in 1918. The number of errors expected during one week were being made on a daily basis, and machine technology was subsequently adopted. Moreover, the bank adopted an efficiency scoring system whereby employees and departments were awarded points for not making, and credit for catching, errors. These scoring systems, developed by the large banks in New York City and Chicago during the 1880s and 1890s, were used to identify deadweight clerks for redundancy and efficient ones for promotion and salary increases.[65]

Accuracy Promotion

One of the more elaborate promotions consisted of a bank publishing in newspapers, on a occasional basis, a complete listing of the balance of every savings account, by account number. Customers could verify balances without visiting the bank, and assurance and confidence were promoted as the bank opened its ledgers to the general public. The Schenectady (New York) Savings Bank was apparently the first bank in America to adopt such a promotional plan. It placed a ten-page advertisement in the *Schenectady Gazette* in February 1907, showing the balance of each of its 22,235 savings accounts. The bank's treasurer, who prepared the advertisement, wrote to *The Bankers' Magazine* that "the adding machine has done much to make possible such a detailed statement." Each customer was mailed a pamphlet containing the information in the advertisement. Owing to the interest from other banks, after the 1907 campaign the bank distributed a circular describing the efforts. It explained what the bank attempted to accomplish, how the listing was compiled, and the cost of the campaign (about $1,000). It said, among other things, that "much gratification was expressed and many compliments paid to the bank by those interested, and the public, at home and abroad." W. H. Kniffen described the Schenectady Savings Bank campaign as the "most famous bank trial balance (and verification of pass-books as well) in this country," and said that by 1911 it had been copied by a number of other banks. For example, in 1910 the Salem Five Cent Savings Bank (Salem, Massachusetts) published an eight-page newspaper advertisement listing the balances of 24,751 savings accounts.[66]

Accuracy and Customer Addresses

Finally, in 1912 the German-American Trust & Savings Bank (Los Angeles) printed "change of address" pads. To attract attention and use, they were on bright yellow paper and prominently placed on the customers' desk beside deposit tickets. In bold print across the top was written "It is IMPORTANT to you." Tellers also kept pads at their cages. Over 2,000 cards were completed by bank customers during a two-month period, and a clever West Coast salesman sold over 50,000 of the standard forms to other banks "in a very short time."[67]

NOTES

1. Louis J. Millett, "The National Farmers' Bank of Owatonna, Minn.," *AR*, 24 (October 1907): 249–58; "An Architecture of Democracy: Three Recent Examples from the Work of Louis H. Sullivan," *AR*, 39 (May 1916): 437–65; State Street Trust Company, *The Log of the State Street Trust Company* (Boston: State Street Trust Company, 1926); for a detailed history of bank architecture, see *Money Matters: A Critical Look at Bank Architecture* (New York: McGraw-Hill, 1990).

2. "Costly Savings-Bank Structures," *NYT*, 24 March 1867; A. C. David, "Private Residences for Banking Firms," *AR*, 14 (July 1903): 13–27; Montgomery Schuyler, "The New National Park Bank," *AR*, 17 (April 1905): 319–28; A. C. David, "The Building of The First National Bank of Chicago," *AR*, 19 (January 1906): 49–58; "The Chemical National Bank, New York," *AR*, 22 (July 1907): 61–65; "The Bank Buildings of Baltimore," *AR*, 22 (August 1907): 79–101; "Recent Bank Buildings of the United States," *AR*, 25 (January 1909): 3–66.

3. "Banking Publicity," *BMa*, 91 (December 1915): 821; J. E. Montague, "Getting Light to Help Your Depositors," *BMo*, 34 (November 1917): 16–18; John W. Harrington, "The Importance of Better Lighting," *BMa*, 120 (June 1920): 789–95+.

4. Ronald A. Fullerton, "Art of Public Relations: U.S. Dept Stores, 1876–1923," *Public Relations Review*, 21, 3 (1990): 68–79.

5. Arthur W. Ingalls, "Advertising a Bank and a Building," *BMa*, 90 (March 1915): 469–71; Edwin P. Lamphier, "How a Connecticut Bank Capitalized on the Opening of Its New Bank Building," *BMa*, 116 (March 1927): 615–19; Lorne Clemes, *A Century of Leadership: The Story of the Bank of Lenawee County* (Adrian, MI: Bank of Lenawee County, 1969), 19–23.

6. "Bank Advertising Emblems," *BMa*, 73 (August 1906): 299–302; "Banking Publicity," *BMa*, 75 (November 1907): 737; "How Banks Are Advertising," *BMa*, 76 (January 1908): 82; "How Banks are Advertising," *BMa*, 76 (March 1908): 402; "A New Emblem," *BMa*, 77 (July 1908): 90; "Advertising Criticism," *BMa*, 79 (August 1909): 276. Advertisements reprinted in *BMa*, 79 (July 1909): 119; *BMa*, 79 (August 1909): 276; Noel M. Loomis, *Wells Fargo* (New York: Bramhall House, 1976), 250.

7. "Fidelity National Bank, Spokane, Washington," *BMa*, 73 (November 1906): 812; T. D. MacGregor, *MacGregor's Book of Bank Advertising* (New York: Bankers Publishing Co., 1921), 82. Advertisements reprinted in *BMa*, 72 (February 1906): 307; *BMa*, 73 (September 1906): 473; *BMa*, 73 (December 1906): 1007; *BMa*, 74 (January 1907): 98; *BMa*, 74 (March 1907): 426; *BMa*, 74 (June 1907): 992; *BMa*, 77 (November 1908): 784; *BMa*, 80 (March 1908): 508; *BMa*, 83 (September 1911): 379; *BMa*, 87 (September 1913): 223; *BMa*, 87 (November 1913): 547; W. R. Morehouse, *Bank Deposit Building* (New York: Bankers Publishing Co., 1918), 175.

8. "Advertising in the Panic," *BMa*, 75 (December 1907): 917; "The Man Behind," *BMa*, 76 (March 1908): 390–91. Advertisement reprinted in *BMa*, 76 (April 1908): 584.

9. Advertisement reprinted in *BMa*, 86 (June 1913): 722. Advertisements in *BMa*, 121 (July 1930): 34, 85, 76.

10. "Portland Trust Co. of Oregon," *BMa*, 74 (June 1907): 990; "Largest on the Honor Roll," *BMa*, 75 (September 1907): 411; "How Banks Are Advertising," *BMa*, 76 (January 1908): 82; "Chicago History Dramatized," *BMo*, 45 (May 1928): 27. Advertisements reprinted in Morehouse, *Bank Deposit Building*, 197; *BMa*, 91 (October 1915): 534. Letter reprinted in *BMa*, 91 (October 1915): 535.

11. Henry S. Henschen, *A History of The State Bank of Chicago from 1879 to 1904* (Chicago: Lakeside Press, 1905), preface.

12. Advertisement reprinted in *BMa*, 80 (June 1910): 964.

13. Robert G. Cleland and Frank B. Putnam, *Isaiis W. Hellman and the Farmers and Merchants Bank* (San Marino, CA: Huntington Library, 1965), 31–42, 58–65. Part of the material concerning the crisis of 1873 is from a description, written at that time by Walter C. McQuillen, that appeared in the book. See also Ira B. Cross, *Financing an Empire: History of Banking in California* (Chicago: S. J. Clarke, 1927), 618–19.

14. Marquis James and Bessie R. James, *Biography of a Bank: The Story of Bank of America N.T, & S.A.* (New York: Harper & Brothers, 1954), 37–39, 119–24.

15. James M. Smallwood, *An Oklahoma Adventure of Banks and Bankers* (Norman: University of Oklahoma Press, 1979), 25.

16. "How Banks Are Advertising," *BMa*, 76 (March 1908): 399.

17. Morehouse, *Bank Deposit Building*, 32.

18. Stoddard Jess, "Uniting the Work of the Receiving and Paying Tellers," *BMa*, 75 (July 1907): 117–18.

19. "New Unit System of Third National Bank, St. Louis," *BMa*, 96 (April 1918): 488; C. R. Smelser, "Handling Savings Accounts by the Unit Teller System," *BMo*, 39 (July 1922): 14–15+; Franklin Hamilton, "Houston Bank's New Quarters Designed for Service," *BMo*, 41 (February 1924): 78–81; C. P. Walker, "A Unit Teller System That Cut Operating Costs," *BMo*, 42 (October 1925): 16–17+.

20. "How Banks are Advertising," *BMa*, 86 (June 1923): 725.

21. B. C. Clarke, "Customers' Payroll Service Doubles Deposits," *BMo*, 43 (October 1926): 22+. Advertisement in *BMa*, 114 (February 1927): 267.

22. Will Payne, "The Workings of a Model Bank," *The World's Work*, 9 (February 1905): 5872–75; W. R. Morehouse, "The New Account Teller and the New Account Department," *BMa*, 86 (March 1913): 334–36; Arthur D. Welton, *The Making of a Modern Bank* (Chicago: Continental and Commercial Banks of Chicago, 1923): 50; H. N. Stronk, "Operating Policies," *BMo*, 45 (September 1928): 19–20+.

23. Albert R. Barrett, *Modern Banking Methods and Practical Bank Bookkeeping*, 5th ed. (New York: Bankers Publishing Co., 1907), 38; John Ring, "Filing Correspondence in a Large Trust Company," *BMa*, 91 (October 1915): 539–40; P. H. Siddons, "A Central Authority File," *BMo*, 44 (July 1927): 13.

24. Thomas D. Lockwood, "Forerunners and Genesis of the Telephone Exchange" (1915) repr. in Members of the Technical Staff, Bell Telephone Laboratories, *A History of Engineering and Science in the Bell System: The Early Years (1875–1925)*, M. D. Fagen, ed. (Murray Hill, NJ: Bell Telephone Laboratories, 1975): 727–79.

25. "Banking Publicity Notes," *BMa*, 73 (September 1906): 476; Arthur A. Ekirch, "Modern Appliances Used by Our Progressive Banks," *BMa*, 80 (March 1910): 417–19; "Peoples Trust Company, New York," *BMa*, 81 (July 1910): 111; Alvin F. Harlow, *Old Wires and New Waves* (New York: Appleton Century, 1936), 505; George D. Smith, *The Anatomy of a Business Strategy: Bell, Western Electric, and the Origins of the American Telephone Industry* (Baltimore: Johns Hopkins University Press, 1986), 38–40.

26. "Telephotographic Aid in Banking Transactions," *BMa*, 119 (July 1929): 129; Members of the Technical Staff, Bell Telephone Laboratories, *A History of Engineering and Science in the Bell System*, 785–86.

27. "Banking by Machinery," *The Review*, 6 (May 1909): 4–5; "Banking by Machinery," *The Review*, 6 (October 1909): 86–87 (FNBC archives). Advertisements reprinted in *BMa*, 78 (February 1909): 297; "How Banks Are Advertising," *BMa*, 84 (February 1912): 229.

28. Laurence J. Davis, "Telling the Story of Your Mechanical Aids," *BMo*, 36 (November 1919): 28; Martha Evans, *History of Fremont Bank and Trust Company (Fremont State Bank): 1904–1979* (Fremont, MI: Fremont Bank and Trust Company, 1979), 4.

29. "A New World Record," *BMa*, 82 (May 1991): 682–83.

30. K. T. Rood, "A New Messenger for the Banker," *BMa*, 119 (August 1929): 227+; A. Trigge, *A History of the Canadian Imperial Bank of Commerce*, Vol. III (Toronto: Canadian Bank of Commerce, 1934), 46; Members of the Technical Staff, Bell Telephone Laboratories, *A History of Engineering and Science in the Bell System*, 743–46. Advertisement in *NYT*, 15 March 1930.

31. "Economical Device for Handling Outgoing Mail," *BMa*, 95 (September 1907): 419–20; William H. Kniffen, *The Practical Work of a Bank* (New York: Bankers Publishing Co., 1919), 526.

32. "Mailing the Bank's Correspondence," *BMa*, 100 (May 1920): 727–79.

33. T. D. MacGregor, *Bank Advertising Plans* (New York: Bankers Publishing Co., 1913), 31–32. Advertisements in *BMa*, 110 (May 1925): 845; *BMa*, 110 (June 1925): 1010; *BMa*, 111 (July 1925): 39; *BMa*, 111 (September 1925): 363.

34. Susan Porter Benson, *Counter Cultures: Saleswomen, Managers and Customers in American Department Stores, 1890–1940* (Urbana: University of Illinois Press, 1988), 88.

35. Joseph F. Rehme, "Over $60,000 in Savings on Saturday Night," *BMo*, 43 (July 1926): 21–22; Larry Schweikart, *A History of Banking in Arizona* (Tucson: University of Arizona Press, 1982), 39. Advertisement reprinted in *BMa*, 77 (August 1908): 249.

36. Cross, *Financing an Empire*, 67; Cyril F. James, *The Growth of Chicago Banks* (New York: Harper & Brothers, 1938), 371; Thomas J. Noel, *Growing Through History with Colorado: The Colorado National Banks, the First 125 Years, 1862–1987* (Denver: Colorado National Bank, 1987), 30.

37. Neil Munro, *The History of the Royal Bank of Scotland* (Edinburgh: R.& R. Clarke, 1928), 105, 214–15; Charles A. Malcolm, *The History of the British Linen Bank* (Edinburgh: T. and A. Constable, 1950), 64, 99; Merrill Denison, *Canada's First Bank*, Vol. I (New York: Dodd, Mead, 1966), 2. See also Merchants' Bank of Halifax, *Rules and Regulations* (Halifax, Nova Scotia, Merchants' Bank, 1885), 20 (RB archives).

38. Olin W. Hill, "The Night and Day Bank of New York City," *The Business World*, 8 (September 1907): 827–35.

39. "An Automobile Bank to Call at Your Door," *NYT*, 10 November 1906; "The New Science of Business: A Night Bank on Wheels," *The World's Work*, 13 (February 1907): 8586; "Electric Vehicles for Banks," *BMa*, 83 (December 1911): 732–36.

40. "Night Bank for St. Louis," *NYT*, 5 October 1908; "Night Bank Opens in Times Square," *NYT*, 5 September 1910; "All-Night Bank for London," *NYT*, 5 August 1912; "Largest Day and Night Bank Opens New 20 Story Building," *BMa*, 109 (August 1924): 337. Advertisement reprinted in *BMa*, 84 (May 1912): 708. Information about the Day and Night Bank (Oklahoma City) was provided by Laura Cupp by telephone. See also advertisement in *Daily Oklahoman*, 3 July 1910.

41. Charles A. Goddard, "Productive Advertising Policy of a 24-Hour Bank," *BMa*, 98 (February 1919): 15; Cross, *Financing an Empire*, 633, 709, 713. Advertisements reprinted in *BMa*, 91 (November 1915): 708; *BMa*, 92 (January 1916): 82.

42. Barry Provorse, *The Peoples Bank Story* (Bellevue, WA: Documentary Book Publishers, 1987), 54–55. Advertisement reprinted in *BMa*, 114 (March 1927): 455.

43. "A Day and Night Deposit Venture That Is Meeting with Success," *BMa*, 80 (June 1910): 942–45.

44. "Night Depository Makes Shorter Hours," *BMa*, 115 (October 1927): 529+; "Curb Depository New Bank Service," *BMa*, 119 (November 1929): 870.

45. "From Current Bank Advertising," *BMa*, 74 (May 1907): 804; Erie County Savings Bank, *An Historical Sketch of the Erie County Savings Bank: 1854–1909* (Buffalo, NY: Erie County Savings Bank, 1909), 71; "Progressive Advertising," *BMa*, 86 (February 1913): 182–84; "How Banks Are Advertising," *BMa*, 87 (September 1913): 325; T. D. MacGregor, "Pertinent Points," *BMa*, 88 (May 1914):   496; "The Cash Value of Courtesy," *BMo*, 35 (June 1918): 15; Morehouse, *Bank Deposit Building*, 16; L. L. Hall, "Flashing a Welcome to the New Customer," *BMo*, 36 (August 1919): 16; Osgood Baley, "A Million a Year Growth in a Country Bank," *BMo*, 37 (March 1920): 17–19+; James and James, *Biography of a Bank*, 45; Vincent P. Carosso, *The Morgans: Private International Bankers, 1854–1913* (Cambridge, MA: Harvard University Press, 1987), 436.

46. "Keeping the Customer Waiting," *BMa*, 117 (December 1928): 948–49; R. H. Mottram, *Miniature Banking Histories* (London: Chatto and Windus, 1930), 97.

47. "How Banks are Advertising," *BMa*, 76 (January 1908): 82; Edwin G. Booz, "The Best Bank Location," *BMo*, 47 (May 1930): 44+.

48. Victor Ross, *A History of the Canadian Bank of Commerce*, Vol. II (Toronto: Oxford University Press, 1922), 294–95, plates 44, 45, 48; G. E. Mills and D. W. Holdsworth, "The B. C. Mills Prefabricated System: The Emergence of Ready-made Buildings in Western Canada," in *Canadian Historic Sites*, Occasional Papers in Archeology and History, No. 14 (Ottawa: Indian and Northern Affairs, 1975), 127–69; Noel, *Growing Through History with Colorado*, 18.

49. "How Banks Are Advertising," *BMa*, 81 (December 1910): 884; MacGregor, *Bank Advertising Plans*, 25; "A 'Get Acquainted' Counter," *BMa*, 101 (September 1920): 398; H. H. Smock, "How Lobby Signs Help to Hold Customers," *BMo*, 39 (February 1922): 74–75; Mahlon D. Miller, "Some of the Reasons Why Banks Lose Business," *BMo*, 39 (April 1922): 42; Frank L. Beach, "How It's Done – A Tabloid of Productive Ideas," *Burrough's Clearing House*, 7 (March 1923): 9; Jules C. Smith, "How We Doubled Our Deposits in Three Years," *BMo*, 46 (April 1929): 9–12+.

50. Susan P. Benson, "The Cinderella of Occupations: Managing the Work of Department Store Saleswomen, 1900–1940," *Business History Review*, 55 (Spring, 1981): 1-25.

51. An Old Cashier, "Advice to Bank Clerks," *BMa*, 39 (April, 1885): 736–37; D. M. Stewart, "Duties of the Teller in a Canadian Bank," *BMa*, 48 (December 1893): 436–40; I. L. Jones, "The Duties of a Bank Employee," *BMa*, 59 (July 1899): 73–75; "A Model Bank Cashier," *BMo*, 18 (September 1899):   251–53; Lucius Teter, "Savings Bank Advertising," *BMa*, 67 (November 1902): 845; J. H. Griffith, "Ought Bank Clerks to Be Good-Natured," *BMa*, 74 (January 1907): 87–88; Barrett, *Modern Banking Methods*, 286–88; "Unwavering Politeness," *BMa*, 76 (April 1908): 595; "Backing up Advertising," *BMa*, 81 (October 1910): 558; Arthur A. Ekirch, "Courtesy – The Basis of Success," *BMa*, 83 (November 1911): 586–87; "Courtesy," *System*, 28 (August 1915): 202–03; Charles D. Jarvis, "The Human Element in Banking," *BMa*, 91 (November 1915): 609–12; "Politeness in Banking," *BMa*, 93 (December 1916): 535; "Seven Principles of Courtesy," *BMa*, 95 (November 1917): 677–79; "The Cash Value of Courtesy," *BMo*, 35 (June 1918): 15; Harris A. Dunn, "The Cash Value of a Smile," *System*, 33 (April 1918): 565–67; "Courtesy," *JABA*, 12 (August 1919): 66; Edward J. Phelps, "Good Service and Good Servers," *JABA*, 13 (September 1920): 110–12; William G. Rose, "Why the Teller is Able to Make or Break Friendships," *BMo*, 39 (March 1922): 22; "What's All This Talk About Bank 'New Business'?" *BMo*, 41 (October 1924): 9–10;

Arthur J. Peel, "Double-Barreled Service from the Man Behind the Wicket," *BMo*, 42
(July 1925): 12; Henry A., "Letters Which Help the Bank," *ABAJ*, 18 (September 1925):
183–86+; Rollin H. Cross, "Our Lobby Man Makes Bank Service Real," *BMo*, 43 (July
1926): 32; Eugene C. Glasgow, "Grouchy Tellers?" *BMo*, 45 (May 1928): 11; W. H.
Burch, "Tellers Control Bank Growth," *BMo*, 30 (January 1930): 11–13+.

52. David R. Forgan, "Courtesy," *The Review*, 1 (April 1905): 93–94 (FNBC archives).

53. Charles D. Jarvis, "The Human Element in Banking," *BMa*, 91 (November 1915):
611; Franklin J. Lewis, "How Politeness Counts at the Teller's Window," *BMo*, 38
(January 1921): 15–17. Advertisements reprinted in *BMa*, 78 (June 1909): 1004; *BMa*,
84 (February 1912): 229; *BMa*, 87 (September 1913): 325.

54. Rollin G. Osterwies, *Charter Number Two: The Centennial History of the First
New Haven National Bank* (New Haven, CT: First New Haven National Bank, 1963), 37;
Haas, *A History of Banking in New Haven*, 52; "A Currency Washing Machine," *The
Review*, 11 (July 1914): 42–43 (FNBC archives).

55. "Reducing Noise in Bank Buildings," *BMo*, 41 (October 1924): 70; John S.
Parkinson, "Noise Control and Banking Efficiency," *BMa*, 119 (December 1929):
1077–78.

56. Gerald H. Bradford, "Enclosing the Machinery in a Sound-Proof Room," *BMo*, 41
(October 1924): 64–67.

57. "Scientific Lighting for Banks," *BMa*, 84 (April 1912): 590–93. Advertisements
in *BMa*, 118 (February 1929): 192; *BMa*, 84 (January 1912): 92.

58. "Banking by Machinery," *The Review*, 5 (November 1908): 97–99; "Banking by
Machinery," *The Review*, 6 (March 1910): 168–69 (FNBC archives); "Checks for the
Busy Customer," *BMo*, 36 (June 1919): 76.

59. "Photography in French Banks," *BMa*, 40 (October, 1885): 310; Harris Croswell,
"Accurate Method Saves Time in Copying Trust Statements," *BMo*, 41 (May 1924): 30.

60. Trigge, *A History of the Canadian Bank of Commerce*, Vol. III, 421; C. H. Bible,
"A New Labour-Saver," *Royal Bank Magazine*, 10 (January 1930): 12–13 (RB archives).
Eastman Kodak documents: "The Recordak Corporation," *The Kodak Magazine*, 9
(January 1929): 3–4; *Recordak Corporation Summary* (1954, rev. 1956); *Highlights of
Microfilming History* (1953); public relations release on the death of George L. McCarthy
(1954). Promotional documents distributed by Recordak Corporation: *Improved Banking
with the Recordak* (late 1920s); *Use and Care of the Recordak* (October 1929); *Recordak:
A Banker's Invention that Saves Time and Money* (early 1930s); *Recordak: An
Indisputable Record That Protects the Bank Against Fraud* (early 1930s) (Eastman Kodak
Company archives).

61. Harry T. Jones, "How the Clerk's Time Helps to Pay Dividends," *BMo*, 35 (January
1918): 13; Ralph P. Anderson, "What Is this Thing Called Service," *BMo*, 39 (December
1922): 30.

62. "Machinery in Banks," *BMa*, 92 (April 1916): 543–46.

63. "A Successful Mechanical Appliance for Bank Clerical Work," *BMa*, 84 (February
1912): 233–37.

64. H. R. Crock, "Reducing Errors in the Accounting Routine," *BMo*, 35 (July 1918):
18–19.

65. James A. Murphy, "An Efficiency Marking System for the Bank Clerk," *BMa*, 99
(July 1919): 18–20.

66. "A Radical Departure in Savings Bank Advertising," *BMa*, 74 (May 1907): 800–02; W. H. Kniffen, "Testing Time in the Savings Bank," *BMa*, 82 (March 1911): 339–47; "How Banks are Advertising," *BMa*, 81 (September, 1910): 402.

67. W. R. Morehouse, "Correcting Customers' Addresses," *BMa*, 86 (February 1913): 151.

3

Service Thought

The final chapter on service discusses service marketing thought. "Thought" may be taken to mean the organized views and principles or the intellectual product of a group of individuals. In this case, the producers were not intellectuals but bankers, and the principles were not organized in one text but spread across sources. The themes discussed in this chapter concern the distinction between functional service and service delivery, service properties, the similarity of product versus service marketing, and gap theory.

First, bankers clearly understood the difference between functional service and service delivery. James I. Clarke, second vice president of the National Bank of Commerce in New York, observed in 1920 that "Under the term 'service,' he [a banker] includes a number of auxiliary activities calculated to assist his own customers and other business men, and he also has in mind the way in which these various functions, banking and others, are performed." Furthermore, the use of the term "quality" by Edward H. Kittredge, publicity manager of the Old Colony Trust Company (Boston), in 1923 implicitly acknowledges the inestimable importance of how a service is conducted: "The external house organ seeks to sell not only the many definite services your bank has to offer, but the *quality* of its service and facilities."[1]

Second, service properties are those traits that distinguish a service from a physical good: intangibility, perishability, heterogeneity, and inseparability of production and consumption. Economists had long grappled with service and its properties: Adam Smith (1723–1790) considered some services unproductive, and Jean-Baptiste Say (1767–1832) said that services are activities consumed at the time of production (i.e., inseparability) and coined the term "immaterial

Table 3.1
Service Characteristics

Intangibility:

He [a bank salesman] is selling something which is intangible. (L. R. Dean, unidentified, 1914)

A bank has not the concrete articles and prices to advertise that a merchant has. (Ralph P. Anderson, advertising manager, Sacramento Bank, 1920)

They [banks] have nothing physical to sell. (Everett Currier, Charles Everett Johnson, Co., 1920)

Financial advertisers have a particularly hard and impregnable problem in the intangibility of the goods which they offer. (C. H. Handerson, publicity manager, Union Trust Company, Cleveland, 1923)

Heterogeneity:

If a large paint concern manufactured paint with as uneven results as the average bank gives service, then the paint concern would soon fall by the wayside. (William O. Rose, unidentified, 1922)

But it [bank service] is not like a commodity that is fixed in nature and quality when it leaves the factory. It is, on the contrary, dependent from day to day and week to week on the continuous support of the operating personnel. (W. W. Douglas, vice president, Bank of Italy, San Francisco [later Bank of America], 1922)

[A bank] . . . is not offering a standardized, machine-made article, but a slighly personalized, confidential service. (G. Prather Knapp, first vice president, Bankers Service Corporation, New York, 1925)

Perishability:

When a service is ready for delivery, it at once begins to depreciate. Service cannot be stored. Neither can it be salvaged. Service is perishable—sell it quickly. (L. A. Downs, president, Illinois Central Railway, 1929)

Sources: For intangibility: L. R. Dean, "Selling Bank Service," *BMa*, 89 (November 1914): 514; Ralph P. Anderson, "A Bank Strengthens Friendship by Advertising," *PI*, 111 (April 29, 1920): 154; Everett Currier, "Selecting the Dress for Your Printed Message," *BMo*, 37 (July 1920): 25; C. H. Handerson, "Merchandising 'Save-at-Shop' Banking to Employers and Employees," *PI*, 125 (25 October 1923): 97. For heterogeneity: William G. Rose, "Why the Teller Is Able to Make or Break Friendships," *BMo*, 39 (March 1922): 22–23+; W. W. Douglas, "Does Your Bank Force Read Your Copy," *BMo*, 39 (July 1922): 23; G. Prather Knapp, "Controlling the Bank's New Business Department," *BMo*, 42 (April 1925): 12. For perishability: L. A. Downs, "Service Is Perishable: Sell It Quickly," *BMo*, 46 (January 1929): 15.

Table 3.2
Product Versus Service Marketing Similarity

Bank advertising is subject to the same laws as any other advertising, because it is intended to react upon the same objects—namely, people—in the mass and class. (C. H. Handerson, publicity manager, Union Trust Company, Cleveland, 1923)

The bank has just as clearly defined a selling problem to meet as has the manufacturer or distributor of any article of commerce . . . . There is, therefore, nothing intangible about the problem of bank advertising. (J. H. Puelicher, president, American Bankers Association, 1923)

It is coming to be generally agreed that banking service is a commodity, to be offered for sale in fundamentally the same way as hosiery, automobile tires or radios. The business of handling people's money does, and should, have a greater air of dignity than most businesses have, but, none the less, the basic principles underlying the sale of commodities are the same. (Wayne L. Thieme, new business manager, Tri-State Loan & Trust Company, Fort Wayne [IN], 1928)

The same fundamental rules of marketing apply with equal force to selling trust accounts as to selling any product no matter what it is. (Oliver J. Neibel, Commerce Trust Company, Kansas City, 1930)

The one certain point is that conditions, styles, and outlooks change with securities, just as they change in the field of commodities. It is just as essential for the dispenser of securities to study and analyze his markets as it is essential for the manufacturer or distributor of soap, a perfume, a food, or an automobile. These questions and the scores of others which could be raised concerning financial advertising, when stripped of their shop language are seen to be singularly like ordinary marketing problems for commodities. (Paul Cherington, director of research, J. Walter Thompson, in a speech before the fifteenth annual convention of the Financial Advertisers' Association, 1930)

Sources: C. H. Handerson, "Why Not Advertise Banks like Soaps or Soups," *PI*, 123 (7 June 1923): 97; J. H. Puelicher, "What Have Banks to Sell?" *PI*, 122 (15 February 1923): 33; Wayne L. Thieme, "The 'New Business Problem' for the Averaged Sized Bank," *BMa*, 117 (August 1928): 233; Oliver J. Neibel, "Five Basic Sales Policies and Their Application to Banking," *BMo*, 47 (April 1930): 9; Paul Cherington, "Fifteenth Annual Convention of the Financial Advertisers' Association," *TC*, 51 (September 1930): 373.

product" (i.e., intangibility). Table 3.1 presents quotations demonstrating bankers' awareness of three of the four service properties. Intangibility was mentioned as early as the 1910s, and heterogeneity and perishability as early as the 1920s. The only reference to perishability in the bank trade press was written by the president of a railroad. No reference to inseparability was

Table 3.3
Product Versus Service Marketing Dissimilarity

Bank advertisers have a specialized problem. They have nothing physical to sell. (Everett Currier, Charles Everett Johnson Co., Chicago, 1920)

The friendly attitude toward customers is far more important in a bank than in a merchandising establishment. A customer may sometimes purchase merchandise of merit from an indifferent sales person, but he will seldom or never recognize the merit of bank service if it is rendered by uninformed, unenthusiastic or unhappy men and women. (S. C. Stallwood, vice president, Northern Trust Company, Chicago, 1923)

Methods employed in commercial advertising cannot be adopted bodily to financial institutions because of the intangibility of the "product." (G. A. O'Reilly, unidentified, 1924)

Sources: Everett Currier, "Selecting the Dress for Your Printed Message," *BMo*, 37 (July 1920): 25; S. C. Stallwood, interviewed by G. Prather Knapp, "Is the New Business Manager Interested in Employees?" *BMo*, 40 (March 1923): 16; G. A. O'Reilly, "Taking a Novel Slant on Bank Merchandising," *BMo*, 41 (July 1924): 40.

identified in any sources. These seeming contradictions may be explained by the combination of service properties characterizing bank service. Bank service is intangible and heterogeneous, but it is not perishable or inseparable. Rail passenger service is produced while consumed, and empty seats in a car cannot be stored for use another day. The rail president, in stressing perishability, was concerned with what is perhaps the most important service property in the passenger rail industry. Bankers do not produce a service in anticipation of demand, but manufacture their product only when demand arises. Thus loans are evaluated only upon demand, and interest is calculated only for those accounts on the books. Furthermore, the production of the service does not accompany consumption. Loans are not evaluated, and interest on accounts is not calculated, contemporaneously with customer access to funds. The origin of the heterogeneity idea is not known, but it would seem unlikely that bankers were the first to document the concept. Nevertheless, they understood the importance of the idea in their service industry. Thus, the concepts of perishability and inseparability were available to bankers, but they spread the word on intangibility and heterogeneity because it was applicable to their special case.[2]

Third, Tables 3.2 and 3.3 present quotations clearly showing that a debate over the similarity of product versus service marketing existed during the 1920s. Paul Cherington, director of research at J. Walter Thompson, and J. H. Puelicher, president of the American Bankers Association, took part in the debate. A similar debate that took place among marketing professors during the 1970s was a more sophisticated repetition of the theme stated more than half a century earlier.[3]

Table 3.4
Gap Theory Statements

When a bank spends a lot of money in advertising to solicit accounts and new business promising courteous attention at the hands of officers and employees, it is very poor business policy, to say the least, if the men of the bank do not do their part in fulfilling these promises . . . . The men of the working staff should know just what advertising their institution is doing, what promises are made and what facilities and information are placed at the disposal of the public, and then prepare themselves to work in harmony with the advertising for the good of the institution. (*The Bankers' Magazine*, 1908)

. . . the advertising must be sufficiently conservative, so that every promise which it makes can be fulfilled by the equipment and organization of the bank. It would manifestly be unwise to describe, in an advertisement, some equipment or facility which the bank does not possess . . . . when special [advertising] emphasis is being placed upon any one facility, those persons on the force, who have care of the department, or line of business, should be carefully informed with regard to all the details. (A. M. Ingraham, unidentified, 1912)

Good advertising backed up by poor service will lose practically all of its effect. (W. D. Vincent, cashier, Old National Bank of Spokane [WA], 1913)

It is recognized everywhere that no matter how attractive a bank's advertisements may be, profitable business will not result unless the bank's services meet the promises implied. (Fred G. Heuchling, vice president, North-Western Trust & Savings Bank, Chicago, 1925)

Advertising may pave the way, may even bring a certain business to the bank, but unless the bank's employees live up to the advertising ideal, there is a lack of coordination that seriously handicaps the bank and acts as a positive brake upon all forward progress of any consequence. (M. E. Tate, vice president, Security State Bank, Keokuk [IA], 1927)

Sources: "Backing up Advertising," *BMa*, 76 (April 1908): 594; A. M. Ingraham, "Backing up Advertising," *BMa*, 85 (September 1912): 269; W. D. Vincent, "Service as an Advertisement," *BMa*, 87 (June 1913): 49; Fred G. Heuchling, "Reaching out for Business Among the Foreign-Born," *BMo*, 42 (September 1925): 11; M. E. Tate, "More Profitable Accounts," *BMo*, 44 (June 1927): 9.

Fourth, Table 3.4 presents quotations on gap theory. A gap is a difference between two constructs. Many gaps exist in service marketing: a difference between what is communicated to consumers about a service and what consumers receive; a difference between what managers believe consumers expect and what consumers actually expect; and so on. Gaps are important because they may impact the performance of the firm. If consumers expect more than they receive—because of exaggerated communications — then perceptions of service quality may decline and business volume may follow suit. The quotations in

Table 3.5
Gap Theory in Use

. . . [employees] must be familiar with circulars and advertising literature sent out and the promises therein contained; must be familiar with statements and promises made over the counter, and, largely, those made in correspondence, and in faithfully redeeming those promises in . . . service to that patronage. (excerpt from a letter from management to employees of a Cedar Rapids [IA] bank, 1911)

The fact that it is impossible for the officers to meet and deal personally with the many who come daily in the transaction of business, places upon employees the responsibility of properly reflecting the ideals of the institution. In order that you may do this you are urged to follow carefully the advertising and to do your part in seeing that patrons find here the atmosphere and the service which will be promised in the bank's publicity. You are asked to read in the newspapers all the advertising of the bank and keep yourselves "in tune" with it.   (excerpt from letter to employees by Joseph F. Sartori, president of the Security Trust & Savings Bank, Los Angeles, on the eve of a major advertising campaign, 1915)

The bank is continually advertising these [new] services and using them as selling points in securing new business. Imagine the impression a new customer would receive who came in and found it only newspaper talk. (excerpt from an item in the First National Bank of Fort Wayne [IN] employees' magazine, 1928)

Sources: "Co-operation of Employees," *BMa*, 82 (June 1911): 799–800; "Banking Publicity," *BMa*, 91 (December 1915): 821–22; "Living the Services Advertised," *BMa*, 4 (May 1928): 63.

Table 3.4 are much less sophisticated than current discussions on gap theory. In particular, they concentrate on one gap—a difference between consumers' expectations as influenced by communications (e.g., advertising) and realized service. Gap identification occurred as early as 1908. Table 3.5 presents quotations that are excerpts from internal bank documents directed to employees. For example, Joseph F. Sartori's letter instructed employees to adjust their behavior in accordance with the bank's newspaper advertising. This plainly illustrates that gap theory was more than an idealist concept incapable of being operationalized. During the 1910s, Sartori was the acknowledged leader of banking in Southern California and the Security Trust & Savings Bank was the largest in the Los Angeles area.[4]

Finally, consider a classification of advertising that appeared in *The Bankers' Magazine* in 1902.

It [advertising] may all be divided into two general classes— voluntary and quasi-voluntary advertising. Voluntary advertising includes the use of periodical, handsome stationery, useful souveniers, the handy pamphlet and instructive statement. In a measure, involuntary advertising is the successful conclusion of important transactions, an exemplary administration, the courteous treatment of customers, luxurious quarters, social representation and, incidentally, the fact that clean money is paid out over the bank's counters.[5]

What we have here is the idea that a set of factors exists that is separate from but equally important to advertising, and that the factors in the set bear some similarity to contemporary determinants of service quality (e.g., tangibles, courtesy).

In summary, bankers understood how products differed from services, but were unable to resolve whether this led to material differences in marketing. They were aware of gap theory and institutionalized the concept. They understood that the service performed was different from how the service was performed, and that how the service was performed could materially affect the customer's perception of the quality of service received. In the factor of how a service was performed were variables that included tangibles, transaction velocity, accessibility, and security. The total sum of service thought as formally articulated by bankers of the early twentieth century, combined with what they actually practiced, yields the inescapable conclusion that bankers were highly sensitized to basic service marketing principles.

NOTES

1. James I. Clarke, "The Spirit of Service," *JABA*, 13 (September 1920): 136; Edward H. Kittredge, "House Organs for Banks," *The Printing Art*, 41 (July 1923): 455.

2. Adam Smith, *An Inquiry into the Nature and Causes of the Wealth of Nations* (1776; repr., New York: Random House, 1937); Jean-Baptiste Say, *A Treatise on Political Economy* (1821; repr., New York: A. M. Kelly, 1964).

3. Perhaps the most comprehensive review of the services marketing literature, where literature is defined as written work produced by university professors, is in Raymond P. Fisk, Stephen W. Brown, and Mary Jo Bitner, "Tracking the Evolution of the Services Marketing Literature," *Journal of Retailing*, 69 (Spring 1993): 61–103. They identified three periods: (1) crawling out (pre-1980), (2) scurrying about (1980-85), and (3) walking erect (1986-present).

4. Marquis James and Bessie R. James, *Biography of a Bank: The Story of Bank of America N.T. & S.A.* (New York: Harper & Brothers, 1954), 62.

5. R. M. Richter, "Bank Advertising," *BMa*, 64 (April 1902): 569–70.

II

Segmentation

4

Age Segmentation

This chapter concerns children and youth. In some instances, the distinction between child and adult appears quite natural. In apparel and footwear, size and design are dependent on both age and gender. In reading material, children's tastes and abilities differ from those of adults. In other instances, such as banking, insurance, and transportation, the child–adult distinction may appear unwarranted and artificial. Yet some bankers paid considerable attention to the child market (through school savings programs), although these efforts never eclipsed those directed to adult segments. Providing banking service to children was almost never profitable in the short run, a fact well understood by bankers. Two explanatory motives are apparent for their involvement. First, banks were interested in cultivating children (and youth) for their long-run potential. The argument made sense at the end of the nineteenth century, when American mobility was deterred by the infant but developing transportation infrastructure. Second, inculcating thrift, particularly among children, was a morally right cause. A minority reasoned that indoctrinating children in thrift would "turn them into little sordid, cold-hearted economists," but popular sentiment leaned toward thrift as a virtuous trait that could eradicate poverty and destitution, and provide for families in time of illness or unemployment. This chapter begins with a description of European antecedents to American school savings and thrift education efforts. The unprofitability of children savers is discussed along with government involvement. Brief mention is made of the Canadian experience. Other promotions and services for children are then discussed.[1]

The second focus of this chapter is youth segmentation, which is comprised of two distinct yet related activities: (1) marketing to youth or selecting youth as a target market and (2) imbuing a product with youthful attributes, and marketing that product to both youth and older age groups. Youth segmentation

was critical to Pepsi's 1960s campaign, but recent research has traced the practice
back to the 1880s and established that it became an increasingly popular strategy
during the early part of the twentieth century. While suppliers of health and
beauty aids, apparel, footwear, automobiles, soft drinks, and tobacco products
were keenly alert to youth marketing opportunities by 1930, suppliers of financial
services clearly were not. The insurance, banking, and securities industries—
where safety, security, experience, and conservatism are hallmarks of
success—could hardly be criticized for not wanting to introduce the recklessness
of acne-faced youth into advertising and promotions. Rather, the financial
industry continues to this day to project images of experience and solidity.
Selecting the youth market as worthy and potentially profitable is another matter
altogether. What is clear, and will be demonstrated, is that banks carefully
divided the youth market into subsegments to ferret out only those perceived as
profitable. This is similar to Filene's college town outlets, operated before 1940,
that sought out a youth subsegment wealthier than the average emancipated
youth.[2]

EUROPEAN ROOTS OF SCHOOL SAVINGS BANKING

The roots of providing banking service to children in America can be traced
back to European school savings banks, the first of which were created by
teachers in small, German mountain towns during the 1820s. Initial school bank
operators did not require or desire the involvement of incorporated banks: rather,
children's deposits were held in government-sponsored postal banks. The
sentiments of the populace concerning thrift among children were favorable and
reached the upper echelons of German society. During the 1890s, Prince
Bismark described the virtues of thrift.

> This new branch of educators, *die Schulsparcasse*, as being the apprenticeship
> of economic and moral life for the laboring people, the seminary of all other
> popular institutions, and as one of the forces of moral education, which
> beginning at the tractable age, trains the new generation to a sober and regular
> life, to self-control, and in those domestic and social values which in the adult
> constitute a strong, virile character.

By the end of the nineteenth century, with the aid of national nonprofit
organizations, parents, educators, and government, school savings banking in
Germany was widespread. By 1896, deposits totaled $1.2 million from 1,728
school banks. In some kingdoms and provinces every community reportedly had
a school savings bank.[3]

During the 1870s, school savings banking spread to France, Belgium,
England, and Wales, and the practice was widespread by the end of the
nineteenth century. In France in 1886, there were some 24,000 school savings
banks with $2.5 million in deposits from 500,000 students; in Italy in 1891, there
were over 100,000 school savings depositors; in Belgium in 1893, 5,282 school
savings banks had about 240,000 depositors; and in England and Wales in 1894,
8,548 schools promoted thrift and savings.[4]

Just as the virtues of thrift were recognized by German royalty, so they were recognized by other European political and religious figures. In 1888 the wife of the French president, Madame Carnot, held a Christmas party at the Elysée Palace for 200 destitute children and gave each a bank account containing ten francs. In the same year, Pope Leo XIII gave a number of children bank accounts containing 100 francs. The activities of these and other well-known figures could not go unnoticed among the population of Europe or America, and the seeds had been sown for transplanting the practice across the Atlantic.[5]

U.S. SCHOOL SAVINGS BANKING

There were one or two abortive efforts to organize school savings banks in America prior to the establishment of the first "permanent" plan by Jean H. Thiry in 1885. Originally from Belgium, Thiry was a retired businessman who sponsored thrift education after becoming a Long Island City (New York) school commissioner. He did much to popularize the adoption of school savings banking across the nation by writing brochures and collecting and distributing statistics.[6]

There was one critical difference between European and American school savings banks. In Europe, children's deposits were normally held by government-backed postal savings banks. But postal savings banks, while discussed in America for more than forty years and recommended by more than ten postmasters general, did not come into being until 1910. In Europe, banks, if educators desired, could be kept out of schools to protect children from capitalism ideas; but in America, thrift educators, if they wanted deposits to earn interest (which they did, because it was a major lesson of thrift) had to seek out the active involvement of banks.[7]

Table 4.1 lists municipalities adopting school savings banks in America. For each location, the number of schools in the plan, the number of depositors, and total deposits are provided. The region with the greatest early adoption was the Northeast, notably New York and Pennsylvania. There were also pockets of thrift education in Nebraska and in southern California. A few schools participated in the plans in North Dakota and Ohio. Total deposits as of February 1892 were $136,515.

Table 4.2 presents data at the national rather than the school level. Most of the data in Table 4.2 come from the annual reports of the American Bankers Association. The Association was somewhat slow in promoting thrift education, not forming a Committee on Education to promote school thrift until 1919. Concurrently, it began publishing annual reports on the state of school savings banking in America. The lag of almost 35 years between the establishment of school savings banking in America and involvement by the American Bankers Association suggests a reluctance by the Association to dedicate resources to the cause.

Table 4.1
Pre-1893 School Savings Banking in America

Year	Institution/ Location	Number of Schools	Number of Savers	Student Savers (%)	Total Deposits ($)
1885	Long Island City, NY	14	2,385	46	14,348
1886	Rutland, VT	6	834	64	3,215
	Islip, NY	1	70	26	1,013
	Elmira, NY	4	1,226	55	5,180
1887	Lincoln, NE	12	1,500	29	5,214
	Amsterdam, NY	6	815	32	10,733
1888	Horneville, NY	4	822	33	4,264
	Y.M.C. Institute, NYC	1	175	29	16,103
	Jamestown, NY	10	673	24	2,600
	Buffalo, NY	5	954	45	2,052
1889	Kingston, NY	2	212	38	960
	Olean, NY	7	835	52	3,738
	Cazenovia, NY	1	175	55	1,317
	Winfield, NY	1	60	36	255
	San Diego, CA	12	750	27	2,151
	National City, CA	5	105	34	431
	Brooklyn School 31, NYC	1	170	12	488
	Pottstown, PA	20	967	45	10,000
1890	Norristown, PA	6	1,204	47	6,405
	Shannonville, PA	1	23	33	98
	Cheltenham, PA	1	70	54	485
	Brookline, MA	12	818	41	4,702
	Chester, PA	13	1,025	31	8,285
	West Chester, PA	3	449	50	3,084
	Williamsport, PA	14	2,500	55	9,000
	Conshohocken, PA	2	384	52	1,329
	West Grove, PA	2	50	32	260
	Wilkes-Barre, PA	5	—	—	—
	Omaha, NE	37	4,547	32	6,449
	Juniata, NE	2	85	46	110
	Philmont, NY	1	137	49	653
	Schuyler, NE	4	175	29	1,465
	Greenville, OH	2	286	32	830
	West Whiteland, PA	4	44	28	123

Table 4.1 Continued

1891	Phillipsburg, PA	1	385	58	1,400
	Doylestown, PA	1	180	60	1,107
	Campello, MA	1	200	38	717
	Rockland, MD	1	92	53	365
	North Wales, PA	1	120	60	505
	Warren, PA	15	300	39	2,960
	Waveland, IN	1	155	67	133
	Lock Haven, NY	4	684	55	1,111
	Y.M.C.A., Troy, NY	1	20	53	6
	Corry, PA	4	401	44	380
	Guide Rock, NE	1	34	29	32
	Mendocino, CA	1	66	37	167
	Brookville, PA	2	183	34	221
1892	Mayville, ND	1	37	31	69
	Camden, NJ	1	48	53	2
	Phoenixville, PA	23	—	—	—
	Parkesburg, PA	5	—	—	—
Totals		285	27,430	—	136,515

Source: Adapted from Sara L. Oberholtzer, "School Savings Banks," *Annuls of the American Academy of Political and Social Science*, 3 (July 1892): 14–29.

As seen in Table 4.2, the number of schools, depositors, and total balances for all school savings banks grew slowly during the late nineteenth century. The 1920s was a period of tremendous growth in student depositors and total balances. The decline during the 1930s, the result of the Depression, was equally pronounced. Financial pressure forced banks to abondon marginal products, and many school savings departments were closed. And parents had children withdraw funds to cover expenses.

Table 4.2 also presents the number of individuals in the United States between 5 and 19 years of age and the ratio of this figure to the number of student depositors. The ratio rose from 0.12 percent in 1890 (about one in 835) to 0.73 percent in 1910 (about one in 137). Between 1920 and 1930, the ratio leapt from 1.47 percent to 12.7 percent (from about one in 70 to about one in 8).

School Savings Bank Operationalization

Technological and administrative innovations adopted between 1885 and 1930 eased educator burdens. School savings bank systems developed from ones where teachers both taught thrift and recorded transactions to ones where teachers just taught thrift.

The Grand Rapids (Michigan) Savings Bank operation was fairly typical of late-nineteenth-century programs. Teachers bought $5 worth of penny stamps

Table 4.2
School Savings Banking, 1889–90 to 1939–40

	School Savings Banking: Total for United States				U.S. Population Aged 5–19	Depositors ÷ U.S. Population Aged 5–19 (%)
Year	Schools	Depositors	Deposits	Total Balance ($)		
1889–90	220	24,525	—	127,340	21,165,070	0.12
1894–95	—	30,921	402,020	157,164		
1909–10	1,168	203,458	—	870,696	27,921,375	0.73
1914–15	1,925	398,540	—	1,792,640		
1919–20	2,736	462,651	1,800,301	4,200,872	31,469,768	1.47
1924–25	10,163	2,869,497	16,961,560	25,913,531		
1929–30	14,610	4,597,731	29,113,063	52,049,849	36,164,601	12.71
1934–35	8,940	2,836,595	12,598,076	30,786,473		
1939–40	8,427	2,539,477	13,111,312	33,910,682	34,746,040	7.30

Sources: Schools, depositors, and deposits from: Sara L. Oberholtzer, "School Savings Banks," *Annals of the American Academy of Political and Social Science,* 3 (July 1892): 14–29; "School Savings Banks," 1 (no. 5, part 1), *Report of the Commissioner of Education* (Washington, D.C.: U.S. Government Printing Office, 1898), 160–64; American Bankers Association, *School Savings Banking, Sixteenth Annual Report* (New York: American Bankers Association, 1935), 5; "A Quarter Century of School Savings Banks," *BMa,* 80 (June 1910): 897–89; American Bankers Association, *School Savings Banking, Twenty-Second Annual Report* (New York: American Bankers Association, 1941), 22; U.S. population figures: *Historical Statistics of the United States, Colonial Times to 1970: Bicentennial Issue, Part 1* (Washington, D.C.: U.S. Government Printing Office, 1975), 15.

from the bank and sold them to students after weekly thrift lectures. Students pasted stamps in manila envelopes and opened interest-bearing savings accounts once 50 cents had been accumulated. On specific days, bank representatives arrived at schools, exchanged stamps and funds with teachers, and dropped off promotional material. Even after an account had been opened, students continued to purchase stamps from teachers, who updated passbooks and ledgers. Students vistited the bank only when making withdrawals.

One means to lighten educators' workload was to give students credit hours for operating a school bank. The Alameda (California) school savings plan, instituted in 1914, had a sizable student staff who not only operated a bank at their high school but also visited elementary schools, where they collected and entered deposits in ledgers. Another involvement reduction mechanism was stamp vending machines, called "automatic tellers" by supporters and "bank slot machines" by detractors. They first appeared in New York City during the mid-1910s, and by the early 1920s had spread to schools throughout the nation.[8]

A unique development in school savings banking occurred in Louisville, Kentucky. In 1919 the Liberty Insurance Bank, in conjunction with educators, began cultivating children's accounts. But community activists had a much more aggressive plan than a single institution's cultivating thrift among children. The bank's officers, along with members of the Louisville Board of Education and the Louisville School Thrift Association, approached the leading banks of the city and suggested that a distinct institution be created to handle children's accounts. The result was the School Savings Bank, begun in 1921 with capital of $100,000 contributed by 14 leading banks in the city, with deposits safeguarded by bonds. Managed by a woman, it was at that time the only bank in America devoted solely to servicing children's accounts. As in most other school savings systems, children were encouraged to make deposits after weekly thrift lectures. To accommodate working youth, depositors could bypass educational institutions and deal directly with the bank. On the basis of grades and deportment, outstanding students were given the honor of delivering deposits to the bank in a miniature safe. The bank did not engage in advertising, yet was able to boast deposits totaling $150,000 by the end of 1925 and almost as many accounts as school-aged children in the city. The creation of a separate bank for children fulfilled two purposes: (1) it relieved banks of direct involvement in a less than profitable practice and (2) because of the guaranty bonds, it presumably protected children depositors from defalcation.[9]

A final operationalization perhaps most relieved teachers. In 1922, 11 Los Angeles banks and a number of educators formed the Los Angeles School Savings Association. Home safes were distributed to schoolchildren, and when approximately one dollar had been saved, an interest-bearing account was opened at whichever participating bank parents chose. The banks were not allowed to solicit accounts, nor were they allowed to stimulate dormant or inactive ones, these activities being the responsibility of the Association. Aside from teaching thrift, teachers were eliminated from the process. Curiously, the Association hired a Dutch Cleanser salesman to promote the program.[10]

We can question the extent to which peer pressure and subtle coercion were inadvertently or advertently used to encourage thrift among children. Certainly, it would be obvious to students who in their class made a deposit after a thrift lecture and who did not. Parents not wanting their children to appear less privileged would find some money, no matter how little, for them to deposit. Coercion was not unknown in the sale of World War I Liberty Bonds; teachers were said to have called out in class the names of families not having purchased bonds, suggesting a lack of patriotism.[11]

Motives: Profitability and Thrift Legislation

Before describing the Canadian experience with school thrift, two points alluded to earlier are elaborated upon. The first centers on the profitability of school savings plans. Before 1902, nationally chartered banks in America were not allowed to accept savings accounts, a situation explaining the lack of involvement of large, nationally known banks such as The First National Bank of Chicago and the National City Bank of New York. In other cases, the savings banks linked with schools often found themselves in the minority. For example, Charles W. Garfield organized school banking in Grand Rapids, Michigan, during the 1890s. His request for a monopoly on school banking was initially rejected by educators; they later acquiesced when other banks in the region declined to participate. Garfield optimistically estimated that 1917 school savings operations added a paltry $805 to profits from deposits of $85,000. Yet the department consumed as much in resources one responsible for millions of dollars in commercial assets, and stationery and equipment expenses were the largest of any department in the bank. Garfield said:

> As soon as children reach the age when they leave school they take up their school savings business and transfer it to the regular savings department and if they go into business they stay with us in the commercial department. . . . if we shut our eyes to the indirect values that come to the bank it would be a losing game.

Garfield thus understood, as did many other bankers, that school banking was not immediately profitable. Research conducted during the 1920s provided empirical support of a different sort.

Table 4.3 summarizes account profitability research conducted by Paul Hardesty, publicity manager of the Union Trust Company, Chicago. It presents the percentage of profitable accounts by age group and gender. The pattern is quite clear: as age increases, so does profitability. Although the youngest age group in the study is 21–25, it is not difficult to extrapolate backward and see that juvenile accounts must have been unprofitable, primarily because of low balances. Hardesty observed:

Table 4.3
Percentage of Profitable Accounts, by Age and Gender

	Age Group (%)					
	21–25	26–30	31–35	36–40	41–45	
Female	21	37	40	39	40	
Male	18	23	26	29	34	

	Age Group (%)					Sample Size
	46–50	51–55	56–60	61–65	66–70	
Female	59	65	47	67	75	1,023
Male	37	33	47	60	57	1,002

Source: Paul L. Hardesty, "Are the Women Better Savers Than Men?" *BMo*, 41 (May 1924): 9–10+.

The practical question is whether to concentrate on young people at the age when they are most impressionable but when earning power and property accumulation are usually small; or upon the older people who have made some progress in both earning power and accumulation, but have become set in their habits of saving and spending. . . . evidently different motives can be used in appealing to youth and age. And with the adjustment of the appeal, the percentage of profitable accounts among younger people might show a healthy increase.[12]

The second point that requires elaboration centers on the reaction of lawmakers to thrift education efforts. In some cases they adjusted laws and fees to facilitate thrift education. For example, during the 1910s and 1920s, New Jersey, Ohio, and New York made it lawful for superintendents and principals to collect school savings deposits, and during the early 1920s California waived branch certificate fees for bank branches doing a majority of business in school savings. In other cases, legislators mandated the inclusion of thrift in educational curricula. Following enactments of this sort by East Coast states during the 1910s, a 1920–21 Nevada statute provided the following:

It is hereby the duty of all teachers in the public schools in the State of Nevada to teach in their respective schools lessons on the subject of thrift. These lessons shall emphasize the importance of industry, production, earning, wise spending, regular savings, and safe investment; also the importance of thrift in time and material. It shall also be the duty of the state board of education to prepare courses on the subject of thrift as outlined in Section 1 [previous paragraph], the same to be a part of the state courses for study for elementary and high schools.[13]

CANADIAN SCHOOL SAVINGS BANKING

The way in which Canadian bankers approached school-aged savers illustrates well their conservative nature relative to their American counterparts. In Canada, as in Europe and the United States, school savings banking had philanthropic origins. During the 1870s, several nonprofit "penny banks" were organized in Toronto by religious institutions. During the 1890s, one of these, the Fred Victor Mission, cooperated with local schools in cultivating thrift among children. Unfortunately, these banks lacked the skill and enterprise to handle deposits. The situation was exacerbated by the reluctance of Canadian banks to become involved. The Toronto penny banks sought relief from the federal government, which took the form of the Penny Bank Act (1903).

The Act established a range of requirements. A penny bank was required to have the words "Penny Bank" in its name, bank directors were unpaid, profits were retained by the bank (and not paid to directors or members who subscribed to the bank's guaranty fund [the minimum was $100]), deposits were accepted from any individual of any age (up to a maximum account value of $300), interest on deposits could not exceed the rate paid by the Canadian Post Office Savings Bank, loans were prohibited, and a penny bank could absorb an extant "savings association" operated for benevolent purposes.

The Penny Bank Act was designed so that Canadian bankers could assist the poor and the young without committing bank resources to marginally unprofitable segments. In 1905 the Penny Bank of Toronto was organized and assumed the liabilities of Toronto's earlier penny banks. Initial guaranty fund members included Sir Edmund Walker (president of the Canadian Bank of Commerce), D. R. Wilkie (president of the Imperial Bank), E. B. Osler (president of the Dominion Bank), and Duncan Coulson (president of the Bank of Toronto). Well-known financiers and Canadian senators also participated and the guaranty fund far exceeded minimum legal requirements. Deposits were $81,000 after one year, and grew to $172,000 by 1911, much of the increase coming from school-aged children. By 1911, operations had spread to Ottawa, London, and many small Ontario communities. To better describe the scope of operations, the bank changed its name in 1922 to the Penny Bank of Ontario. Deposits peaked at about $1.5 million during the mid-1930s. World War II siphoned small change toward the war effort, and in 1943 deposits were no longer accepted. When the Act was repealed in 1948, unclaimed deposits of less than one dollar—which totaled $80,000—were donated to Toronto's Hospital for Sick Children. The remaining $2.7 million, from some 79,000 depositors, was still on the books of the Post Office Savings Bank as of 1983.[14]

PROMOTIONS AIMED AT CHILDREN

A range of promotions was used by banks to socialize children in banking methods. Many were outside the auspices of school banking authorities as banks sought to reach children in and out of school. The practices are reviewed and categorized in the sections that follow.

Contests

Bank-sponsored contests for children began shortly after the start of the twentieth century and became increasingly popular. An early example was a contest run by the Century Banking Company (Jackson, Mississippi). In 1907 it sponsored an essay contest on "Why Deposit with Century Banking Co.?" that was open to public school students. The first prize was a choice of season tickets for the local baseball team, season tickets to a theater, a nickel a week for life, or a trip to the Jamestown Exposition. Essay contests on banking, thrift, or economy were perhaps the most popular. By 1920, banks had asked students to write bank advertisements and submit birdhouses for evaluation and prizes.[15]

Novelties

Banks distributed novelties such as specially designed children's books, folders, and blotters. By 1920, banks had given away thousands of novelties encouraging thrift among children or encouraging parents to teach thrift to their children. In many cases, demand outstripped supply. The Continental & Commercial National Bank of Chicago in 1920 published a book titled *Thrift After Mother Goose*. Over 17,000 copies were distributed in a one-week period during December 1920. In 1913 the St. Louis Union Trust Company distributed a booklet, "directed at the child," titled *The Primer of Thrift*. The back of the booklet was a slotted postcard that stored ten dimes. When the slots were filled, customers could open an interest-bearing savings account.[16]

Premiums

Premiums were one of the most popular promotional mechanisms directed to children. During the 1910s, the Central Trust Company of Illinois (Chicago) gave boys and girls between nine and 19 years of age who opened an account a copy of *Oh, Skin-nay!*, a popular juvenile book. During the early 1920s the Calumet Trust & Savings Bank (Chicago) celebrated the opening of a special children's teller by giving new and current children account holders a brightly colored cap (3,000 caps costing $450 were gone within two and a half days). The bank also ran a contest in which prizes of up to $20 were awarded to boys and girls securing new accounts, and a similar contest in which bicycles were given away. Other banks donated one dollar to a child's account when it was opened. In local newspapers, the Sacramento Valley Trust Company promoted April 4, 1911, as the day on which schoolchildren presenting the bank's advertisement would be given a passbook containing one dollar. At the end of five years, the one dollar plus accumulated interest could be withdrawn, regardless of whether the account had been used. Anticipating a large crowd, the bank announced that it would be open until 8 P.M. and would honor the offer for several days afterward if customer traffic required it. During the 1910s, the Union County Trust Company (Elizabeth, New Jersey) gave passbooks containing one dollar to local churches that distributed them as Sunday school prizes. Other banks scanned birth announcements and promoted the dollar premium through direct mail or paid-for advertising. The Bank of Barnegat (New Jersey) in 1913 sent the following letter to new parents:

> We understand that you have added another member to your family. Will you be so kind as to let us know the name and sex of the baby? We have placed $1.00 to its credit and have opened an account which will be compounded semi-annually with interest at three percent as the account is increased. Kindly call the bank and a home safe will be given to you for the baby.[17]

School-Directed Promotions

Some banks published house organs that were distributed to schools to complement school savings programs. These house organs first appeared early in the twentieth century. During the mid-1910s, *Thrift Magazine*, a house organ distributed by the Portsmouth (New Hampshire) Trust & Guarantee Company, was described as "especially valuable to the younger generation, but older persons will find on its pages much that will be helpful." During the 1920s, the Rochester Savings Bank published *The Thrift Advocate* to "encourage thrift in the school and home," the Poughkeepsie (New York) Savings Bank published *The Thrift Messenger*, the Rockaway (New York) Savings Bank published *School Savings Bank Journal*, the Home Savings Bank (Boston) published *The Busy Bee*, and the East New York Savings Bank published *The School Savings Bank Monitor*. During the 1910s and 1920s, banks placed advertisements in high school newspapers, offered tours of bank facilities, and provided blank report cards to schools at no charge. In the case of the latter, banks used the back page of the report card for their advertising because this "gets right into the homes—several thousand of them—and at the same time is quite a saving to the schools."[18]

Physical Accoutrements

Some banks went further than adjusting channels of distribution (e.g., using schools) or promotions to socialize and attract children: they physically adjusted the bank to better suit children. One of the more popular means was a special teller for children. Operationalizations ranged from the simple—a box on the floor with a sign above saying "Children's Teller"—to the complex—a miniature banking room for children. During the early 1920s, the Calumet Trust & Savings Bank (Chicago) and the Union Trust Company (Cleveland) opted for the simple operationalization to better serve children. The New Jamaica Plain branch of the Boston Five Cent Savings Bank in 1930 decided something more elegant was required.

> A miniature bank has been arranged inside of the bank building to take care of this youthful business. A small foyer is separated from the main banking room by eight Roman arches and their accompanying columns. Here is a counter twelve feet long and thirty inches high, which differs from a regulation bank counter only in size. It is equipped with grilles, tellers' cages, etc., and furnished with the usual equipment necessary to do a banking business. . . . Three clerks are seated behind the counter and work comfortably, dispatching "business as usual."

The First Trust & Savings Bank of Canton (Ohio) also created a special banking room for younger customers. In its new 1919 quarters, it operated a 28 × 128-foot banking room exclusively for boys, reported to be the only boys' department in the United States. The department had six cages, one reserved for Boy Scout accounts. Other special cages were planned; the bank hoped that other institutions for young men would encourage thrift among their members. The department had special passbooks printed with the words "Boys' Department" on them.[19]

Farm Clubs

Banks also cultivated the children of farmers, which served to improve relations with the farmers themselves. One of the more common promotions, a club for children, arose during the 1910s. For example, the Citizens State Bank (Jewell, Kansas) in 1916 organized a Pig Club. Forty boys between the ages of 10 and 16 within the bank's territory were selected for membership, each receiving a pig "immune from cholera." Parental approval was required. After a period, the pig was sold and its initial value was repaid to the bank. Ten percent of the selling price was deposited in the bank and could be withdrawn only to purchase more livestock. Accurate recordkeeping was required of club members, and a story of each pig's life was submitted to the bank for inclusion in *Our Booster*, the bank's house organ (first published 1912). *Our Booster* also promoted the bank's agricultural library, open to all county residents. Other bank-sponsored farm clubs at various locations were open to boys and girls and concentrated on sheep, baby beef, bees, dairy animals, and poultry.[20]

Canadian Banks

It was noted earlier that Canadian banks avoided school savings banking. Their conservatism did not, however, lead them to discourage all children's accounts. What they apparently avoided was school thrift accounts. Parents opening an account for a child was a different matter. Thus an advertisement by the Bank of Toronto during the 1920s said, "A Savings account for Christmas," and continued, "fortunate is the lad who receives a Bank of Toronto Savings Account for Christmas. It will appeal to the boy, whether son, nephew or grandchild—at the impressionable age when the lesson of saving will be retained." Other Canadian banks followed a similar strategy.[21]

YOUTH

Young Entrepreneurs

One youth subsegment of particular interest to bankers was young entrepreneurs. In 1907 newspaper advertisements, the First National Bank of Boston said, "Young men will do well to investigate the advantages offered them by this bank in financing their business," and the National Bank of the Republic (Chicago) said, "The young business man who has demonstrated ability successfully to conduct a small business will receive attention and consideration."

"The Young Man in Business," *The Bankers' Magazine* article that discussed these advertisements, said, "A bank that has helped a [young] man build up his business from small beginnings is in a position to reap the advantages that follow when business has grown to large proportions." The Peoples Bank & Trust Company (New Haven, Connecticut) in 1908 told "Ambitious Young Men" that a growing savings account gave one a "reputation" among bankers and businessmen and forged a solid path toward opening a business or buying into an established one.[22]

Newlyweds

Newlyweds comprised a second category of youth sought through "June appeal." These advertisements often played on the fear of young women about to enter matrimony with a less than frugal man. For example, a 1908 newspaper advertisement by the Houston National Bank said that a savings account created security at home, and a Citizens First National Bank (Albany, New York) advertisement directed to young women said, "After you are married, be sure to have a bank account," and "No man can be his best cramped by poverty." These appeals sprang up across the nation every June during the early twentieth century.[23]

College Students

Although much smaller proportionately during the early part of the twentieth century than now, college students were a particularly attractive youth segment because of their higher-than-average current and expected earning power, especially those attending prestigious universities. The efforts of banks located in college towns to attract college students did not go unnoticed in the trade press: in 1908 *The Bankers' Magazine* said that "financial institutions in college towns often make particular effort to secure the business of students and faculty." Banks advertised in college newspapers and used direct mail. For instance, the Stillwater State Bank and the Farmers & Merchants Bank (Stillwater, Oklahoma) advertised in the first issue of *The College Mirror* (May 15, 1895), the student newspaper of Oklahoma State University. In 1908 Percy D. Haughton, assistant secretary of the City Trust Company of Boston, wrote to Harvard University students from the company's Bunker Hill branch.

> If you propose being in the vicinity during the coming year, it would be a most excellent plan to become identified with a prominent Boston bank. We address you in the interests of City Trust Company, because we have noted that there is hesitancy on the part of young men in opening an account with a large banking institution. We wish you to feel, however, that your account, irrespective of its size, will be most welcomed at this Trust Company. As you may observe from the enclosed statement, many of our officers are Harvard graduates, and, for this reason, we take interest in those Harvard men who are about to start their business or professional career. With this end in view, the writer would be glad to see you at any time, and to advise you on all financial matters. Trusting that we may be of service to you.

Banks also delivered services on campus. Early attempts were undertaken by students and college administrators. The Women's College of Baltimore opened an on-campus private bank during the 1890s. Later efforts consisted of joint ventures. In 1915 the Middletown (Connecticut) National Bank opened a branch at Wesleyan University with student employees.[24]

Some promotions spanned both high school and college students. In 1924 the Union Trust Company of Detroit began sponsoring a university scholarship contest. Every year five $1,000 scholarships were awarded to high school seniors. Contest promotion involved bankers visiting high schools, high school newspaper advertising, awards to all entrants, and elaborate banquets. In 1928 every entrant was awarded a copy of Herbert Hoover's book, *American Individualism*. Not only did the bank receive widespread publicity among high school students, but some winners found summer or full-time employment at the bank.[25]

Gap Theory

Gap theory was applied not only in a general sense but also in relation to segment-specific efforts. A 1921 advertising campaign by the Equitable Trust Company of New York focused on attracting youth (not children). One newspaper advertisement said, "There is a young man in this city who is looking for a friendly bank." The bank president addressed gap theory in a letter on the campaign to employees:

> The success or failure of the campaign rests with all of us who make up the Equitable. Moreover, with the appearance of this first message we are under obligation to make good our representations. We must give to all attracted by the series the friendly and cordial reception and the personal attention they will expect.

In addition to the letter, staff were exposed to the advertisements as they were displayed throughout the bank.[26]

NOTES

1. *Canadian Journal of Commerce*, repr. in "Thrift," *BMa*, 41 (December 1885): 459.

2. Susan P. Benson, *Counter Cultures: Saleswomen, Managers and Customers in American Department Stores, 1890–1940* (Urbana: University of Illinois Press, 1988), 33; Stanley C. Hollander and Richard Germain, *Was There a Pepsi Generation Before Pepsi Discovered It? Youth-Based Segmentation in Marketing* (Lincolnwood, IL: NTC Business Books, American Marketing Association, 1992).

3. "School Savings Banks," 1 (no. 5, part 1, *Report of the Commissioner of Education*, Washington, D.C.: U.S. Government Printing Office, 1898), 160–64; "School Savings Banks," *BMa*, 55 (August 1897): 211–13.

4. Carobel Murphy, *Thrift Through Education* (New York: A. S. Barnes, 1929), 10.

5. Sara L. Oberholtzer, "School Savings Banks," *Annuls of the American Academy of Political and Social Science*, 3 (July 1892): 14–29.

6. Ibid.; American Bankers Association, *School Savings Banks, Sixteenth Annual Report* (New York: American Bankers Association, 1935).

7. Edwin W. Kemmerer, *Postal Savings: A Historical and Critical Study of the Postal Savings Bank System of the United States* (Princeton: Princeton University Press, 1917), 1–2.

8. Lawrence Dalton, "Children the Best Publicity Agents," *BMo*, 37 (April 1920): 24; C. J. Du Four, "How Alameda Has Educated Children," *BMo*, 38 (November 1921): 25; T. D. MacGregor, "A Step Toward Universal Thrift," *BMa*, 106 (May 1923): 843–50.

9. Ray E. Harrington, "How Louisville Bankers Are Winning School Savers," *BMo*, 34 (January 1926): 18+.

10. W. R. Morehouse, "The Los Angeles School Savings Plan," *BMa*, 106 (June 1923): 997–1001; F. A. Stearns, "Los Angeles Children Deposit $298,000 in School Savings," *BMo*, 40 (July 1923): 30–31.

11. Donald F. Dixon, "Advertising U.S. War Bonds in the First World War," *Journal of Nonprofit and Public Sector Marketing*, 3, 1 (1995): 65–80.

12. William Avery, "$90,000 in Deposits from the Children," *BMo*, 34 (October 1917): 15; Paul L. Hardesty, "Are the Women Better Savers Than Men?" *BMo*, 41 (May 1924): 9–10+.

13. American Bankers Association, *School Savings Banking* (New York: Ronald Press, 1923), 49–50.

14. W. A. Craick, "The School Savings Bank in Canada," *BMa*, 84 (March 1912): 325–28. A copy of the Penny Bank Act (passed October 24, 1903, by the Canadian federal government) was forwarded to the author (TD archives).

15. "Banking Publicity Notes," *BMa*, 75 (November 1907): 735.

16. T. D. MacGregor, *Bank Advertising Plans* (New York: Bankers Publishing Co., 1913), 55–56; "Thrift After Mother Goose," *The Four Cs*, 1 (January 1921): 28.

17. "Interesting the Children," *BMa*, 82 (June 1911): 797; C. L. Edholm, "Banks a Dollar for Every Baby," *The Illustrated World*, 19 (July 1913): 722–23; MacGregor, *Bank Advertising Plans*, 9–10; "How Banks Are Advertising," *BMa*, 88 (February 1914): 203; James R. Rhoades, "Novel Appeals That Always Gain the 'Kids' Attention," *BMo*, 38 (June 1921): 76–77.

18. MacGregor, *Bank Advertising Plans*, 23; "About a House Organ," *BMa*, 90 (March 1915): 349; American Bankers Association, *School Savings Banking*, 134–35.

19. Gilbert O. Gilbert, "Reaching out for Boys' Accounts," *BMo*, 36 (July 1919): 13; "How Banks are Advertising," *BMa*, 109 (August 1924): 238; "Five Cents Savings Bank Takes Nickels," *BMa*, 121 (July 1930): 140.

20. A. W. Shaw Company, *Advertising and Service* (Chicago: A. W. Shaw Company, 1918), 156–59.

21. 1924 advertisement by the Bank of Toronto appearing in *The Farmer's Almanac* (TD archives).

22. "The Young Businessman," *BMa*, 74 (April 1907): 630. Advertisement reprinted in *BMa*, 77 (August 1908): 249.

23. Advertisements reprinted in *BMa*, 76 (February 1908): 239; *BMa*, 77 (August 1908): 252.

24. "A College Bank," *BMo*, 18 (November 1899): 533; "How Banks are Advertising," *BMa*, 77 (August 1908): 258; "Students to Run a Bank," *NYT*, 16 October 1915. The author conducted a personal search of *The College Mirror* (Oklahoma State University student newspaper).

25. "A Bank Offers College Scholarship in Essay Contest," *PI*, 126 (24 February 1924): 124.

26. Arthur de Bebian, "Advertising Within the Bank," *BMa*, 102 (February 1921): 244.

5

Gender Segmentation

Segmenting the market on the basis of gender is a task complicated by social custom and the extent to which the opposite gender dominates any given consumption arena. Upwards of 80 to 90 percent of department store customers were women during the late nineteenth and early twentieth centuries, so special efforts were required to attract male customers. To this end, some department stores segregated menswear from the remainder of the store, and by the 1920s many had established all-male-staffed Christmas shops. Both offered fewer services than were afforded to women customers, on the premise that men were more businesslike and busy than women. In an opposite vein, automotive suppliers targeted men first and later designed special appeals for women (Cadillac's first advertising campaign directed to women, in 1919, was also the first automobile advertisement to appear in *Ladies Home Journal*), and cigarette suppliers during the 1920s had a difficult time convincing women of the acceptability of smoking in public. Despite the presumed dominance of financial matters by males, the insurance and banking industries were quick to realize that both men and women were important markets for their products. Insurance organizations were already playing on the loss of a spouse and playing on fear when targeting women during the mid-nineteenth century.[1]

Providing a specialized marketing mix for female customers in banking and for men in department store retailing in the nineteenth or early twentieth century was more difficult than providing a mix in the insurance industry (for either gender), because in banking and retailing the customer, with the exception of mail order and telephone business, visited the institution. A mix for women in banking was more difficult than providing one for men in the department store industry because in both cases the institutions were male-dominated at senior levels. What the department stores did for men (by the 1920s) was create a homogeneous environment for male customers at specific times of the year (e.g., male-staffed Christmas departments). Bank managers' first efforts at creating a more homogeneous environment for women occurred almost a century earlier, during the 1830s, when they reserved a limited number of banking hours for female customers. During the 1870s, homogeneity was increased by providing "women's departments," special banking rooms exclusively for women. A third phase in the development of banking for women further homogenized women's departments around the start of the twentieth century, when banks hired women to staff and manage the departments. These became known as a "women's bank within a bank." The remainder of this chapter is devoted to banking for women.

RESERVED BANKING HOURS (1830s–1870s)

Prior to the 1830s, there is little to suggest that banks offered women special services. Of course, bankers probably treated women customers differently than they served men, but there is no evidence of any special service that could be characterized as gender segmentation. In 1833, however, the Greenwich Savings Bank was organized in Greenwich Village, New York. It was open for two hours two days a week: Monday and Friday from 5 P.M. to 7 P.M. In a special effort to service women, the Friday hours were reserved exclusively for female patrons. No account was given for the rationale of the policy, but it appears to have been born out of a Victorian attitude that women, the weaker sex, should be protected and shielded from men. A second bank that reserved special hours for women was the Mariners' Savings Institution, organized in 1853 in New York City. The bank's initial passbook said that Thursdays from 10 A.M. to 2 P.M. were reserved for women and that "persons doing business with the Bank, must take their regular turns; and females who make deposits on any other day than Thursday, must observe the same rule." Women were welcome to bank at any time. A third example of this policy is provided by the Boatman's Savings Institution, begun in 1847 in St. Louis and now called the Boatmen's National Bank. When it was organized, Friday was declared the day when women only were welcome in the bank. A thousand copies of a handbill announcing the opening of the bank, hours of operation (10 A.M. to 4 P.M.), and the Friday, women-only policy were distributed around the community. The first woman depositor, Mrs. Eliza Cotton, entered the bank five days after its opening, a Saturday, and deposited $100. Only three of the first ten female depositors transacted their initial business on a Friday. Many men made deposits on Fridays, probably because rural visitors and men working on Mississippi River boats were unable to time their arrival to satisfy the bank's owners. The bank was relatively successful in attracting female customers. By the end of the first year of operation, 22 of 186 depositors were women. But the "Friday" policy, while well-intentioned, was unsuccessful and difficult to enforce without offending male customers who were unable to visit the bank on other weekdays. No hard data exist of the proportion of banks reserving banking hours for women. However, I suspect that it was not very common.[2]

SPECIAL BANKING FACILITIES (1870s–1900s)

The next phase in the development of banking for women was the dedication of a special banking room for their use. Three distinct types of rooms are identifiable: (1) women's departments or special banking rooms with direct teller access; (2) ladies' rooms or special rooms for women without direct teller access; and (3) safety deposit inspection booths reserved for women. In all three cases, women were treated as customers distinct from men whenever they entered the bank, not just at special times. Moreover, the earlier women's departments were located in wealthier metropolitan areas. As time progressed, a trickle-down effect can be observed; some later banks adopting women's departments served women from a broader spectrum of society. Finally, the lack of mention of women's facilities in European bank retrospectives may mean that many of these practices were of American origin.

Women's Departments

Sometime during the 1870s the Second National Bank of New York opened the first women's department in a bank in the United States. The bank was located at the corner of 23rd Street and 5th Avenue, where fashionable shops and elegant residences met. In spite of the fact that only five women held accounts in their own names, Joseph S. Case convinced bank directors to operate a distinctively furnished room with its own teller and maid. By the early 1910s, the department had over 3,000 customers and deposits in excess of $3 million. In 1911 *The Bankers' Magazine* reported:

> The substantial growth in the deposits made by women and the talk of the matter, attracted the attention of other banks, not only in New York but in other cities, which sent representatives to look into the matter, and the Second National's plan, widely copied everywhere, met with success.

Soon afterward, the Fifth Avenue Bank of New York organized a similar department.[3]

A number of other metropolitan banks adopted an upper-class orientation to serving women. The women's department of The First National Bank of Chicago, begun in 1882, had about 1,300 accounts in 1905. About one-third of them were "men accounts"—that is, they were accounts maintained by women on behalf of husbands or employers. A 1913 blotter (i.e., memorandum book) promotion of The First's women's department provides insight into the department's orientation.

> The Department for Ladies of the First National Bank is devoted exclusively to their use and to the care of their accounts. The Bank, located at the Northwest corner of Monroe and Dearborn streets, is convenient to the shopping district, and affords a pleasant place where they may rest, attend to correspondence, transact their business or meet their friends. A maid is constantly in attendance, and telephone service is at hand. New bills and silver are paid out at the window. There is no charge for the care of accounts in this department. Deposits may be made by mail if more convenient. A most cordial invitation

is extended to the ladies, as our guests, to use this department and its conveniences, whether or not an account is kept in this bank.

The promotion also described how current customers could recommend a new customer either in person or by mail, suggesting that the bank screened potential customers. The women's department of the Boulevard Bridge Bank, founded in 1921 and located in Chicago's Wrigley Building on Michigan Avenue, was managed by Mrs. Frederick Countiss, "one of Chicago's foremost club women." She designed the department's interior and had staff pay customers' bills, examine legal documents, and organize home finances. Also provided were stenographic and social secretary services—the latter to organize meetings for social and charitable institutions. The Centre Bank (New York City) in 1924 chaperoned children returning from boarding school; purchased and delivered wedding gifts, fruit, or flowers; sublet apartments; and interviewed servants at employment agencies.[4]

Bank architects commented on the orientation of these upper-class women's departments.

> The arrangement and furnishing of a banking room are also dependent upon the class of customers. Thus some banks in fashionable parts of the large cities have luxuriously appointed ladies' rooms, whereas the downtown banks are arranged with a special purpose allowing the work of downtown customers to be dispatched with as much speed as possible. (W. J. Hoggson, 1906)[5]

Trade press comments between 1890 and 1920 to the effect "most of the important banks in the United States have 'ladies' departments'" and "the modern bank building does not seem complete without a ladies' retiring room" suggest that the spread of women's departments throughout America was relatively quick. Table 5.1 lists banks that operated a women's department prior to 1930. The list includes well-known, large banks that have survived in some form, including the Northern Trust Company, the Bank of Italy (Bank of America), the Guaranty Trust Company of New York (Morgan Guaranty Trust), the Continental & Commercial National Bank of Chicago, The First National Bank of Chicago, and the Cleveland Trust Company. But not all the banks are situated in metropolitan areas of sufficient population to warrant an upper-class women's department. Women's departments in Portland, Winnipeg, Fort Wayne, Spokane, Omaha, Salt Lake City, and Wichita could hardly have survived on the concentration of wealthy females in their districts. The women's department of the Omaha National Bank in 1911 had "plenty of chairs and tables," and was finished in Circassian walnut, making the "department a pleasant place for milady to transact her business." Yet in 1910, Omaha's population was only 124,096. The town of Plainfield, New Jersey, supported a women's department of the State Trust Company during the 1910s, depite a 1910 population of 20,500. The features of the department—telephone, stationery, writing desks, paying and receiving tellers, booths connected to safe deposit vault service—are similar to those provided by metropolitan, upper-class departments.[6]

Table 5.1
Women's Departments (Direct Teller Access)

Institution	Location	Year
Second National Bank of New York	New York City	1870s[a]
Fifth Avenue Bank of New York	New York City	1870s[a]
The First National Bank of Chicago	Chicago, IL	1882[a]
American Security & Trust Company	Washington, D.C.	1895[a]
First New Haven National Bank	New Haven, CT	1895
Mercantile Trust Company	St. Louis, MO	1905
Crown Bank of Canada	Toronto, Ontario	1906
Night & Day Bank	New York City	1906[a]
Detroit Savings Bank	Detroit, MI	1906
Portland Trust Company of Oregon	Portland, OR	1907
Columbia Trust Company	New York City	1907[a]
Rochester Trust & Safe Deposit Co.	Rochester, NY	1907
Cleveland Trust Company	Cleveland, OH	1908
Union Trust & Savings Bank	Washington, D.C.	1909
First National Bank	Kansas City, MO	1909
Northern Crown Bank	Winnipeg, Manitoba	1909
Old National Bank of Spokane	Spokane, WA	1909
Home Trust Company of New York	New York City	1910
Peoples Trust Company	Brooklyn, NY	1910
First National Bank of Fort Wayne	Fort Wayne, IN	1910
Omaha National Bank	Omaha, NE	1911[a]
Peoples National Bank	Charleston, SC	1911
District National Bank	Washington, D.C.	1911
First National Bank of Syracuse	Syracuse, NY	1913
Third National Bank	Buffalo, NY	1913
Continental & Commercial National Bank of Chicago	Chicago, IL	1913
Utah Savings & Trust Company	Salt Lake City, UT	1913
Fulton Trust Company	New York City	1913
First National Bank of Los Angeles	Los Angeles, CA	1914
Peoples Trust & Savings Bank	Chicago, IL	1914[a]
Marine National Bank	Albany, NY	1914
Lincoln Trust Company	New York City	1914
First & Security National Bank	Minneapolis, MN	1915
Northwestern National Bank of Minneapolis	Minneapolis, MN	1915
Fourth & First National Bank	Nashville, TN	1915

Table 5.1 Continued

Park Trust Company	Worcester, MA	1916[a]
State Trust Company	Plainfield, NJ	1918
Guaranty Trust Company (16th Street)	New York City	1918
Lowry National Bank of Atlanta	Atlanta, GA	1921[a]
Bank of Italy	San Francisco, CA	1921[a]
Lake Shore Trust & Savings Bank	Chicago, IL	1922
Boulevard Bridge Bank	Chicago, IL	1922
Fourth National of Kansas	Wichita, KS	1923
Northern Trust Company	Chicago, IL	1924[a]

[a] Year during which department was initially installed. Year without superscript is the year of the citation.

Sources: "Two Rochester Banks," *AR*, 21 (January 1907): 18–31; "Recent Bank Buildings of the United States," *AR*, 25 (January 1909): 3–66; Olin W. Hill, "The Night and Day Bank of New York City," *The Business World*, 27 (September 1907): 827–35; "The Cleveland Trust Company," *BMa*, 79 (October 1909): 628; "The Peoples Trust Company of Brooklyn," *BMa*, 81 (July 1910): 111; "The Home Trust Company of New York," *BMa*, 81 (August 1910): 245; "Modernly Equipped House of the First National Bank of Fort Wayne, Indiana," *BMa*, 81 (September 1910): 407; "Peoples National Bank, Charleston, South Carolina," *BMa*, 82 (May 1911): 652; "The District National Bank of Washington, D.C.," *BMa*, 82 (May 1911): 662; First National Bank of Syracuse, *The First National Bank of Syracuse: The Story of Fifty Years* (Syracuse, NY: First National Bank of Syracuse, 1913), 46; "Buffalo's Remodeled Third National Bank," *BMa*, 86 (January 1913): 85; "Utah Savings & Trust Company, Salt Lake City," *BMa*, 87 (October 1913): 465; "The First National Bank of Los Angeles, California," *BMa*, 88 (March 1914): 363–73; "First and Security National Bank, Minneapolis, Minn.," *BMa*, 90 (May 1915): 600; N. Y. Carter, "Women as Bankers for Women Customers," *BMo*, 34 (May 1917): 16; R. W. Sexton, *American Commercial Buildings of Today* (New York: Architectural Book Publishing Co., 1928), 256, 282; American Security & Trust Company, *Growing with the Nation's Capital: 75th Anniversary, 1889–1964* (Washington, D.C.: American Security & Trust Company, 1964), 18–19; Arthur M. Woodford, *Detroit and Its Banks: The Story of the Detroit Trust & Bank* (Detroit: Wayne State University Press, 1974), 138.

Three additional points concerning women's departments need to be made. First, some bank managers believed that a differential advantage could be obtained by cultivating female commercial customers rather than female consumers. The Continental & Commercial National Bank (Chicago) during the 1910s established a women's department in its commercial institution rather than in the Continental & Commercial Trust & Savings Bank, its savings affiliate targeting individual consumers.[7]

Second, multiple-site banks operating a women's department did not establish them at each branch. The Bank of Italy (San Francisco) in 1921 began a women's department in the bank's newly erected head office. In that year, none of the the bank's 61 branches featured a women's department. The Bank of Italy also illustrates the scale attained by some women's departments. In 1925, a Mrs. Knight was given responsibility for the women's department and managed to attract 12,000 female depositors and $5 million in deposits over a two-year period. The department, which had no male employees, handed out home budgeting booklets and offered free English lessons to the foreign born—the latter suggesting a less than upper-class orientation. In 1927, the department accounted for 0.81 percent of the bank's $616 million in deposits, an impressive figure, considering it was over twice the deposits of the bank's average branch.[8]

Third, the five sisters of Canada (the large Canadian banks, such as the Royal Bank, the Canadian Bank of Commerce, and the Bank of Nova Scotia) appear never to have established women's departments. Canadian examples do exist, but these were in small regional banks. The Crown Bank of Canada (Toronto) and the Northern Crown Bank (Winnipeg) established them between 1900 and 1910. Both banks were later absorbed by the Royal Bank.

Ladies' Rooms and Other Special Rooms

A second type of facility for females was a ladies' room, similar to a women's department except that it lacked direct teller access. Just like a women's department, the furnishings were comfortable, the decor soft, and the natural lighting ample. In these rooms, women could write letters on a desk and with paper and pen provided by the bank, meet friends, relax, or sew. For example, the ladies' room in the new Tootle, Lemon and Co.'s Bank (St. Joseph, Missouri), constructed in 1899, was described as a place where women could "write letters, meet friends and make themselves generally at home," but there was no teller service. Table 5.2 provides a list of banks that operated a ladies' room.

A third and less frequent type of special female facility was female safety deposit booths or booth areas. Of course, some banks that operated a women's department or a ladies' room also featured female safety deposit booths. For instance, the Provident Savings Bank (Baltimore) in 1907 operated safety deposit booths reserved for female customers.[9]

Just as multiple-site banks did not operate a women's department in every branch, so some banks operated different types of women's facilities at different branches. In newly erected structures, the Guaranty Trust Company of New York featured a women's department at its 16th Street branch in 1918 and a ladies' room at its 5th Avenue head office in 1921. The difference in orientation probably arose from the location of each building. The women's department was in a branch located in a shopping district; the ladies' room was located in the commercial head office on 5th Avenue. Male management may have perceived a lack of demand for a women's department at the head office. In contrast, the entrance to the women's department at the 16th Street branch was situated beside the branch's main doors, allowing access without entering the bank's main room. It featured separate paying and receiving tellers, white woodwork, a fireplace, two large windows, comfortable furniture, and an elevator down to the vault in

Table 5.2
Ladies' Writing, Relaxation, or Consultation Rooms

Institution	Location	Year
Tootle, Lemon and Co.'s Bank	St. Joseph, MO	1899
Colonial Trust Company	Baltimore, MD	1907
International Trust Company	Baltimore, MD	1907
Ohio Savings Bank & Trust Company	Toledo, OH	1908
National Shawmut Bank	Boston, MA	1908
Old Colony Trust Company	Boston, MA	1908
Second National Bank	Wilkes-Barre, PA	1909
Savings Bank of Baltimore	Baltimore, MD	1909
Commonwealth Trust Co. of Boston	Boston, MA	1909
La Grange Trust & Savings Bank	La Grange, IL	1909
Continental Bank & Trust Company	Shreveport, LA	1910
Washington Trust Company	Westerly, RI	1911
First National Bank of Joliet	Joliet, IL	1911
Southwest National Bank of Commerce	Kansas City, MO	1912
Union Bank & Trust Company	Jackson, TN	1912
Guaranty State Bank & Trust Company	Dallas, TX	1912
Central State Bank	Des Moines, IA	1913
Syracuse Trust Company	Syracuse, NY	1913
Security Trust & Savings Bank	Los Angeles, CA	1914
J. P. Morgan & Co.	New York City	1915
Guaranty Trust Co. (5th Avenue)	New York City	1921
Fidelity National Bank	Oklahoma City, OK	1924
Roxborough Trust Company	Philadelphia, PA	1928
Danbury National Bank	Danbury, CT	1928
First National Trust & Savings Bank	Los Angeles, CA	1928
American Bank & Trust Company	Hazelton, PA	1928
Vermont Peoples National Bank	Brattleboro, VT	1928
Chevy Chase Savings Bank	Washington, D.C.	1928
Second National Bank	Nashua, NH	1928

Sources: "Recent Bank Buildings of the United States," *AR*, 25 (January 1909): 3–66; "The Continental Bank & Trust Company, Shreveport, Louisiana," *BMa*, 81 (November 1910): 253; "The Old National Bank at Home in a New Building," *BMa*, 82 (March 1911): 416; "The Washington Trust Company of Westerly, Rhode Island," *BMa*, 83 (August 1911): 253; "First National Bank of Joliet, Illinois," *BMa*, 83 (August 1911): 260; "Guaranty State Bank and Trust Co., Dallas, Texas," *BMa*, 84 (June 1912): 824; "Central State Bank, Des Moines, Iowa," *BMa*, 86 (April 1913): 482; "Security and Trust Savings Bank, Los Angeles, Cal.," *BMa*, 88 (March 1914): 386; "Some Recent Bank Plans," *AR*, 37 (February 1915): 97–115; advertisement in *Daily Oklahoman*, 6 December 1924; R. W. Sexton, *American Commercial Buildings of Today* (New York: Architectural Book Publishing Co., 1928), 267–91.

the basement. The elevator was connected to a buzzer, alerting an attendant in the basement to open the elevator door for customers. In the basement, there was a special ladies' room for inspecting safety deposit box contents.[10]

The Guaranty Trust Company approach of different facilities at different locations is consistent with a 1917 observation of *The Bankers' Magazine*: "Location of the bank is an important element affecting the adaptability of the institution to women's needs." Bank proximity to fashionable neighborhoods or retail centers was an advantage, while proximity to manufacturing, wholesaling, or commercial districts was a disadvantage for the cultivation of female customers. Regardless of the chauvinism implied, there is evidence of a customer orientation and an understanding of the linkage between urban location and ability to meet the needs of a specific demographic market segment.[11]

FEMALE-OPERATED WOMEN'S DEPARTMENTS (1900–1930)

The last phase in the development of banking for women began when banks started to employ women to staff and manage women's departments. Previous to 1900–1905, very few women were employed by banks in general, and women's departments were staffed almost exclusively by men. In 1883 *The Bankers' Magazine* said that just two females were bank presidents; each had inherited majority stock from her deceased husband. Lenore D. Montgomery reported in 1893 that nationally chartered banks employed 346 women. Those holding prominent positions were related to male bankers or had inherited a private bank or bank stock. Evalyn Tome, for instance, was a director of the Cecil National Bank (Maryland). Her husband owned the bank and two others. Other women were employed as clerks, tellers, cashiers, and treasurers. But the connection between women's departments and the employment of women had not yet been made.[12]

The most common argument given by women at the beginning of the twentieth century for staffing a women's department with females centered on male insensitivity. Male tellers generally treated male customers with respect, even when the customer was ignorant of banking methods. The same could not be said when the customer was female. D. M. Stewart of the Canadian Bank of Commerce branch in New York City in 1893 alluded to this: "When they [women] come to do business at the bank they should not be stared at or in any way or made to feel uncomfortable. The rule should be to pay their checks, and receive their deposits, and act toward them in a gentlemanly manner."[13]

Starting in about 1905, banks began to hire women to work in women's departments. Some banks went even further, and allocated responsibility to the department for bookkeeping, advertising and promotion, hiring and firing, departmental training, and account opening and closing, thereby creating a "women's bank within a bank." These responsibilities led to a flurry of special products and promotions created by women for women and coincided with overall more aggressive banking policies. The hiring of a woman to manage a newly formed or extant women's department was often the focus of an advertising campaign, suggesting that bankers sought as much value as possible from a woman manager. Women's departments of a significant size often had a marked increase in the proportion of female subordinates within the department. Female women's department managers were in a unique position to attract—which they did—the accounts of members of feminist or other women's associations. The paragraphs that follow provide documentary evidence for these claims.

Female-Staffed and -Managed Women's Departments

As early as 1905, Mrs. R. Graham Frost was managing the Mercantile Trust Company's (St. Louis) women's department. In a trade press article she did not state when the women's department was established or when a female was first appointed to manage it. The department had 12,000 customers by 1905, each given equal "earnest attention" regardless of account size. Her justification for the existence of the department was the following:

> A women has many little worries which she cannot well impart to a man, but which she finds easy to tell another woman. Much that she cannot tell, and may not herself altogether recognize, will be sufficiently apprehended by a sympathizing women manager possessed of that intuition for which the sex is justly famed.[14]

In 1906, within two years after its founding, the Crown Bank of Canada (Toronto) appointed Mrs. E. B. B. Reesor as advertising manager. By year's end she was responsible for the bank's savings and women's departments. In 15 months under Reesor's stewardship, the number of female customers swelled from 200 to about 8,000 and female employees increased from eight to 18. The women's department was comprised of three rooms: a banking room with two tellers and two ledger keepers; a resting room; and a dressing room. In the latter were a full-length mirror and a sewing table.[15]

The new 1906 Detroit Savings Bank building had a women's department with its own street entrance. It was staffed by a female. The only other female in the bank was the president's secretary.[16]

In her 1924 book, *The Women's Department*, Anne Seward said that Columbia Trust Company (New York City) had the first women's department to be managed by a woman and provided 1907 as the year. Seward's error may have been the result of limiting her analysis to New York City. The manager of Columbia's department, Virginia Furman, was a longtime depositor at the bank and was the daughter of a prominent New York banker. Her position gave her easy access to the city's wealthy community and to various women's organizations. The New York State Suffrage Party and the Women's City Club called on members to transfer accounts to the bank in a show of support. The innovation was quickly copied by other New York City banks. By 1921, the Bankers Trust Company had appointed Jean Arnot Reid to manage its women's department, Central Union Trust Company had appointed Mina M. Bruere as assistant secretary, and the United States Mortgage & Trust Company had appointed Nathalie Laimbeer as assistant secretary. They, along with Furman and others, founded the National Association of Bank Women in 1921. By 1925 the Association had 172 members.[17]

According to bank president Benjamin I. Cohen, the women's department of the Portland Trust Company of Oregon was the first in the Pacific Northwest. In 1907 it was managed by Harriet E. Moorehouse, previously the cashier "of a large company" with over 15 years of business experience. In 1909 the bank distributed a booklet titled *The Bank Lady*, written by Anna Docking, a newspaper reporter. In it she wrote:

> While money troubles, with all their manifold complications, have no terrors for her [Moorehouse], yet she understands well the attitude of the feminine mind unfamiliar with these things. The business world welcomes her as one who fills a long-felt need, and the hosts of women who are aiding and encouraging her work by their confidence and patronage wonder how they ever got along without the Bank Lady.[18]

In 1908 Mrs. E. B. B. Reesor of the Crown Bank of Canada, in an open letter published in *The Bankers' Magazine*, asked other female women's department managers to write to her. Mrs. Moorehouse (of Portland) replied thus:

> The results have been more than satisfactory. A women's department in a bank appeals to every class of women, from one of wealth to the maid in the house. Each needs a place where she can go over business matters in confidence and in an informal way with one of her own sex; where she can be frank; where she can display ignorance (and many of them feel it keenly) without embarrassment. She would hesitate to go to the window, stand in line and ask questions that a busy clerk could only answer briefly, and in all probability, in a way that she would not comprehend—not being familiar with business and business terms. Many women who have wholly depended upon their husbands or some male relative to do their banking, are suddenly left to their own resources and find themselves almost helpless in their ignorance of business methods, and to this class a women's department of a bank most strongly appeals.

Reesor responded by saying, "The foregoing gives a reason, and a powerful one, for the establishment of women's departments with women managers."[19]

In 1911 the First & Security National Bank (Minneapolis), which had had a women's department in operation for at least two years, separated the women's accounts and brought the department under the charge of a Miss Heslup. She was made responsible for female business, including opening new accounts and direct mail. Depositors grew from 1,500 to 5,500, and departmental deposits from $400,000 to $1,564,832, between 1911 and 1915.[20]

The Fourth & First National Bank (Nashville) had a male-staffed women's department in operation for some time. In 1915 May Selley was appointed teller and manager of the department. Given complete freedom to develop the department, she wrote to current customers and announced her new position. She stated that women "were not being segregated by any nuisance of law," and asked for their support in making the women's department a success. In subsequent direct mail appeals, she enclosed premiums such as blotters and pencils. She ordered new checkbooks, but only in one color, which went against the normal practice of offering women checkbooks in an abundance of colors. She did, however, order them in two different sizes: larger ones with large print for elderly customers who carried large purses and who possibly had failing sight, and smaller ones for younger customers who followed the current fashion of carrying petite purses.[21]

In 1925, Nathalie Laimbeer was appointed to the "executive staff of National City Bank, New York, in charge of women's banking department." *The Bankers' Magazine* note from which the quotation was taken and retrospectives of the National City Bank do not state whether this "women's department" was visible to customers—that is, was it a back-office department that coordinated efforts directed to women, or was it a front-office department patronized by female customers? In the same year, the Farmers Loan & Trust Company, then owned by National City Bank, organized a women's department and appointed Anne H. Houghton as manager. In 1926, the United States Mortgage & Trust Company (New York) hired Miss Elanor Goss to work in its women's department. A 1916 graduate of Vassar, she was a nationally recognized tennis player before her entry into banking. In 1925 Caroline Olney was the manager of the Chemical National Bank's women's department.[22]

Male Women's Department Employees

A number of banks retained males to staff and manage their women's department throughout the period. Many male bankers and some female bankers were under the impression that males provided females a different and perhaps better type of service. For many years, social strictures no doubt prevailed, and those men who worked in women's departments were probably married. During the 1910s, the First National Bank of Syracuse picked a man, probably young and probably good looking, "particularly for his politeness and ability in dealing with our women customers." Sex appeal may have been at work.[23]

Some women recommended that a women's department be staffed by men. A female employee of the Night and Day Bank (New York) wrote a report that upper management implemented. A women's department was created with its own street entrance, carpeted floors, tapestry-covered walls, and mahogany furniture. The *New York Times* reported in 1906 that the female employee "particularly insisted that there must be nothing gaudy, but that the whole effect must convey the idea of established and certain wealth." Two dressing rooms were planned: one in the safety deposit vault to facilitate access to jewels before and after evening outings; and one adjacent to the women's department, outfitted with a full-length mirror. Smelling salts were kept on hand for "when a woman finds that her account is overdrawn." The female employee who helped establish the women's department recommended that a male teller be used, as "women would be convinced by his figuring."[24]

Despite the pathbreaking adoption of a women's department by The First National Bank of Chicago in 1882, departmental staff remained male during the 1920s: "There are men tellers, another unusual idea for a women's 'bank.'" The manager of the department was a male vice president, and his desk was located in the open in the department. Thus, by 1920, the transition to women-staffed women's departments was complete, and those retaining the older employment practice were a novelty.[25]

Women's Banks

A rare extension of the women's department was banks reserved solely for women customers. In a 1910 article, the *New York Times* said, "A novel departure in British banking will be inaugurated on Monday next with the opening of a women's bank officered and conducted exclusively by women and catering only to women customers." The bank planned for an initial base of about 500 businesswomen and society members. It hired one man to act as a messenger and as a security guard to chase away men. The *Times* article did not provide the name of the institution, but it may have been the Farrow's Bank for Women, an institution reserved exclusively for female patrons, which operated in Knightsbridge (across from Hyde Park). An advertisement for the bank in 1914 said that "the advent of this branch was received with general acclamation and its progress has been rapid. Here ladies find a courteous and obliging staff of their own sex, ready to assist them in any and every detail of banking and finance." In 1914 *The Bankers' Magazine* was unaware of a similar bank or bank branch in the United States.[26]

Organized by Mrs. F. J. Runyon in 1919, the First Women's Bank of Tennessee (Clarkesville) was reportedly the first women's bank in the United States. She (the president) and her only employee, cashier Mrs. M. G. Lyle, trained at a bank 16 miles away. All six bank directors were female. While the bank's name and the staff's and directors' sex suggest a gender-based segmentation strategy, the bank sought out the town's prominent businessmen to purchase the initial stock offering and apparently was willing to provide service to all comers.[27]

PROMOTION

The flurry of promotions (and special products) directed to women that began early during the twentieth century coincided with the appointment of female women's department managers. The pattern was accelerated when these managers were given responsibility for advertising. The promotional campaigns directed to women fall into four distinct yet related types: mass, product, housewife, and other class advertising.

Mass Advertising

There were, first, the mass appeal advertisements that sought women as a general class of customer. These advertisements were mostly informative, describing basic services and, perhaps most important, heralding the social acceptability and welcome of women dealing with banks. An early example of an advertisement that attempted to inform women of the acceptability of banking is that provided by the Northern Trust Company (Chicago). A 1909 advertisement said "It might surprise you to know how many of our depositors are women." One for the East Orange Bank (New Jersey) in 1924 said, "This bank welcomes the business of women. It is always glad to add to its growing number of women customers." The large Canadian banks, although they did not establish women's departments, advertised in a similar manner. A 1911 advertisement for the Traders Bank of Canada (Toronto) said, "Women's accounts always receive courteous treatment at this bank. . . . Every assistance is offered in making up the deposit or cheque forms." A 1926 newspaper advertisement by the Royal Bank of Canada showed a women at a bank desk (possibly writing a check). After a brief thrift message, it added, "Ladies will receive courteous, helpful attention from our staff." Direct mail was also used. C. L. Munn, advertising manager of the Wachovia Bank & Trust Company (Winston-Salem, North Carolina) wrote in a 1911 letter to potential female customers:

> Every women owes a duty to herself and to her children as well in learning something of business and business methods. Banks are the only institutions helpful to women in the careful and prudent handling of her money matters. Banks are easily reached and glad to co-operate and serve.[28]

Product Advertising

Second, there were advertisements that concentrated on specific products. One product of particular focus was demand deposit service. For example, the Colonial Trust Company (Boston) in 1907 advertised that "many women now keep banking accounts. Many more should, and would if they realized the convenience and economy of paying bills by check." A 1925 campaign by the Equitable Trust Company of New York directed to women listed the difficulties of dying without a will. The Equitable continued using fear throughout the 1920s: a 1927 newspaper advertisement said, "To make a will is a woman's privilege as well a man's," and directed interested women to write to the bank for a brochure on will writing. A third service promoted in advertising was safe deposit service. In 1913 the Union Trust & Savings Bank (Spokane, Washington), for example, promoted its recent safe deposit service in a direct mail campaign specifically targeting women.[29]

Housewives

Third, there were advertisements directed to housewives. Banks understood that women were likely to control a household's budget:

> Women do the greater part of the buying in this country and nine times out of ten, they have the deciding vote in the choice of a home site and are the power behind the throne when it comes to domestic economy. So if you are wise you will always bear the women in mind not only when preparing your copy, but in choosing your medium. (*The Bankers' Magazine*, 1908)

The Des Moines Savings Bank in 1907 said "Let the Wife Try," and explained that "some men cannot save, but the family prospers because the wife keeps a savings account"—perhaps as much an appeal to men as to women. A 1909 advertisement by the Hampden Trust Company (Massachusetts), headed "To Springfield Housewives," informed women of the benefits of paying household bills by check. The main copy of a 1924 Bank of Italy (San Francisco) advertisement was headed, "To the Housewives . . ." and stated that the women's department at the bank's head office "is a strong tangible expression of the bank's attitude toward the countless women who are in business—as managers of the Home, or as participants in the commercial activities of California."[30]

Other banks printed and distributed checkbooks designed to help manage household finances. The First Wisconsin National Bank (Milwaukee) in 1921 distributed elaborate home financing material, titled *Simplified Home Budget System*, consisting of a Kitchen Kalendar, a Budget Book, and a Pocket Expense Book. The bank's president was personally involved in the design of the handout, and it was pretested before distribution to the public. The home economics drive of the early twentieth century resulted in a number of banks offering free budgeting and home economics services, in some cases provided by university-educated women. Between 1920 and 1925 the Peoples Savings & Trust Company (Pittsburgh), the Commonwealth Trust Company of Boston, the New York Trust Company, the First National Bank of Detroit, the Montclair Savings Bank (New Jersey), and the Savings Bank of New London (Connecticut) offered the service. Bank efforts to instill efficient home economics was of sufficient scope that it received attention in academic home economics periodicals such as *The Journal of Home Economics*.[31]

Another special service for female customers was the payment of multiple household bills from a single check. As early as 1915, the Citizens National Bank of Englewood and the Montclair Savings Bank, both in New Jersey, offered such a service. The Fifth Avenue Bank of New York, which had operated a women's department since the 1870s, began a similar service in 1911 that was described as being "in the interest of its women depositors." In 1930 the Shawmut National Bank, Boston, on the advice of a female advisory board, further refined the multiple-bill-paying service. Customers signed a power of attorney and in essence were given overdraft protection. At the end of the month, the bank billed the customer for the amount of checks paid plus a service fee.[32]

Other Classes of Women

Fourth, and last, there were several special classes of females whom banks sought. In 1912 the Edmonton (Alberta) branch of the Traders Bank of Canada, in an advertisement that probably appealed to parents as well as daughters, said, "The girls on the farm. Let your girls at home take up some hobby—bee keeping, poultry farming, dairying, gardening, etc.—thus earning some money for themselves. Encourage them to open a savings account in this bank with the profits." A 1916 advertisement by the National Bank of Commerce (St. Louis) sought to attract female treasurers of social and charitable organizations. The bank explained that if the patron, on behalf on the organization, used the bank exclusively, the bank in return would show her how to "keep the books" and make the annual report. The Meyer-Kiser Bank (Indianapolis) in 1920 undertook a campaign directed to employed or self-employed women under the rubric of "businesswomen" (but the campaign attracted many females in general). This campaign consisted mostly of a series of streetcar cards featuring longtime bank employee Blessing Fischer. One had the following text next to her image: "I am a woman banker. It is my business to help you women who are wage-earners." Fischer had been with the bank since its opening, as assistant to the president, and this gave her wide experience in banking matters, especially legal affairs. The bank put this to good use in her contact with employed women.[33]

VACATION CLUBS

Tangentially related to banking for women, but related to promoting thrift among them, was the work of the Vacation Bureau, established in 1908. Its initial goal was to screen and compile a list of reputable country boardinghouses accessible to single, younger New York City working women. Substandard retreats failed to maintain acceptable levels of cleanliness, or they held prizefights, sold alcohol, or harbored men of dubious qualities who were apt to prey on young women. Modest discounts were arranged for women referred by the Bureau. Under the guidance of Gertrude Robinson Smith, a Vacation Savings Fund was established in 1911 to help less thrifty, lower-paid young women (many were retail workers) accumulate money for one or two weeks of recuperative country air. The Fund was unable to reach the 400,000 single, working women of New York City from its central office, so local branches were established with the cooperation of retailers and other businesses that employed large numbers of women. A branch, of which over 100 existed by 1913, was in reality a reliable woman who sold stamps and deposited receipts with the Fund. Stamps ranging in value from five cents to one dollar were sold to women, who collected them in a Fund passbook. In 1912, 4,000 women took vacations owing to the efforts of the Fund, and it was estimated that stamp sales of about $100,000 would allow 10,000 women to take vacations during the summer of 1913. The Metropolitan Life Insurance Company allowed Fund organizers to hold monthly meetings at one of its assembly halls. Spring and summer tours of parks, botanical gardens, and museums were organized, and classes in gymnastics, sewing, and acting were offered. One of the more interesting out-growths of the movement resulted from complaints women made about feeling obliged to give large Christmas gifts to retail floorwalkers in order to remain in good stead, described as "a shameless system of graft." Mrs. August Belmont publicly reproached the practice, and the women formed the Society for the Prevention of Useless Giving: "The idea was fresh and welcome, and, under the abbreviated name "the Spugs," the association has become widely known."[34]

EMPIRICAL RESEARCH

Empirical research conducted during the 1920s justified what banks had practiced for many years. One study by Paul Hardesty of the Union Trust Company (Chicago) revealed that 32 percent of 1,288 accounts operated by females were profitable. This contrasts with 23 percent of the 1,138 accounts operated by males. A test of difference between proportions (t = 4.84; $p < .01$) agrees with Hardesty's "eyeball" conclusion that females were more profitable customers than males.[35]

In 1925 Amy Hyde, advertising manager of the Union Bank of Chicago, studied gender. She reported that 43 percent of 1,000 randomly selected accounts were opened by women, but that they accounted for 60 percent of total deposits (average balance of $109 for women versus $55 for men). She asked the Northern Trust Company, a Chicago bank that typically sought a wealthier clientele, to conduct a similar study. It reported that women opened 44 percent of the new accounts during one month. The 44 percent accounted for 67 percent of total deposits (average balance of $482 for women versus $189 for men).[36]

CONCLUDING COMMENTS

There may have been chauvanistic overtones to the original gender-based segmentation efforts of the 1830s, but these and subsequent segmentation plans improved service to women. Media stereotypes of female inferiority in dealing with finances, reinforced by the prevailing culture, led some women to desire dealing with a bank that employed sympathetic women. The *New York Times* in 1906, for instance, after explaining that the Fifth Avenue Bank had long sought female customers, provided derogatory examples of why female patrons were not worth the bother.[37]

The employment of women to manage and staff women's departments was one means used to signal the female populace that banks were sensitive to their unique needs. Because banks did not provide personal consumption credit until the late 1920s, women's departments were not a mechanism that siphoned credit from the female consumer segment. That occurred after World War II.

As of the early 1990s, The First National Bank of Chicago operated a women's department, mostly for an elderly, wealthy clientele. Aside from isolated and very specialized departments of this type, women's departments have all but disappeared. The key explanatory factor is one of cost. Women were increasingly hired by banks as the early twentieth century progressed, but World War I siphoned off a considerable portion of many banks' younger male workforce. In contrast to marginal numbers before World War I, the National City Bank of New York employed 525 women in 1918 (out of a total staff of about 1,500), and the Guaranty Trust Company of New York employed more than 500 women (out of a staff of about 2,000). The infusion of illtrained personnel resulted in hastily organized banking seminars for women by the Wall Street division of New York University in 1917. William K. Kniffen, the author of banking textbooks, led several sessions. Women were employed by banks as stenographers, telephone operators, librarians, translators, credit investigators, and machine operators. Bank managers quickly realized that women could be paid less than men, and this, in combination with technology that reduced skill levels required to perform some jobs adequately, meant that women employees offered a low-cost alternative. During World War I, the Fidelity National Bank & Trust Company (Kansas City), for instance, replaced its office boys with office girls. When the war ended, they retained the female errand girls through the 1920s because, as explained by a bank vice president, girls were "steadier" and "soberer," and they "are not always asking for fifty cents or a dollar a week more in their pay envelopes."

Through the 1920s and 1930s female opportunities were limited to lower-paid positions. World War II saw a repetition of the World War I experience. During World War I, the proportion of women employed by the United States National Bank of Oregon (Portland), for instance, rose to about 30 percent and remained at that level through the 1920s and 1930s. During World War II, the proportion rose to about 65 percent and remained at that level through the 1950s and 1960s. For the first time women were employed as tellers in main banking halls, and as a consequence, women did not have to bank in the women's department to be served by females. Women's departments still created a homogeneous environment for women, but the cost and advantage of operating them were questioned. The answer was obvious: as long as women were tellers in the main lobby, a women's department was cost inefficient.[38]

NOTES

1. "Pebeco Advertises to Women Who Smoke," *PI*, 145 (25 October 1928): 89–90+; Shepard B. Clouch, *A Century of American Life Insurance: A History of the Mutual Life Insurance Company of New York, 1843–1943* (New York: Columbia University Press, 1946), 93–94; Susan P. Benson, *Counter Cultures: Saleswomen, Managers, and Customers in American Department Stores, 1890–1940* (Urbana: University of Illinois Press, 1988), 99–100.

2. Joseph Husband, *One Hundred Years of Greenwich Savings Bank* (New York: Greenwich Savings Bank, 1933), 55; W. G. Rule, *The Story of the Oldest Bank West of the Mississippi* (St. Louis: Boatmen's National Bank of St. Louis, 1947), 21–25; Meyer Berger, *Growth of an Idea 1850–1950: The Story of the Manhattan Savings Bank* (New York: Manhattan Savings Bank, 1950), 29.

3. "The Bank's Appeal to Women," *BMa*, 82 (March 1911): 389.

4. Otto C. Brodhay, "The Ladies' Department," *The Review*, 2 (June 1905): 23–24 (FNBC archives); "How Banks Are Advertising," *BMa*, 86 (February 1913): 188; Osgood Baley, "What Chicago Banks Are Doing for Women Depositors," *BMo*, 39 (July 1922): 18–19+; Anne Seward, *The Women's Department* (New York: Bankers Publishing Co., 1924), 65–66.

5. W. J. Hoggson, "Laying out a Banking Room," *BMa*, 72 (February 1906): 315.

6. "The Omaha National Bank Improves Its Quarters," *BMa*, 82 (May 1911): 671; Warren M. Avery, "The Kind of Bank a Woman Likes," *BMo*, 35 (February 1918): 20. Population estimates: *Fourteenth Census of the United States Taken in the Year 1920*, Vol. 1, *Population* (Washington, D.C.: U.S. Government Printing Office, 1921), 78, 84.

7. "How Banks Are Advertising," *BMa*, 86 (February 1913): 188; Baley, "What Chicago Banks Are Doing for Women Depositors."

8. Mrs. Edward D. Knight, "Service for Women," *BMo*, 44 (February 1927): 20–21; Marquis James and Bessie R. James, *Biography of a Bank: The Story of Bank of America N.T. & S.A.* (New York: Harper & Brothers, 1954), 131.

9. "The Bank Buildings of Baltimore," *AR*, 22 (August 1907): 79–101.

10. "The Sixteenth Street Branch of the Guaranty Trust Company of New York," *AR*, 43 (June 1918): 491–504.

11. "Banking Service for Women," *BMa*, 94 (April 1917): 387–88.

12. "Women as Presidents," *BMa*, 37 (June 1883): 956; Lenore D. Montgomery, "Women in Banking," *BMa*, 48 (May 1894): 833–37.

13. D. M. Stewart, "Duties of the Teller in a Canadian Bank," *BMa*, 48 (December 1893): 436–40;

14. Mrs. R. Graham Frost, "The Women's Department," *TC*, 2 (July 1905): 545.

15. E. B. B. Reesor, "How to Get Women to Bank at Your Bank," *BMa*, 74 (June 1907): 959–62; "Manager of the Women's Department. The Crown Bank of Canada," *BMa*, 74 (July 1907): 963–64.

16. Arthur M. Woodford, *Detroit and Its Banks: The Story of the Detroit Bank and Trust* (Detroit: Wayne State University Press, 1974), 138, 143.

17. Seward, *The Women's Department*, 9; "Helping the Men to Carry the Load," *BMa*, 111 (September 1925): 411–12; Genieve N. Gildersleeve, *Women in Banking: A History of the National Association of Bank Women* (Washington, D.C.: Public Affairs Press, 1959).

18. Benjamin I. Cohen, "New Methods for Advertising and Their Results," *TC*, 5 (October 1907): 691–93; "The Bank Lady," *BMa*, 78 (March 1909): 504–05.

19. E. B. B. Reesor, "Women as Bankers," *BMa*, 79 (October 1909): 511–14.

20. "Experience with the Women's Department," *BMa*, 95 (August 1917): 187–91.

21. May Selley, "Women and the Bank," *BMa*, 91 (October 1915): 494.

22. "Banking and Financial Notes," *BMa*, 110 (March 1925): 547–48; "Banking and Financial Notes," *BMa*, 111 (October 1925): 638; "Banking and Financial Notes," *BMa*, 111 (November 1925): 798; "Banking and Financial Notes," *BMa*, 113 (December 1926): 925.

23. "Experience with the Women's Department," *BMa*, 95 (August 1917): 190.

24. "A Bank for Women All to Themselves," *NYT*, 23 September 1906.

25. Baley, "What Chicago Banks Are Doing for Women Depositors."

26. "Bank for Women Only," *NYT*, 13 March 1910; "British Bank Advertising," *BMa*, 88 (June 1914): 690–92.

27. Vonnie R. Griffith, "First Woman President of the First Women's Bank in the United States," *Ladies Home Journal*, 37 (June 1920): 149.

28. "How Banks Are Advertising," *BMa*, 83 (October 1911): 502. Advertisements reprinted in *BMa*, 78 (July 1909): 1006; *BMa*, 109 (August 1924): 235; *BMa*, 113 (September 1926): 376. Traders Bank of Canada 1911 advertisement from TD archives.

29. "How Banks Are Advertising," *BMa*, 87 (July 1913): 56. Advertisements reprinted in *BMa*, 75 (December 1907): 923; *BMa*, 114 (February 1927): 295.

30. Advertisements reprinted in *BMa*, 74 (January 1907): 98; *BMa*, 76 (February 1908): 227; *BMa*, 78 (February 1909): 297; *BMa*, 109 (August 1924): 235.

31. Mrs. Clarence Renshaw, "The Home Service Department," *JABA*, 12 (January 1920): 356–57; R. E. Wright, "A Novel Budget Plan to Help Teach Community Thrift," *BMo*, 38 (March 1921): 27–28; Baley, "What Chicago Banks Are Doing for Women

Depositors"; Frank L. Campbell, "A Home Economics Department That Builds Savings," *BMo*, 39 (September 1922): 28+; E. Lillian White, "Analyzing the Work of the Service Department," *BMo*, 42 (May 1925): 13–14. Regarding *The Journal of Home Economics*, see A. Agnes Donham, "Home Service in Boston Banks," 13 (September 1921): 440–42; Sarah J. MacLeod, "Home Economics and Banks," 16 (April 1924): 177–80; Leo D. Woodworth, "Home Service Departments in Banks," 20 (September 1928): 405–08.

32. "To Help Women Pay Bills," *NYT*, 23 (November 1911); "Banks Pay Family Bills," *BMa*, 92 (May 1916): 621–23; "Financial Service for Women," *BMa*, 121 (August 1930): 190.

33. Murray E. Crain, "How the Face on a Card Gets the Women Depositors," *BMo*, 37 (October 1920): 18–19. Advertisements reprinted in *BMa*, 84 (January 1912): 71; *BMa*, 92 (March 1916): 413.

34. Hugh Thompson, "The Vacation Savings Movement," *Munsey's Magazine*, 49 (May 1913): 257–59.

35. Paul L. Hardesty, "Are the Women Better Savers Than Men?" *BMo*, 41 (May 1924): 9–10.

36. Amy R. Hyde, "Are Women Eclipsing Men as Bank Depositors?" *BMo*, 42 (November 1925): 30–31.

37. "Women Depositors," *NYT* (25 June 1906).

38. "Bank Training in Wall Street for Women," *BMa*, 95 (October 1917): 493–94; Leroy A. Mershon, "Filling the Gaps in the Clerical Force," *BMo*, 35 (May 1918): 22–23+; "More Women in Banks," *NYT* (14 August 1918); "Office Boys are Girls in Kansas City Bank," *BMa*, 121 (September 1929): 422.

6

Nationality and Race Segmentation

The central properties of segmenting on nationality or race are the title and location of the institution, the makeup of its staff and management, and transacting business and communicating in various languages. In insurance, because of reliance on agents, transacting business in foreign languages and the ethnicity or race of the agent, but not the location of physical facilities, were key. The department store industry appealed to the masses, and its central city locations were consistent with that approach. Early in the twentieth century, some personal-service departments provided translators for immigrants or non-English-speaking visitors, but department stores never avowedly favored any given nationality group. If anything, the money, but not the manners of working-class immigrants, were welcome. In banking, restrictive location regulations propelled nationality banking. German, Scandinavian, Hibernian, Oriental, and Italian banks existed at different times and at different locations in America. These began as local, community banks and were thus akin to small retail and hotel establishments operated by individuals for those of their own ethnic group or race. The first part of this chapter deals with nationality banks.

Race here is treated in relation to African-Americans. An outgrowth of mutual aid societies formed after the Civil War was a spirit of enterprise that resulted in the formation of African-American banks and insurance organizations. These financial institutions built upon African-American-operated businesses primarily in personal service industries (such as barbershops, livery stables, caterers, taverns, and inns) and fostered expansion into retailing. The second part of this chapter deals with African-American banking.[1]

NATIONALITY BANKING

For the purpose of discussion, nationality banks are divided into two types: state or national chartered banks, and private "immigrant" banks. Nationality banks, as discussed here, do not include branches of foreign-based banks. After discussing each type, attention is turned to the effect of World War I on German banking and to targeting multiple nationality groups.

Chartered Banks

German banks were among the earliest and most frequently organized nationality banks in America. They were formed during the 1850s in St. Louis; the 1860s in Philadelphia, St. Paul, Chicago, and San Francisco; and the 1870s in Washington, D.C. By 1901, there were 23 nationally chartered banks with "German" or a close variant thereof (e.g., Germania) in their title. This rose to 30 by 1916.[2]

Hibernian banks were formed during the 1850s in San Francisco, during the 1890s in Portland (Oregon), and during the 1900s in Los Angeles. Scandinavian banks were formed during the 1870s in Chicago and during the 1900s in San Francisco and Oregon. Asian banks, notably Japanese and Chinese banks, were organized primarily in California around 1900. Italian banks were formed during the 1890s in California. Table 6.1 presents a sample of chartered nationality banks, and the location and year of organization for each.

Several observations can be made about nationality banks, the first of which concerns the link between the development of nationality banks and immigration patterns. Chartered nationality banks emerged during and just after the 1846–55 immigration wave of three million. About 50 percent of the wave originated from Great Britain and Ireland and about 30 percent from Germany, so the first German and Irish banks appeared at this time. A number of Germans had settled in America during the seventeenth century. They were, like the Scotch-Irish, "pushed" to the frontier, away from established eastern seaboard communities. William Penn promoted Pennsylvania as tolerant, and this attracted many Germans: in 1766, Benjamin Franklin estimated that one-third of Pennsylvania was peopled by individuals of German birth or descent. Germantown, outside of Philadelphia, was founded in 1763 by a Frankfurt lawyer. The dearth of immigration during the early nineteenth century led to strong assimilation pressures. When the Bank of Germantown (later called the Germantown National Bank) was organized in 1814, the names of the organizers, officers, and directors did not reflect German ancestry (the first president and cashier were Samuel Harvey and John F. Watson, respectively). In 1813, an unnamed German lamented that German was no longer the language of the "legislative halls and courts of justice" in Germantown, and by the mid-nineteenth century the language of worship in the American Lutheran Church was English, a fact resented by more recent German immigrants. German immigration societies sought to congregate Germans in specific geographic regions to stem assimilation tides. During the 1830s the *Giessener Gesellschaft* (which loosely translates into "Giessen's Society") lured Germans to the Missouri River near St. Louis, which

Table 6.1
Sample of Nationality Banks

Institution	Location	Year
German		
German Savings Institution	St. Louis, MO	1853
German Trust & Savings Bank	Philadelphia, PA	1860
German American Bank	St. Paul, MN	1863
German Savings & Loan Society	San Francisco, CA	1868
German Savings Bank	Chicago, IL	1869
German National Bank	Chicago, IL	1870
German American Bank	New York City	1870
German National Bank	Chicago, IL	1871
German American Savings Bank	Washington, D.C.	1872
German American Bank of Rochester	Rochester, NY	1875
German National Bank	Denver, CO	1877
German American Loan & Trust Co.	New York City	1882
German National Bank	Lincoln, NE	1886
German-American Savings Bank	Los Angeles, CA	1890
German American State Bank	Chicago, IL	1904
German-American Bank	Anaheim, CA	1905
German State Bank	Cottonwood, ID	1907
German American Bank	Chicago, IL	1912
German Bank	Chicago, IL	1915
Asian		
Japanese Bank	San Francisco, CA	1903
Nichi Bei Ginko	San Francisco, CA	1904–05
Japanese Bank of Sacramento	Sacramento, CA	1904–05
Fuso Ginko of Vacaville	Vacaville, CA	1906
Kimmon Ginko	San Francisco, CA	1906
Japanese Bank	Oakland, CA	1907
Nippon Savings Bank	Sacramento, CA	1907
Canton Bank of San Francisco	San Francisco, CA	1907
O'Fu Savings Bank	Oakland, CA	1908
Kamikawa Bros. Bank	Fresno, CA	1908
Irish		
Hibernia Savings & Loan Society	San Francisco, CA	1859
Hibernia Savings Bank	Portland, OR	1892
Hibernia Savings Bank	Los Angeles, CA	1909

Table 6.1 Continued

Italian		
Columbus Savings & Loan Society	San Francisco, CA	1893
Italian-American Bank	San Francisco, CA	1899
Bank of Italy	San Francisco, CA	1904
Nordic		
Scandinavian National Bank	Chicago, IL	1872
Swedish-American National Bank	Minneapolis, MN	1901
Swedish American National Bank	Jamestown, NY	1901
Scandinavian-American National Bank	Sioux Falls, SD	1901
Swedish-American National Bank	Rockford, IL	1901
Scandinavian-American Bank	Astoria, OR	1907
Scandinavian-American Bank	Portland, OR	1908
Scandinavian-American Bank of Marshfield	Marshfield, OR	1914
Scandinavian Trust Company	New York City	1917
Hungarian		
Hungarian American Bank	New York City	1907

Note: Year refers to the year in which the bank was organized.

Sources: Ira B. Cross, *Financing an Empire: History of Banking in California* (Chicago: S. J. Clarke, 1927), 233–34; Frank P. Donavan and Cushing F. Wright, *The First Through a Century, 1853–1953: A History of the First National Bank of Saint Paul* (St. Paul, MN: First National Bank of St. Paul, 1954), 61–72; O. K. Burrell, *Gold in the Woodpile: An Informal History of Banking in Oregon* (Eugene: University of Oregon Press, 1967), 265. See also *Report of the Comptroller of the Currency* (Washington, D.C.: U.S. Government Printing Office, 1901, 1916).

explains the organization and strength of German banks after 1850 in the region. At that time, German banks had little difficulty promoting their existence in German. The number of German-language newspapers declined between the late eighteenth century and 1840, but rose dramatically from about 40 in 1840 to over 125 in 1853.[3]

Owing to the dominance of the English language among the nation's 20 million inhabitants, Anglo, non-Irish immigrants must have felt little need to establish English nationality banks. Many Anglo immigrants were linked to established English institutions in America and Canada before leaving Europe. In 1833 the Edinburgh-based British Linen Bank provided emigrants to the new world with letters of credit for deposited money that were accepted by Quebec City, Montreal, Toronto, and New York City banks. Newspaper advertisements told of two percent interest paid on deposits left with the bank for 39 days or more.[4]

The emergence of Oriental and southern European banks (Italian ones in particular) toward the end of the nineteenth century and early in the twentieth century reflects the proportionately small number of immigrants from these regions earlier in the century and their larger movement into the country later in the century. Between 1820 and 1855, about 7,000 Italians, 100 Greeks, 2,000 Portuguese, and 16,000 Chinese landed in America, hardly a sufficient base to establish nationality banks. In 1882, about 87 percent of European immigrants were from northern and western Europe, compared with 13 percent from southern and eastern Europe. In 1907 the proportions were reversed, with about 80 percent from the south and east and 20 percent from the north and west.

Immigration from the Orient was virtually nonexistent before 1850, but between then and 1882, over 300,000 Chinese entered the nation, mostly through San Francisco. This ended abruptly in 1882 with the passage of the Chinese Exclusion Act, renewed in 1892, which limited immigration from China. Chinese immigration was halted altogether in 1902. In 1885, Japan lifted the ban on emigration, and a number of Japanese went to Hawaii. They were allowed to enter the continental United States after the islands were absorbed in 1898, and did so at a rate of about 10,000 per year.

The emergence of Oriental and Italian banks in America thus reflects the changing source of immigrants over time. It was especially in California between 1880 and 1910 that Italian banks, and between 1900 and 1915 that Oriental banks, arose, indicating the popularity and later settlement of the region. The lack of the emergence of Chinese and Japanese chartered nationality banks in California prior to 1900 was also the result of virulent anti-Oriental sentiment that manifested itself in exclusionary laws, labor union protests, attempts to segregate schoolchildren, and mob violence. No doubt, private banks among these groups flourished.

A second observation about nationality banks concerns their acceptance by the public. In some localities, nationality banks, especially German ones, were very successful. In 1901 the German National Bank was the seventh largest of 13 national banks in Cincinnati, the German National Bank was the larger of two national banks in Little Rock (Arkansas), and the National German-American Bank was the larger of two national banks in Wausau (Wisconsin). In 1901, the National German-American Bank was the second largest of five national banks in St. Paul (Minnesota), and in 1915 it was the third largest bank in the city. From the 1860s on, the bank's credo suggests a concern with service quality:

> Strict adherence to general rules of legitimate banking. Abstaining from all transactions of a speculative nature. Close and prompt attention to all business entrusted to our care. Liberality to customers as far as is consistent with due safety. Upon the foundation of these principles, we beg leave to tender you the services of this bank and to solicit your business in this city and vicinity.

Banks representing other nationalities also were successful. By 1869, the Hibernia Savings & Loan Society had 14,060 depositors, more than the combined total of the other savings banks in San Francisco. The safety and security of

such a jewel was a source of nationalist pride. During a run in 1870, "speculators and money brokers" offered 50 to 80 cents on the dollar to nervous
depositors outside the bank. The bickering ended an hour later when several
wealthy Irishmen offered one dollar for every dollar in a passbook. In 1915 the
Scandinavian American National Bank was the third largest of four national
banks in St. Paul (Minnesota). The Hibernia National Bank was the fourth
largest of eight national banks in New Orleans. In 1928 the Hibernia Savings
Bank was the fourth largest bank in Portland (Oregon). The most successful of
all nationality banks was the Bank of Italy: by the late 1920s, it was the largest
bank in California and the tenth largest bank in the world.[5]

Third, nationality banks were organized almost exclusively by members of
the particular nationality group, many originally as private banks. The National
German-American Bank (of St. Paul) was chartered in 1863 but for the previous
decade had been a private bank called Meyers and Willius. The German Savings
& Loan Society (San Francisco) was organized in 1868 by leading German
citizens of the city (the first president and secretary were C. F. Mebius and G.
Wertzlar, respectively). In 1879 two Norwegians started a private bank called
Haugen & Lindgren, Bankers. The bank was reorganized in 1891 with a state
charter as the State Bank of Chicago. The lack of ethnic identification in the
new name reflected a broadening of the bank's customer base. The Nichi Bei
Ginko (Golden Gate) in San Francisco, the first bona fide Japanese bank in
California, was a private institution organized several years before 1905 by T.
Nakamura; the Japanese Bank of Sacramento was organized as a private bank by
Japanese residents of the city in 1904 or 1905; and the Canton Bank of San
Francisco, chartered in 1907, was organized by Look Tin Eli and other leading
Chinese citizens.

Fourth, although nationality banks may sound like altruistic endeavors, they
were not immune from mismanagement or fraud. When the 1877 crisis struck
Chicago, the panic engulfed Henry Greenbaum's German National Bank,
organized in 1871, and its affiliate, the German Savings Bank. Greenbaum
eventually faced more than 20 charges of fraud and embezzlement. The German
American Savings Bank (Washington, D.C.) was organized in 1872—its
"principal business was among the Germans of the District"—and failed in 1878.
The reason listed by examiners was "fraudulent management and depreciation of
securities." The California Bank Act of 1909 created the superintendent of
banks, who had the power to close unsafe banks. Of the ten banks closed by the
first superintendent in 1909 and 1910, five were Japanese. According to Ira B.
Cross, these banks had been "simply looted." To facilitate government
supervision of the industry, the superintendent required that all California banks
keep records in English.[6]

Fifth, it must be stressed that nationality banks did not exist in every locale
in America. In Massachusetts, for example, in 1901 no national nationality
banks existed. The paucity of nationality banks in any particular region was
probably a function of (1) an established banking system in that region, which
may have included a number of private "immigrant" banks (described in the next

section); (2) a lack of concentration of immigrants from a particular ethnic group; and/or (3) special efforts by extant nonnationality banks to meet the needs of immigrant customers. In the case of the latter, a number of nonnationality banks in New York City and in other major metropolitan areas were able to transact business in multiple languages.

Finally, special efforts to reach immigrants were not the exclusive domain of banking. In the insurance industry, for example, parallels exist. The Germania Insurance Company of New York began operations in 1860. (It changed its name to the Guardian Insurance Company of New York during World War I.) During the 1870s, the Mutual Benefit Life Insurance Company distributed German-language reports and prospectuses, and the Prudential Life Insurance Company printed policies in German as late as 1892. The most aggressive company regarding German customers was Metropolitan Life. In 1867 about half the customers of the National Travelers Insurance Company (which became Metropolitan Life in the following year) were German, due largely to the efforts of two German agents. The liberal policy of continuous coverage while traveling in Europe attracted more Germans. In 1869 Metropolitan Life formally established a German department to cultivate customers in and around New York City. The head of the department, Abraham Kaufmann, earned more in commissions that year than any other employee. To alleviate the difficulty of collecting small policy payments on a weekly basis, in 1869 Kaufmann seems to have organized the *Hildise Bund* (formed from the German saying *Hilf dir selbst*, or "Help Yourself"), a fraternal association that collected weekly dues and remitted them to Metropolitan on a quarterly basis. The suspicion that Kaufmann played a major role in organizing the *Bund* is based on two *Bund* rules: (1) officers, agents, or employees of all insurance providers except Metropolitan were barred from holding executive office positions; and (2) life insurance of some value (even if small) from Metropolitan was a requisite for membership. The *Bund* spread to German communities in the Midwest relatively quickly. Local chapters operated club rooms, and the association operated a sickness and disability fund on its own accord. The first mover advantage of Metropolitan was not easily overcome: during the early 1870s, New York Life organized a competing German association, but little headway was made. The success of Metropolitan with the *Bund* took a difficult turn during the economic crisis of 1877. Metropolitan raised the rates on *Bund* members; in response, about 80 percent of lapsed policies that year belonged to Germans. Abraham Kaufmann ran into personal financial difficulties and was forced to leave the company.[7]

Private Immigrant Banks

The second type of nationality bank was the private immigrant bank. From a legal perspective, these banks were identical to J. P. Morgan & Co. (New York City). From a social position, they were of considerably lower status. State laws regarding private banking were a hodgepodge: during the early 1910s, 19 states required all banks to have state or federal operating authority (e.g., Oklahoma,

California, Idaho, Nevada, California); nine states allowed private banking but regulated it (e.g., Arizona, Washington, North Carolina); and the remaining states, most notably New York, did not regulate private banking. In unregulated states, private banks had no capital reserve requirements. Many had small reserves, some kept substandard records, and others paid no interest on deposits. A few operated at multiple-site locations, and many failed due to lack of control.

General mistrust of private immigrant bankers led to an investigation by the federal government. A 1911 Senate commission noted that many private immigrant banks were in good community standing. The proprietor was of the same ethnic origin as customers, thus creating a bond not reproducible by Anglo banks. In 1910 at least 2,625 immigrants banks operated in America. They were concentrated heavily in Northeast urban areas, most notably in New York City, which contained 38 percent of them. The majority of private immigrant banks were operated by Italians (40.5 percent), followed by Jews (12.9 percent), Poles (11.2 percent), and Hungarians (7.8 percent).[8]

Virtually all of the 116 immigrant banks studied in detail by the Senate commission performed nonbank services. The most common was serving as steamship ticket agent (87 percent). By 1890, the Hamburg-Amerika Line, the Red-Star Line, and the Anchor Line, respectively, had about 3,200, 1,800, and 1,500 agents in America, a number of whom combined the service with private banking. In Europe, the steamship lines promoted emigration to America, as did the land-grant railroads and, after the 1860s, the northwestern states stretching from Wisconsin to Washington. (The latter distributed maps and pamphlets and sent immigration agents to Europe.) The steamship companies planned capacity on the volume of traffic from Europe to America and were thus willing to saturate the American market with agents to utilize that capacity for return voyages. The Senate investigation concluded there were between 5,000 and 6,000 commissioned steamship ticket street peddlers or runners in New York City alone.[9]

Another product sold by private immigrant banks were money orders. By 1910 these banks captured about 50 percent of the market for consumer sales of money orders sent overseas. They were supported by national suppliers. For instance, just after World War I, the American Express Company began an intensive campagin to brand its name within immigrant markets. Foreign-language immigrant newspaper advertising was used liberally, the languages being Greek, Polish, Yiddish, German, Bohemian, Slovak, Hungarian, Slovenian, Croatian, Italian, and Romanian. To overcome the unscrupulous image of many subagents—some of them private immigrant banks—a message of trustworthiness was repeated in advertisments regardless of the foreign language or specific theme: "Insist on an American Express receipt: it is your insurance against loss." A standard sign (i.e., brand) was developed for subagents to display, and posters and brochures were designed for each language group; for instance, Italian subagents received Italian-language display material showing the Bay of Naples, a major embarkation point for emigrants. Promotional foreign-language folders with space for subagents to stamp their names and addresses were provided at no charge. Around 1920, American Express began to sell folders to subagents at cost; these folders were imprinted with the name and address of the subagent.[10]

Private immigrant banks were located in pool halls, hotels, groceries, and drinking establishments, and they were operated by real estate agents, notaries public, labor contractors, and grocers. Some published foreign-language organs; others advertised in local foreign-language newspapers with copy that was to the point: "A stock of the better quality of Tobacco. Italian Grocery. Gold and silver money both foreign and American bought and sold at a good rate." Some advertisements were misleading, especially those that used the word "bank." Chartered banks were concerned with the practice because they saw use of the word "bank" as positioning an institution under regulatory control. The window display was the key way to inform the public of a private bank's existence, and the most common item used was currency. In New York City, it was said that more than $1,000 was necessary in a window to attract customers.[11]

Private immigrant banks were attuned to the special needs of customers. Many were open during evening hours, Jewish and many Italian ones were open Sunday mornings, and others were open all day Saturday. Accessibility of this sort could create problems. During the 1920s, a private Jewish banker of Russian descent in Chicago's Jewish ghetto experienced a run on a Sunday. His reserve was in an incorporated bank that was closed, so he was forced to pay depositors in rubles and promise to exchange them for dollars on the next day.[12]

The Senate commission summarized the situation thus: "His [the private immigrant banker's] willingness to conform to the convenience and peculiar needs of his patrons give [sic] the immigrant banker a distinct advantage over his American competitor."[13]

The failure of the Tisbo brothers private bank about a decade after the Senate investigation illustrates the failure of the commission to materially affect private immigrant bank practice. Rumors of the disappearance of Vincenzo, Vitto, and Francisco Tisbo caused a near riot outside their New York City office in 1923. Police initially estimated that 40,000 depositors owed $2 million were abandoned by the steamship ticket agent private bank. On a tip that they had left the country, Italian authorities guarded their ports; American Express and several steamship companies publicly defended their channels of distribution; and grass-roots committees organized publicity campaigns to encourage Italians to deal with regulated institutions. Eventually, Francisco Tisbo and his wife were arrested in Naples and tried in an Italian court. A fourth brother, Riccardo, was arrested after the failure of an Italian-based bank. The two remaining Tisbo brothers were nowhere to be found. Investigators revised the public loss down to $200,000 and pinned the downfall of the empire on a failed Brooklyn laundry.[14]

THE EFFECT OF WORLD WAR I ON GERMAN BANKING

American involvement in World War I on the side of the Allies had a tremendous effect on German nationality banking. Almost overnight, German institutions were on the wrong side of the war, and they faced a public relations fiasco. By the end of the war, no German nationality banks (by name) remained. Also caught in the fray were German hotels, insurance companies, restaurants, and bakeries. Table 6.2 provides a sample of German nationality banks that changed names after America declared war. The comptroller of the currency quickly granted name change requests during the period. Even banks without "German" in their names that were owned by Germans were forced to respond to the war. In Denver in 1917, the majority owner of the Colorado National Bank, Harold Kountze, felt compelled to hang American flags and 10-foot banners proclaiming "Buy Victory Bonds" on the bank. German banks resisted public opinion and in some cases vigorously defended themselves. In a full-page advertisement in the April 13, 1917, issue of the *Denver Post*, the German American Trust Company said that the bank was controlled by Americans and had no foreign investments. The appeal was insufficient, for within a year the bank had become the American Bank & Trust Company. Even a formidable institution such as the German Savings Institution (of St. Louis), with capital and surplus amounting to $2.5 million (compared with $9.5 million, $6.5 million, and $5.0 million for the Mercantile Trust Company, the Mississippi Valley Trust Company, and the St. Louis Union Bank, respectively), could not navigate against the current of public opinion. It became the Liberty Bank in 1918. In St. Louis, German and non-German banks confronted public relations problems during World War I. At the beginning of the war, when America was not yet involved, the German-American Alliance of St. Louis threatened to withdraw funds from banks promoting Allied war bonds. (Liberty bonds were not created until direct American involvement in the war.) In 1915, a coalition of nine of the city's leading banks announced their subscription to $2.7 million of Allied war bonds. Since the British and French governments had recently procured horses and related supplies in St. Louis markets, the coalition supported the British and French efforts in order to gain their continued business. At the same time, local Germans were mollified by the coalition's promise that none of the bonds would finance the purchase of munitions or arms and that the banks would sell war bonds issued by both the Allied governments and the imperial German government. The official declaration of war against Germany in April 1917 changed all this, however.[15]

CULTIVATING MULTIPLE NATIONALITY GROUPS

Many nonnationality banks sought to meet the needs of multiple nationality groups. The critical factor in attracting nationality groups was offering foreign-language service and information. Fred Heuchling, vice president of North-Western Trust & Savings Bank (Chicago) in 1925 discussed gap theory as it related to nationality groups:

Table 6.2
Sample of German Banks That Changed Names During World War I

Original Name	New Name	Location
German American Trust & Savings Bank	Guaranty Trust & Savings Bank	Los Angeles, CA
German Savings & Loan Society	San Francisco Savings & Loan Society	San Francisco, CA
German-American Trust & Savings Bank	Guaranty Trust & Savings Bank	Los Angeles, CA
German-American Bank	Golden State Bank of Anaheim	Anaheim, CA
German State Bank	Cottonwood State Bank	Cottonwood, ID
German American Bank	Continental Bank of New York	New York City
Germania Bank	Commonwealth Bank	New York City
German Exchange Bank	Commercial Exchange Bank	New York City
German National Bank of Allegheny	National Bank of America at Pittsburgh	Pittsburgh, PA
German Bank of Chicago	Cosmopolitan State Bank	Chicago, IL
German American State Bank of Matteson	State Bank of Matteson	Matteson, IL
German American Bank	American State Bank of Bloomington	Bloomington, IL
German American Bank of East Dubuque	American State of East Dubuque	East Dubuque, IL
German Bank	Stephenson State Bank	Freeport, IL
German-American State Bank of Roanoke	Roanoke State Bank	Roanoke, IL
German Trust & Savings Bank	American Trust & Savings Bank	Rock Island, IL
German State Bank	Hoyleton State and Savings Bank	Hoyleton, IL

Sources: "Rename German Banks," *NYT*, 21 January 1918; "Bank Drops German Name," *NYT*, 2 April 1918; "German Omitted from Bank Names," *NYT*, 8 June 1918.

It is useless to publish an invitation to Germans, for example, to do business with your bank, if you cannot keep them satisfied after you have secured their accounts. If your published invitation appears in the German language, it is natural for them to assume that, if they wish, they can transact their business with you in that same tongue.[16]

Undoubtedly the most successful nationality bank in America was the Bank of Italy. It was organized in 1904 in San Francisco by A. P. Gianinni because of his inability, as a director of the Columbus Savings & Loan Society, to effect changes in the bank's credit policy. He organized the Bank of Italy to focus on small, independent entrepreneurs rather than on the business interests of bank directors. By 1927, Gianinni had transformed a single, insignificant office into a banking empire with over $600 million in deposits. In 1928 it was the tenth largest bank in the world (the bank is now Bank of America). By that time, the bank had in place effective means to attract and handle multiple nationality groups. During the early 1920s, a "foreign department" was organized at the head office with responsibility for Russian, Spanish, Greek, Slavonic, Chinese, and Portuguese divisions. Each division had a staff of one or two, one of whom was an assistant cashier. The staff ensured that branches in ethnic areas were staffed by individuals from that group. They were also responsible for drumming up savings, loan, and foreign exchange business. Norman N. Yue, who headed the Chinese division, monitored operations in San Francisco, Los Angeles, Sacramento, Stockton, and Oakland, and staffed appropriate branches with Chinese employees. The Bank of Italy, in 1926 and 1927, attracted 3,757 Chinese accounts totaling $3.3 million in deposits. By 1926, the bank had 4,155 Greek customers, mostly from San Francisco and Los Angeles, with $5 million in deposits. The Portuguese division concentrated its efforts on towns in central California. The Slovenians were scattered throughout the state, but aggressive efforts yielded a total of 13,543 accounts totaling $6.6 million by 1930. Twenty-five Spanish tellers were deployed in southern California; this effort attracted 1,886 new accounts between 1928 and 1930, with $1.4 million in deposits. The Russian division was started in 1921, and by the end of the following year, it had attracted 585 accounts, totaling almost $500,000 in deposits. The Bank of Italy also printed booklets in each of these languages describing the history of the bank, available services and directions for their use (e.g., banking by mail, in Chinese), American immigration policies, and tips on how to pass the citizenship exam. With the exception of the Italian division, the foreign divisions eventually came under control of the bank's business extension department. As the bank grew to one of the largest in the America, Italians remained the core customer base. In 1928 approximately 20 percent of deposits and 40 percent of share-holders could be traced to individuals of Italian descent.[17]

Another bank that aggressively sought multiple nationality groups was the Dollar Savings & Trust Company (Youngstown, Ohio). It formed a foreign department in 1906 to attract the half of the city that was foreign born. The bank hired a manager who was fluent in several European languages and had experience in foreign exchange. He traveled overseas and arranged connections with English, Italian, German, French, and Russian banks. The bank became a steamship ticket agent to supplement its established banking business. Ancillary services and promotions ensued, such as the provision of lodging and employment information, poste restante service, and free picture postcards of the bank. The department was unprofitable during its first few years, but by 1918 deposits totaled about $7 million from some 10,000 depositors, and the department's nine tellers were fluent in 14 languages.[18]

Many other nonnationality banks, especially those in the Northeast, sought out multiple nationality groups by providing service and promotional material in multiple languages. This was particularly true of many New York City banks (e.g., the Bowery Savings Bank). During the 1900s, the First National Bank of Pittsburgh promoted its ability to transact business in 22 languages. One of its advertisements illustrates how a bank seeking the foreign born adjusted its product offering.

> All languages are spoken at the First National Bank of Pittsburgh, and every detail of foreign business is attended to with promptness and accuracy. Foreign money of all denominations bought and sold. Money remitted to any point abroad, by mail, cable or money order. Steamship tickets sold and berths reserved. Tourists supplied with letters of credit and Travelers' Checks. Passports obtained when necessary, and clients kept informed of the movement of ships. Commercial credits established abroad for importers.

During the 1910s, the savings department of the Second National Bank (Toledo, Ohio) employed physical means of identifying foreign-born customers. Fingerprints and a standardized card that recorded height, weight, eye and hair color, birthmarks, amputations, moles, scars, and deformities assured correct identification of customers, perhaps a necessity when the teller and customer shared no common language. The Fletcher Savings & Trust Company (Indianapolis) employed a translator who spoke nine languages in addition to sign language. Three women solicitors visited factories and large retail stores, distributing foreign-language literature. The Cleveland Trust Company operated a "Departmento Italiano," and the United States National Bank of Portland (Oregon) and the Ladd & Tilton Bank (Oregon) both advertised in Italian in *La Tribuna Italiana*, a Portland community newspaper. During the 1920s, the Union Trust Company (Cleveland) operated "neighborhood" branches with Jewish, Hungarian, and Polish staffs and advertised in these languages in local foreign-language newspapers.[19]

AFRICAN-AMERICAN BANKING

Banking service for African-Americans was initially organized by the military. In 1864 Union generals commanding African-American troops organized banks in New Orleans, Norfolk (Virginia), and Beaufort (South Carolina). Troops were encouraged to deposit a portion of their pay into these banks. Like the Free Labor Bank (New Orleans), these banks were open to all African-Americans. The next year a minister named John W. Alvord proposed uniting these military banks to better promote thrift and economy among African-Americans. As a result of these efforts, the U.S. Congress granted a charter in March 1865 to the Freedmen's Savings Bank & Trust Company to operate in the District of Columbia (the bank is commonly referred to as the Freedmen's Bank). John Alvord was the secretary, and he arranged for 50 prominent individuals to sit on the board of trustees. He was also an inspector and superintendent of schools for the Freedmen's Bureau. The Bureau, organized in 1865 by the federal government and operated by the War Department, attempted to regulate the life and work of newly freed African-Americans, many of whom had congregated around military bases at the end of the Civil War. It engaged extensively in church work and education and provided information to African-Americans on political and social rights, but it failed to improve their material welfare.

John Alvord, along with a former military paymaster who oversaw payments to large numbers of African-Americans during the war and who promoted a similar plan to amalgamate the military banks at the end of the war, began organizing branches throughout the South. The establishment of a head office in New York City and branches outside the District of Columbia contravened the bank's charter, which limited operations to the District. Whether from a fear of undermining reconstruction efforts or a belief that the charter guaranteed the bank's safe operation (Congress could examine the bank's books at any time and required that two-thirds of deposits be held in U.S. securities), Congress mistakenly—in retrospect—turned a blind eye to operational transgressions. Freedmen's absorbed the military savings banks, and bank representatives were present when African-American regiments were paid. The connection between the Freedmen's Bureau and the Freedmen's Bank ran deep. General O. O. Howard, commissioner of the Freedmen's Bureau, endorsed the bank. The bank's passbook contained the usual thrift exhortations of the period, Howard's endorsement, and a statement that the bank was enacted through congressional legislation. Freedmen's Bank trustee George W. Balloch, the "chief disbursing officer" of the Freedmen's Bureau, allowed Freedmen's Bank employees to solicit customers at the Bureau's offices. Some Freedmen's Bureau agents became Freedmen's Bank cashiers, and a number of customers were served by individuals garbed in uniform. The 1870 passbook used in New York City said in English, German, and French that "the government of the United States has made this bank perfectly safe." All of these factors led prospective and current depositors to assume that the bank and the Bureau were connected, that the bank was an official arm of the American government, and that deposits were insured by the federal government. The bank did little to correct these misconceptions.

When the bank moved its head office to Washington, D.C., in 1868, a movement was well under way to train African-Americans for managerial positions. In 1870 the bank was allowed to conduct regular banking business (e.g., to provide loans), but most branches, at least initially, continued to engage primarily in the deposit line of business. Branches retained local African-American property owners, who formed advisory boards to guide policy and promote bank development. The head office distributed regular reports and pamphlets on the bank's progress and on thrift. By 1872, the Freedmen's Bank operated 34 branches in 16 states from Florida to New York City, although the vast bulk were located in Southern states; and in 1874 deposits totaled $3.3 million from approximately 70,000 depositors. Not all depositors were African-

Americans. In New York City, 1,000 of 4,000 depositors, and in Charleston, 300 of 2,790 depositors, were Caucasians.

Shortly after the bank moved its head office to Washington, D.C., difficulties began to arise. The bank drew on little experience, either internally or from other banks, in branch management and control. Inspections were infrequent, accounting procedures were lacking, and ill-prepared African-Americans were promoted too quickly. Some branch cashiers, sensing opportunity, committed fraud. For example, Rev. Philip D. Cory, of the Atlanta branch, encouraged Caucasian depositors while discouraging African-American ones. Evidently he hoped to sever ties with Freedmen's and form his own bank. Cory was sentenced in 1874 to a four-year prison term for embezzlement ($100,000 was missing), but was pardoned in exchange for becoming an Indian agent in the West and the promise to make restitution. More damaging was a "Washington clique" that wrested control of the bank from the trustees. As one historian of the bank explained: "Between 1870 and 1873 the Freedmen's Bank was practically controlled by Jay Cooke and Company and the First National Bank [of Washington]." The Washington clique gained control over the bank's finance committee. There were many questionable transactions: Jay Cooke borrowed $500,000 at five percent interest while the bank was paying six percent on deposits; worthless real estate loans were sold at "full value" to Freedmen's by the First National Bank; unsecured loans or loans against worthless paper were given to contractors and speculators (one public works contractor obtained $180,000 in this fashion); and representatives of the Freedmen's Bank received loans based on worthless paper. When the bank faced severe cash shortages in 1873 and 1874 and was unable to collect on worthless paper, trustees, not liable for losses, began withdrawing from the bank, word spread of mismanagement, runs developed, and the bank was forced to sell viable securities. A national bank examiner in 1874 concluded that the bank had been insolvent for over a year. Now aged and enfeebled, John Alvord was removed as Freedmen's president, a figurehead post for the last few years. Frederick Douglass, a well respected African-American, was named president of the bank in 1876, but he apparently was unaware of the mismanagement that antedated his appointment and of the examiner's report. Three months after Douglass took charge, the bank closed its doors. The bank's affairs were wound up, and as loans collected or written off, depositors received 62 cents on the dollar, the last seven cents paid in 1882. As late as 1910, the possibility of reimbursing depositors was raised in Congress, but at that point there was little interest in the subject.[20]

After Freedmen's, a lull existed in African-American banking; it was 1888 before additional banks were organized. A minimum of 134 African-American-operated banks were organized between 1888 and 1936, and virtually all of the 28 organized between 1888 and 1905 acted as depositories for African-American insurance and burial orders (i.e., fraternal associations organized by African-American ministers and churches). One of the earliest was the Savings Bank of the Grand Fountain United Order of True Reformers, organized in Richmond (Virginia) in 1888. The bank was organized by the Grand Order of the True

Reformers, which had been founded in 1881. In addition to the bank, subordinate to the Order were: (1) the Reformers Mercantile and Industrial Association, operational for some time before its formal organization in 1900; (2) a retirement home; and (3) the Westham Farm, an association to promote the development of an African-American agricultural community. With over 50,000 members in 1901, the Order was successful within the African-American community, but the bank failed in 1910 for long supplying credit to the Order's money-losing interests. (The receiver stated that "The Order wrecked the bank.")

Other African-American banks were organized independently of fraternal associations. Their motives, similar to those ascribed to members of other nationality or racial groups, centered on the need for access to credit and the sense that they were denied such by the current banking system. For example, the Capital Savings Bank (Washington, D.C.) was begun in 1888 as an outgrowth of the Industrial Building & Savings Company. A statement of purpose (1885) said that it was formed "in response to the demand of colored men to be admitted into the channels of business." It continued:

> We saw that we were putting many thousands of dollars into the financial institutions of this city, thereby contributing largely to the support of its business houses. But we were not represented in the management of this business, nor in the clerical force, nor in any fiduciary capacity. In short, as things were, we had no opportunity to learn the art of business. There was need also of an institution for savings that would reach the poorer classes of colored people, teach them the importantness of being industrious, of seeking steady employment, of saving their money and getting homes, giving them an opportunity to pay for their homes in small installments, and teach the importance of fostering and building up strong business interests among ourselves.

In Maryland, Edward B. Taylor helped establish the Taylor & Jenkins Bank. He was frustrated with the current banking system because he was unable to obtain commercial credit despite that fact that his catering business generated nearly $100,000 per year in revenues. Regardless of the orientation of early African-American banks, they were plagued by the nature of their credit portfolios. The lack of industrial and commercial business ownership among the African-American market pressured banks to promote real estate, theatrical, or other amusement enterprises in order to expand their loan base. These customers were riskier than those engaged in manufacturing, a situation leading to a more unsound financial base than those of banks sponsoring production and assembly operations. Despite the difficulties, a number of African-American banks organized prior to 1930 continued to operate during the 1980s. Table 6.3 provides a list.[21]

CANADIAN BANKS

When the Canadian West was opened for settlement during the first decade of the twentieth century, one of the earliest immigrant groups to arrive was Americans. The Canadian Bank of Commerce aggressively sought their business,

Table 6.3
Pre-1930 African-American-Owned Banks

Institution	Location	Year
Berean Savings Association	Philadelphia, PA	1888
Tuskegee Federal Savings & Loan Assn.	Tuskegee, AL	1894
Consolidated Bank & Trust Company	Richmond, VA	1903
Citizens Savings Bank & Trust Company	Nashville, TN	1904
Mechanics and Farmers Bank	Durham, NC	1908
Berkley Federal Savings Bank	Norfolk, VA	1913
New Age Federal Savings & Loan Assn.	St. Louis, MO	1915
First State Bank	Danville, VA	1919
Ideal Savings & Loan Association	Baltimore, MD	1920
Citizens Trust Bank	Atlanta, GA	1921
Victory Savings Bank	Columbia, SC	1921
Mutual Savings & Loan Association	Durham, NC	1921
Columbia Savings & Loan Association	Milwaukee, WI	1924
Mutual Federal Savings & Loan Association of Atlanta	Atlanta, GA	1925
Carver State Bank	Savannah, GA	1927
Imperial Savings & Loan Association of Mobile	Mobile, AL	1929

Note: Year refers to year of founding.

Sources: "Bank Overview," *Black Enterprise*, 22 (June 1987): 193–94; "Savings & Loan Overview," *Black Enterprise*, 22 (June 1987): 211–12.

and its success encouraged it to formulate plans to attract the business of recently arrived non-English-speaking immigrants. Victor Ross, author of a 1922 history of the Canadian Bank of Commerce, explained why the immigrant-related efforts of the Canadian banks lagged that of their American counterparts.

> There was therefore a call to provide banking facilities suited to the needs of these foreigners, many of whom could not speak English, and were unfamiliar with the business methods of this country [Canada]. In the United States a similar problem had presented itself at an earlier date and had in great measure been solved by the organization of small banks for the avowed purpose of catering to the needs of the various nationalities. In any neighbourhood where a colony of one particular nationality of any size had sprung up, one of these banks would be organized, its staff comprising at least one officer who could speak the language and was familiar with the customs of the foreigners. In Canada there was no legal provision for forming such small banks, and the task of providing for the needs of the newcomers had to be taken up by the head offices, if anything was to be done.

The sentiment that the foreign born were an appealing class of customer was echoed in 1926 by an Oshawa (Ontario) branch manager of the Canadian Bank of Commerce: the foreign born were "as a class, hard-working, frugal, thrifty and saving." Despite an appreciation for immigrants and an understanding of the impediments to establishing nationality banks, Canadian bankers never availed themselves of the opportunity to the extent observed in America.[22]

NOTES

1. E. Franklin Frazier, *The Negro in the United States* (New York: Macmillan, 1957), 387–413.

2. These figures were created by analyzing *Report of the Comptroller of the Currency* (Washington, D.C.: U.S. Government Printing Office, 1901 and 1916).

3. John T. Holdsworth, *Financing an Empire: History of Banking in Pennsylvania* (Chicago: S. J. Clarke, 1928), 398–418; Maldwyn A. Jones, *American Immigration* (Chicago: University of Chicago Press, 1960), 124–37.

4. Charles A. Malcolm, *The History of the British Linen Bank* (Edinburgh: T. and A. Constable, Ltd., 1950), 104.

5. Ira B. Cross, *Financing an Empire: History of Banking in California* (Chicago: S. J. Clarke, 1927), 233–34; Frank P. Donavan and Cushing F. Wright, *The First Through a Century, 1853–1953: A History of the First National Bank of Saint Paul* (St. Paul, MN: First National Bank of St. Paul, 1954), 61–72; O. K. Burrell, *Gold in the Woodpile: An Informal History of Banking in Oregon* (Eugene: University of Oregon Press, 1967), 265.

6. Cyril F. James, *The Growth of Chicago Banks* (New York: Harper & Brothers, 1938), 496–503, 1253–54; David M. Cole, *The Development of Banking in the District of Columbia* (New York: William Frederick Press, 1959), 348–52.

7. Marquis James, *The Metropolitan Life: A Study in Business Growth* (New York: Viking Press, 1947), 33–44, 67–68; Mildred F. Stone, *Since 1845: A History of the Mutual Benefit Life Insurance Company* (Newark, NJ: Rutgers University Press, 1957), 74; William H. A. Carr, *From Three Cents a Week . . . The Story of The Prudential Insurance Company of America* (Englewood Cliffs, NJ: Prentice-Hall, 1975), 23.

8. "Immigrant Banks, *Reports of the Immigration Commission*, (Washington, D.C.: U.S. Government Printing Office, 1911), 197–350.

9. William J. Bromwell, *History of Immigration to the United States* (1855; repr., New York: Augustus M. Kelly, 1969); Jones, *American Immigration*.

10. "Immigrant Banks," *Reports of the Immigration Commission*, 197–350; J. Duncan Holmes, "How Foreign-Born Respond to Neat Advertising," *BMo*, 39 (January 1922): 14–15+.

11. "Immigrant Banks," *Reports of the Immigration Commission*, 230; "Overdone Advertising," *JABA*, 12 (August 1919): 77–78.

12. Jones, *American Immigration*, 202.

13. "Immigrant Banks," *Reports of the Immigration Commission*, 234.

14. "Fake Bankers with $2,000,000 Vanish," *NYT*, 14 March 1923; "Tisbo Safes Opened as Italians Riot," *NYT*, 13 March 1923; "Immigrant Inquiry Gets Quick Results: Tisbo Depositors Lose All," *NYT*, 14 November 1923.

15. Timothy W. Hubbard and Louis E. Davids, *Banking in Mid-America: A History of Missouri's Banks* (Washington D.C.: Public Affairs Press, 1969), 141–43; Thomas J. Noel, *Growing Through History with Colorado: The Colorado National Banks, the First 125 Years*, 1862–1987 (Denver: Colorado National Banks, 1987), 25.

16. Fred G. Heuchling, "Reaching out for Business Among the Foreign Born," *BMo*, 42 (September 1925): 13.

17. Franklin S. Clark, "How Seven Foreign Departments Win Foreigners' Business," *BMo*, 42 (December 1925): 26–27+; Marquis James and Bessie R. James, *Biography of a Bank: The Story of Bank of America N.T. & S.A.* (New York: Harper & Brothers, 1954), 211–21.

18.   J. N. Higley, "Banks and the Foreigners," *BMa*, 98 (March 1919): 313–36.

19. "1910 Calendar and New Year's Advertising," *BMa*, 80 (February 1910): 327; A. W. Shaw Company, *Advertising and Service* (Chicago: A. W. Shaw Company, 1918), 187–88; P. J. Slach, "Methods We Use in Winning Foreigners," *BMo*, 43 (February 1926): 26–27+; Burrell, *Gold in the Woodpile*, 258. Advertisement reprinted in *BMa*, 77 (August, 1908): 255.

20. Walter L. Fleming, *The Freedmen's Savings Bank* (Chapel Hill: University of North Carolina Press, 1927).

21. Abram L. Harris, *The Negro as Capitalist* (Philadelphia: American Academy of Political and Social Science, 1936).

22. H. Duncan, "The Foreigner as a Banking Prospect," *Caduceus*, 6 (January 1926): 39–41 (CIBC archives); Victor A. Ross, *A History of the Canadian Bank of Commerce*, Vol. II (Toronto: Oxford University Press, 1922).

7

User Status Segmentation

User status segmentation is taken here to mean splitting the market into new or potential customers, current customers, and past customers, and designing a special marketing mix for each. Certainly much of what has already been discussed (a service quality orientation, market segmentation on the basis of age, gender, and nationality or race) would go a long way toward generating new customers. Here, however, we are interested in mechanisms used to attract new business across a spectrum of the entire market that include personal solicitation, employee new-business campaigns, special savings plans, and related promotions. The first part of this chapter dicusses new or potential customers.

Marketing to current customers means devising special plans to increase sales to and provide better service to those who are already customers. In the department store industry after 1900, managers encouraged suggestion selling, which in part entailed suggesting a tie to go with a shirt, a purse to match shoes, and so on. Suggestion selling bridged the gap between having salespeople specialize in particular wares or departments and interselling, allowing salespeople to lead customers throughout the store and assist in making purchases from multiple departments. Interselling was undesirable because it unbalanced staff levels and made it difficult to allocate selling costs to departments. To increase interdepartmental sales without interselling, some department stores relied on referrals whereby salespeople in pairs referred customers to one another.[1]

Some businesses collect demographic information (e.g., name, age, income, occupation, residence) and service or product usage rates as a matter of normal operations. Banks, insurance organizations, and many industrial goods suppliers may form membership relations with customers. Some retailers may attempt to create membership relations with customers to foster loyalty. Department stores of the late nineteenth and early twentieth centuries formed membership relations with upper-class women, a small but influential portion of their customer base, through charge cards. Manufacturers of consumer nondurables can form membership relations with wholesalers and retailers, but being one or more levels removed from final consumers makes exact identification of current consumers a difficult task. But the close link between bank and customer is unparalleled and affords many unusual opportunities. If bankers desire, they can create a centralized file on all current customers and use it for cross-selling purposes and to identify inactive and dormant accounts. The banking industry did develop such central information files early in the twentieth century. Retailers with customers and items for sale numbering in the thousands could hardly undertake such an effort. Manufacturers could do so for wholesalers, retailers, and industrial markets, but would find the construction and maintenance cost of such files for final consumers inefficient. In banking, where membership relations are naturally formed, where the number of customers could be large but not prohibitive, and where the number of products was small, a centralized file on customers could be profitable.

Because banks could track exactly which services were being used and in what quantity (through central information files), they were able to estimate individual customer profitability. Customer profitability was particularly important for providers of demand deposit service because of high operating costs. In the insurance, department store, and many manufacturing industries, attention was paid to goods because of product standardization, although the number of goods handled was a moderating factor. For example, in department stores, accountants concentrated on product profitability, often treated in departmental terms to reduce the number of units analyzed. As a consequence, departments and buyers, but rarely customers, were analyzed for profitability. But when bankers standardized a product (such as Christmas Clubs) or controlled the source of customers (as in Industrial Savings Clubs), they quickly focused on product rather than customer profitability. The second part of this chapter deals with current customers by discussing central information files, direct mail, and customer profitability.

The final part of the chapter deals with past customers. It was the central information file that most effectively allowed banks to track service usage rates and identify inactive or dormant accounts. Special efforts to reach these customers are discussed.

NEW/POTENTIAL CUSTOMERS

Personal Solicitation

A cardinal feature of pre-1900 banking industry in America and elsewhere was the time-honored custom of not interfering with another bank's established customers, a custom of European origin. For example, in 1839 the directors of the Belfast Banking Company, the Northern Banking Company, and the Provincial Bank of Ireland (Belfast's three largest banks) agreed that:

> In future no solicitation or canvassing for accounts either by public bodies or private individuals is to be permitted on the part of any director, manager or any other person in the pay or employment of any of the above banking companies, that all applications or proposals emanating from the banks are to be considered as solicitations and discontinued accordingly.

Later in the nineteenth century, Irish bankers began determining the pay of branch managers on branch performance rather than strictly on age and tenure. Despite exhortations from the head office to increase business volume and performance-based incentives, the anti-solicitation agreement held throughout the century.[2]

In America, life insurance-trust companies were formed during the early nineteenth century. The Pennsylvania Company for Life Insurers on Lives and Granting Annuities, one of the first in the nation, was organized in 1812 and, like others of its time, adopted a passive new-business stance. Organizers considered, but did not hire, sales agents. They advertised and distributed sales booklets, but sales presentations were made only to those who came to the organization's office. There was no active follow-up of prospects. These American life insurance-trust companies had aggressive models to follow but initially chose not to. English life insurance companies had adopted commissioned agents during the late eighteenth century, and the marine insurance industry in America followed suit by the 1820s. The New York Life Insurance and Trust Company, organized in 1830, was the first American life insurance company to appoint agents. Agents both passed on farm and village property loans, receiving a commission, and sold life insurance. It was not until the mid-1830s that these agents generated substantial revenue from commissioned sales, and for most agents, life insurance sales were secondary to other business and legal affairs. The life insurance industry underwent dramatic change during the 1840s with the organization of the nation's first mutual, which employed commissioned agents who increasingly were to provide for themselves solely on the basis of life insurance sales.[3]

Despite the increasing number of commissioned agents in the life insurance industry and of drummers in general during the mid-to-later nineteenth century, the noninterference tradition was still observed in banking. For example, Junius Morgan was admitted in 1854 to George Peabody & Co., a London-based private bank. While he was finalizing his private affairs, Peabody wrote to Morgan, asking him to make a "complimentary call," a "friendly visit," on Wm. Wilson & Co. of Baltimore, a large shipowner doing considerable trade with India. Wilson was already the client of Brown, Shipley & Co., another private bank. But the purpose of this visit did not cross the fine line because it would be "favorably remembered" should Wilson cease relations with its current merchant bank. Peabody & Co. aggressively sought new business, much more so than Baring Brothers & Co., another London-based merchant bank that during the mid-eighteenth century "because of their position, did not openly recruit business; clients applied to them." The aggressiveness of Peabody & Co. in seeking new business was thought by Junius Morgan and George Peabody to explain in part the firm's 1857–58 financial troubles. But they lived by the solicitation rule. In 1864 George Peabody retired and Junius Morgan took over, renaming the institution J. S. Morgan & Co. Within days Drexel & Co. of Philadelphia shifted its account to Brown, Shipley & Co. In his retrospective on the history of the Morgans, Vincent P. Carosso said:

> Either because of what he had learned from friends in Philadelphia or because Drexel & Co. had failed to explain satisfactorily the reasons for its action, Morgan believed that Brown Brothers, taking advantage of Peabody's retirement, had solicited the account and won it by negotiating a lower rate on commissions. Respectable bankers (then and well into the twentieth century) did not interfere with their competitors' clients. Not only did they eschew such tactics, but when they did accept a customer with an established banking relationship, such as Drexel & Co. had with the Morgan's house, they did so only after the client had informed his banker that he was leaving of his own accord, not because he had been enticed to do by some other firm.[4]

During the latter part of the nineteenth century, the anti-solicitation rule began to break down. In 1898 the New Haven Clearing House Association passed a resolution barring solicitation of other banks' established customers. Such a resolution would hardly have been necessary if the banking community was observing the anti-solicitation rule. Before describing the new form of solicitation at the consumer level, an event that helped dissolve the rule in Canada and impacted America is described.

The Dissolution of the Canadian Rule

In Canada, the Canadian Bankers Association took the lead in enforcing the anti-solicitation rule. But by the end of the nineteenth century, the custom was eroding. In 1899 two representatives of a Winnipeg branch of the Bank of Nova Scotia visited an established customer of another bank, and the matter was brought to the attention of the Winnipeg subsection of the Canadian Bankers Association. The president of the subsection, in an open letter dated April 19, 1899, stated that "such a course has always been considered unprofessional, improper, and unsafe," and that "while all the members of this Sub-Section are desirous of extending friendly and neighborly relations to fellow Bankers, any repetition of such action as now referred to must result in the withdrawal of such friendly relations." The letter, which did not mention any of the involved parties by name, was distributed to the Winnipeg members of the association and to the general managers of all banks doing business in Winnipeg.

Having been informed that it was staff of his bank who had violated the standard, H. C. McLeod, general manager of the Bank of Nova Scotia, responded in a letter dated May 3, 1899. In it he asked for proof of the charges, why no hearing had been held, and why the head office of the bank had not been informed prior to distribution of the subsection president's letter. "The usefulness of the Canadian Bankers Association would seem to depend on avoiding the use of its name to foster prejudice or for personal ends." In a letter of the same date to the secretary of the Canadian Bankers Association in

Montreal, McLeod wrote that "the proceeding [of the Winnipeg subsection] is seemingly most extraordinary and suggests a prostitution of the name of the Association."

The blast–counterblast continued when the president of the Winnipeg subsection acknowledged in a letter that it was Bank of Nova Scotia employees who had committed the infraction. The president explained the process by which the matter was brought to the attention of the subsection and the manner of debate that followed. In stinging rebuke, he wrote: "The members are not aware of the practice which prevails at other places . . . but in this city whenever direct evidence of unprofessional conduct on the part of another Banker is brought to the notice of a member, he has not hesitated to place the matter before the other members."

McLeod's written response to the subsection secretary demanded proof of the accusations, which he claimed was still lacking, and added that the "Winnipeg Sub-Section of the Canadian Bankers Association, supposed to be a deliberative body, did, on mere hearsay, take an action calculated to prejudice the interests of a member thereof." In addition, he stated that the subsection, under the rules of the Canadian Bankers Association, did not possess the right to discipline members for this type of infraction. He demanded the withdrawal of all charges, regardless of their accuracy. On the same day, McLeod sent a letter to the secretary of the Canadian Bankers Association and asked that the Winnipeg subsection resolution be "expunged."

On June 29, 1899, the secretary of the Winnipeg subsection wrote to McLeod and provided more details concerning the accusation. His tone was adamant: the subsection had violated none of the Association's rules. He concluded by saying that it was regrettable that the bank would voluntarily withdraw from the Winnipeg subsection.

The final letter in the series was written by McLeod on July 17, 1899, to the secretary of the Canadian Bankers Association. He expressed his grave dissatisfaction with the manner in which the matter had been handled. That the executive of the Canadian Bankers Association had not overturned the Winnipeg subsection's resolution was considered a serious affront. He informed the Canadian Bankers Association that the Bank of Nova Scotia would withdraw from the Winnipeg subsection and from the Canadian Bankers Association on September 1, 1899. An internal memo dated the following day informed employees of the planned withdrawal and another, dated July 21, 1899, said that as of September 1, 1899, the bank would no longer honor the association's bank money orders. The Bank of Nova Scotia did withdraw from the Canadian Bankers Association on September 1, 1899. It was not until March 1904, when the Canadian Bankers Association apologized to the satisfaction of McLeod, that the bank returned to the fold.[5]

Personal Solicitation of Consumer Accounts

As the barrier to solicitation was dissolving, banks experimented with attracting new business. For example, in 1911 the Garfield Savings Bank

(Cleveland) identified profitable neighborhoods around each of its four East End branches and then instructed branch cashiers, tellers, and bookkeepers to canvas the areas door-to-door. The campaign, the bank's secretary explained, was not supposed to gain customers; rather, it was to "be a campaign of friendly calling by the employees of a branch, upon its own neighbors, to gather information about these neighbors, and to leave a pleasant, personal impression." Because employees lacked solicitation experience, they attended a pep rally at which they were subjected to exhortations from the president and other senior officers. Employees were armed with flyers, assigned specific streets, and told not to return until they had canvassed their assigned area. The key to the canvass was a "statistical" sheet that was used to record the prospect's name, address, occupation, whom (if anyone) they knew in the bank, attitude toward the bank, where they currently banked, and which service they used. The 10-day campaign yielded 890 contacts and 672 full interviews. Of these, 77 percent were cordial, 28 percent banked entirely with Garfield, 12 percent banked with Garfield as well as another bank, and 60 percent banked entirely with other institutions. The campaign cost $50 and resulted in deposits of $527. Over the next nine months, the bank screened new customers and attributed $20,000 in deposits to individuals who had been called upon. This yielded an average new account deposit of over $30 per interview. Ford saw two other benefits from the campaign: a number of employees had gained solicitation experience that could be used from behind the tellers' cages, and the bank gained basic market share information (albeit in relation to nonrandomly selected districts). These types of campaigns led to an even more aggressive system described in the next section.[6]

Employee New-Business Campaigns

Banks wrestled with the problem of how to use solicitation to develop new business from the everyday populace. One solution was new-business contests or new-business campaigns. These rewarded employees for bringing new business to the bank. Contest rules were somewhat uniform across banks: (1) points were awarded on the basis of both the number and value of new accounts obtained; (2) new accounts opened during the contest that were not the result of employee solicitation did not count; (3) solicitation was not allowed in the bank building; and (4) presidents, directors, and in many cases vice presidents did not participate, but virtually all other employees, including janitors, did. There were some compensation problems with early contests—for instance, the winner of the German-American Trust & Savings Bank's (Los Angeles) first contest in 1912 brought in the largest number of new accounts but not the largest dollar value of new accounts. Prizes included cash, trips, paid holiday time, and pay raises.

As seen in Table 7.1, banks began new-business contests during the early 1910s. The table also shows, if available, the number of new customers, the dollar value of new business (usually one month after the close of the contest), the cost/return ratio, the length of the campaign, and the year in which it was

Table 7.1
Employee New-Business Campaigns

Institution	Location	New Customers	New Business ($)	Cost/Return Ratio	Duration	Year
German-American Trust & Savings Bank	Los Angeles, CA	890	231,000	.001	2 months	1912[a]
German-American Trust & Savings Bank	Los Angeles, CA	864	135,000	.001	4 months	1915
Mississippi Valley Trust Co.	St. Louis, MO	1,279	516,478	—	—	1917
Hibernia Bank & Trust Co.	New Orlean, LA	—	—	—	—	1917
Cleveland Trust Company	Cleveland, OH	4,000	400,000	—	—	1918[a]
Garfield Savings Bank	Cleveland, OH	2,217	—	—	1 month	1919
United Banking & Savings Company	Cleveland, OH	1,000	—	—	—	1919
Chicago Savings Bank & Trust Company	Chicago, IL	1,200	40,000	.003	2 months	1920
Winters National Bank	Dayton, OH	—	155,325	.001	3 months	1920
Chicago Trust Company	Chicago, IL	2,145	51,000	—	2 months	1921
St. Paul Trust & Savings Bank	St. Paul, MN	758	224,100	.001	3 months	1921
St. Paul Trust & Savings Bank	St. Paul, MN	773	233,157	.001	3 months	1922
Liberty Central Trust Company	St. Louis, MO	3,023	800,000	—	3.5 months	1922
Union Trust Company	Chicago, IL	12,385	468,102	.012	3 months	1922
Fidelity National Bank & Trust Co.	Kansas City, KS	—	150,000	.003	4 months	1922
First National Bank	Detroit, MI	14,500	—	.011	3 months	1922
Exchange National Bank	Tulsa, OK	—	—	—	2.5 months	1923
Gotham National Bank	New York City	1,830	668,228	.002	2 months	1924
First National Bank	St. Louis, MO	9,800	800,000	.001	2 months	1924
National Bank of Commerce	St. Louis, MO	—	6,786,766[b]	—	1 year	1925

Table 7.1 Continued

Citizens National Bank/Citizens Trust & Savings Bank	Los Angeles, CA	8,737	12,088,995[b]	.0002	1 year	1925
Lake Shore Trust & Savings Bank	Chicago, IL	3,439	1,120,483[b]	.003	—	1925
National City Bank of New York	New York City	45,266	3,359,335	—	2 months	1926
First National Bank of Bradenton	Bradenton, FL	—	275,000	—	1 month	1926
Union Trust Company	Cleveland, OH	28,000	9,425,000	.002	5 years	1930

Note: Cost/return ratio equals cost of prizes divided by new business.

[a]The year represents the first year that the bank operated an employee new-business campaign; otherwise, it represents that during which the contest was operated.

[b]Securities sales, in addition to new demand and savings deposits, and safety deposit sales reported as new business.

Sources: W. R. Morehouse, "Employees' Contest for Securing New Deposits," *BMa,* 87 (July 1913): 17–21; W. R. Morehouse, "Employees' Contest No. 2," *BMa,* 91 (October 1915): 476–81; Gilbert O. Gilbert, "How Employees' Contest Won $2,000,000 in New Business," *BMo,* 34 (December 1917): 20–21; "Contest That Won 1,000 Accounts," *BMo,* 36 (May 1919): 14; "A Contest That Brought 2,217 New Accounts," *BMo,* 36 (October 1919): 24; Arthur F. Synder, "How Employees Secured $155,325," *BMo,* 37 (June 1920): 23; Warren M. Avery, "A Contest That Brought $40,000 in New Accounts," *BMo,* 37 (June 1920): 22; J. Kelly, "How to Conduct an Employees' Savings Contest," *BMa,* 103 (November 1921): 850–52; Paul L. Hardesty, "Winning 12,358 New Accounts at a Cost of 46 Cents Each," *BMo,* 39 (April 1922): 18+; W. R. Snodgrass, "Getting Them All to Work When You Stage a Contest," *BMo,* 39 (May 1922): 18–19+; Vincent J. Corrigan, "Reaching out for New Accounts That Are Profitable," *BMo,* 39 (June 1922): 52–53+; James A. Hoyt, "This Employees' Contest Landed 14,500 New Accounts," *BMo,* 39 (August 1922): 74–76; M. G. Boecher, "Managing a Contest for New Business," *BMo,* 39 (September 1922): 82–83; Grady Triplett, "These Employees Said 'Thanks' with $200,000 Contest," *BMo,* 40 (February 1923): 24; "New Magnets for Idle Dollars," *ABAJ,* 16 (May 1924): 753; Frank Fuchs, "Contest Brought 9,800 Accounts and $800,000 in Deposits," *PI,* 127 (29 May 1924): 133–34+; B. W. Griffin, "Mass Plans for Gaining New Accounts," *ABAJ,* 17 (August 1924): 86–87; W. R. Weisenberger, "Making Salesmen out of Bank Employees," *BMa,* 110 (June 1925): 997–1001; "Successful Campaign Brings in $12,000,000 in New Deposits," *BMa,* 111 (December 1925): 893–97; Mahlon D. Miller, "Getting $1,120,483 in New Business at a Cost of $3087," *BMa,* 112 (April 1926): 589–94; "Four Week Campaign of Employees Brings Bank $275,000," *BMa,* 113 (November 1926): 755–58; Frederick Kerman and Bryant W. Griffin, *New Business for Banks* (New York: Prentice-Hall, 1926), 150–53; J. R. Kraus, "28,300 New Accounts at 79 Cents Each," *ABAJ,* 23 (July 1930): 107–08+; Allard Smith, "A Substitute for the Bonus," *BMa,* 121 (September 1930): 319–22.

operated. The value of new business was the dollar amount of new savings and demand deposit accounts, and, in some cases, the dollar amount of safety deposit sales. With the exception of the Union Trust Company (Cleveland), contest value figures in excess of $1 million included securities sales. The cost/return ratio was calculated as the dollar value of prizes divided by the dollar value of new business. The cost of contest administration is not included in the cost figures, so the actual cost/return ratios are probably somewhat higher than those reported. The length of a campaign was normally three or four months.

The popularity of the new-business campaigns is attributable to their cost-effectiveness. With the exception of the .0002 cost/return ratio for the Citizens National Bank (Los Angeles), the result of including securities sales in estimating total return, the cost/return ratios tend to cluster around .001 or .002. This meant that it cost in the neighborhood of $1.50 to attract every $1,000 in new business.

These plans evolved over time from intermittent, team plans to continuous, individual ones. For example, during the mid-1910s the Union Trust Company (Cleveland) began distributing a portion of profits to employees. The differential advantage of the bonus was erased after the major banks in the city copied the plan. To reward individual effort, the bank started an employee new-business campaign, but this, too, was copied by other leading Cleveland banks and, more important, employees cultivated new business only during those periods arbitrarily set by senior officers. In 1925, the bank started its "Go-Getters plan," a continuous, individually based employee new-business campaign. Names of top performing employees were published in *The Teller*, the bank's employee magazine.

Not all new-business contests were directed to bank employees. During the 1920s, the Fidelity National Bank & Trust Company (Kansas City) wrote to a number of church, charitable, and social organizations, offering one dollar for every new account secured. A minimum of 50 accounts was required before the bank paid out an award. Apparently, just under 1,500 new accounts were opened in this manner.[7]

Special Savings Plans

Special products unique to banking were developed to encourage low- to medium-income individuals to save. Home safes, which appeared during the 1890s, were supplanted around 1905 by Christmas Clubs, a standardized savings plan that substantially reduced back-office operations. During the late 1910s, Christmas Clubs were supplemented by industrial savings plans designed for direct deposit of part of a worker's pay into a savings account. The following sections describe these products and concludes with a brief mention of club proliferation.

Home Safe Campaigns

Home safes were long-lived, rust-resistant, miniature safes constructed of brass or steel-nickel alloy. Money was deposited at home, and recipients opened an account at the sponsoring bank once a minimum of one dollar was accumulated. Small deposits were subsequently made in the safe, thus alleviating the need for frequent bank visits. Although banks advertised the safes as a foolproof saving method because they retained the key, the artful may have had little difficulty cracking the safes. Banks named their safes Day and Night Bank, Fortune Builder, Receiving Teller, and Deposit Builder. Home safes first appeared during the mid-1890s in the American Northeast, and initially banks employed commissioned door-to-door drummers to sell them. Later, they were given away at no cost.

The popularity of home safes was substantial, but their profitability was questionable. Around 1905, a home safe campaign added 20,000 new accounts over two years to the books of the Royal Trust Company (Chicago). When a home safe was given away, the bank's female advertising manager dispatched a letter of congratulations, and if the account grew, a second letter offered a premium if the customer provided additional new business. The bank targeted ten-block areas with direct mail, and if the response was favorable, direct mail, streetcar, and billboard promotional funds were poured into that area. At the same time, the Central Trust Company's (Chicago) campaign resulted in 24,000 active accounts over a two-year period. Using voter registration lists, it mailed a home safe offer to individuals in targeted precincts; 17 percent took advantage. The banks also used the results to more finely target future direct mail expenditures. Around 1905, one unnamed bank in New York City allowed holders of home safe accounts to write checks on their accounts without service fees. The response was fantastic but terribly unprofitable. Moreover, only one teller was equipped to open home safes, and the long line drove customers away.[8]

In summary, home safes were used to attract new customers. The number of new accounts was considerable, but bankers did not, or were unable to, balance volume against profitability. Eventually, home safes disappeared when bank managers realized that more profitable means were available to attract new, small-account customers.

Christmas Clubs

Like home safes, Christmas Clubs were designed for small savers, but unlike them, they could be profitable. Home safes substantially decreased the number of transactions per account, but they did not decrease the required number of interest calculations. Christmas Clubs also controlled the number of transactions, but by standardizing the value and timing of deposits across customers, interest calculations were also controlled. The advantages of Christmas Clubs were so apparent that within a decade and a half of their adoption around 1905, home safes all but disappeared, except perhaps in relation to thrift among children.

To enroll in a Christmas Club, a customer agreed to make fixed or escalating deposits at fixed intervals over a one-year period. The clubs got their name from the fact that payouts were made shortly before Christmas, and banks used the clubs to promote saving for holiday spending. Banks offered plans to suit various budgets: 10 cents per week, 25 cents per week, and so on. For example, in 1911 the Peoples National Bank (Duncannon, Pennsylvania) offered three plans that paid out $6.66, $13.32, and $33.33 in mid-December. If a customer failed to make a deposit, deposits to date were returned without interest. Banks therefore needed to calculate interest only once for each plan. Transaction costs were further controlled by a double coupon system, whereby the customer's dated coupon was matched with that of the bank and both were hole-punched.

Some confusion exists concerning when and where Christmas Clubs began. Part of that may arise from the adoption of similar plans by industrial and service firms for employees, some as early as the end of the American Civil War, and the development of similar stamp plans. Banks began to offer Christmas Clubs to the general public around 1905, after companies such as Standard Oil, Adams Express, Equitable Life Insurance, and New York Life Insurance had established plans for their staff. Another antecedent of Christmas Clubs was provident stamp banks. The Lighthouse Savings Fund of Philadelphia, a private bank begun in 1900, was antedated at the same location by the Theodore Starr Savings Bank, a stamp center bank. The bank paid interest on regular deposits, but not on stamp accounts. Interestingly, regular accounts were popular because nearby mill workers feared that their wages would be reduced if they saved money at their employer-related bank. Stamp sales of this sort were common, since many early savings banks in America refused initial deposits of less than one dollar. They sold stamps until a dollar had been obtained and then redeemed the stamps for an interest-bearing passbook account. Similarly, as part of the Dime Bank's (Pittston, Pennsylvania) Thrifty System—instituted during the 1910s—the bank installed stamp vending machines throughout the community and accepted deposits when one dollar had been accumulated.

Promotion of Christmas Clubs was concentrated between Thanksgiving and the first few weeks of the new year. A host of Christmas Club material suppliers sprang up, offering banks specialized advertising, Santa Clauses, Christmas decorations, promotional booklets, and window displays. Banks also formed cooperatives. For example, five banks in New Orleans banded together and standardized deposit plans, interest rates, and account opening and closing dates. During the mid-1920s, the city of just under 400,000 boasted 75,000 Christmas Club members (about one of every five residents, matched by few other cities).

The Savings Bank Division of the American Bankers Association commissioned a study of 1920 Christmas Club operations in America. In 1920 there were at least twenty Christmas Club material suppliers. A total of 758 banks reported that 1,020,126 individuals became Christmas Club members that year. Of these, 619,240 (60.7 percent) were still members at year's end. The year-end payout was about $39 million, and of this some $5.5 million (14.1 percent) was rolled over into savings accounts. Most banks sought to have members open a savings account at the end of the year. Among four banks considered typical over the 1912–20 period, the average nominal dollar annual growth rate was 30.6 percent (maximum of 41.7 percent and minimum of 24.9 percent). Membership at one bank, probably typical during the period, grew from 800 to 5,300, an annual growth rate of 26.7 percent, between 1912 and 1920.

Others sources also suggest that Christmas Club activity grew tremendously between 1910 and 1925. The total number of banks offering Christmas Clubs grew by an average of 34.4 percent each year between 1913 and 1923 (from 904 to 17,400). World War I depressed Christmas Club activity because banks heavily promoted installment Liberty Bond sales as opposed to installment savings plans. The president of the Empire City Savings Bank (New York) estimated that total U.S. Christmas Club deposits and depositors increased by about $25 million and 600,000 per year, respectively, during the early 1920s, with 25 percent rolling club savings over into savings accounts.

In summary, while home safes and Christmas Clubs allowed banks to form an initial relation with customers, the latter were preferred because of a lower cost structure.[9]

Industrial Savings Plans

The success of Christmas Clubs led banks to cast an eye on the development of other savings plans. In this regard, banks sought the cooperation of employers to reach blue- and white-collar employees. By the turn of the century, employers regularly used bank-provided pay envelopes printed with some sort of thrift message. Typical is that provided by the Naugatuck Savings Bank (Connecticut) in 1909:

> Do you anticipate a pension when the time comes to retire from work? If not, perhaps with the help of Naugatuck Savings Bank you can acquire one. A dollar saved each week amounts to $53 in one year, $300 in five years, $650 in ten years and $1614 in twenty years. One dollar will open an account. Bank open every Wednesday evening (except legal holidays) from 7 to 8:30.

From this, more elaborate links were forged. For example, in 1913 employers in Wonewoc, Wisconsin, replaced part of employee cash wages with interest-bearing certificates, provided by the Citizens State Bank. Another innovation was the direct deposit of a portion of wages into a savings account. One of the earliest systems of this sort was operated in 1913 by the Nassau County Trust Company (Mineola, New York) for employees of Doubleday, Page & Company (Garden City, New Jersey). Upon request, the paymaster deposited a fixed amount each week into a savings account. The plan may have been initiated by Doubleday, since the firm contributed an amount equal to that paid by the employee.[10]

Perhaps the first industrial savings plan on record was that offered to employees of the Crompton & Knowles Loom Works (Worcester, Massachusetts). Under this plan, begun in 1919, employees were able to choose from among the town's five savings banks. By 1921, 65 percent of the company's workers had opened an industrial savings account and deposits totaled $215,000.

A much better record exists of the trademarked Save at the Shop plan of the Union Trust Company (Cleveland), begun during the early 1920s. The plan initially called for an intensive solicitation of employers to gain their cooperation. If they approved, employees were systematically targeted with Save at the Shop direct mail and office posters. A study of Cleveland factories revealed that the percentage of workers saving a portion of their wages rose from 33 to 56 percent with adoption of the Union Trust plan. Average savings of $64 per year, divided by the $3.50 that it cost to attract each new plan member, led to a cost/return ratio of 0.05. This was less effective than employee new-business campaigns, but still sufficient.

An additional benefit of an industrial savings plan was that it allowed bank solicitors to approach a commercial enterprise and establish a relationship with managers. Later, that relationship might develop into commercial business. For example, the individual in charge of the Bank of Italy (San Francisco) Industrial Savings Division during the late 1920s was an assistant vice president (suggesting the importance of the plan). Of industrial savings plan, he said, "A high spot in the work not often considered is the effect of the contact by the bank with large organizations. The continual intercourse is in effect and results of value to the bank, and has resulted in the bank securing commercial accounts."[11]

Other Clubs

Banks developed several club-type savings plans in addition to Christmas Clubs and industrial savings plans. Steady savers clubs first appeared during the early 1910s. They were similar to Christmas Clubs except that they were not tied to the holiday season and the minimum weekly or monthly deposits were substantial, indicating a middle- or upper-class orientation. For example, during the early 1910s the Union Bank & Trust Company (Jackson, Tennessee) began its $50 Savings Club, referred to as a "forced" savings plan. As a matter of convenience, or perhaps to pressure customers, bank representatives collected deposits at the customer's residence. Similar plans were in place by the mid-1920s in Chicago, Sacramento, and Memphis.

Another type of club that appeared at about the same time focused on vacations. Some were operated independently of banks (e.g., the Women's Vacation Bureau, established in New York City). Banks also collected savings for summer vacations or trips to exotic destinations, such as the 1915 World's Panama-Pacific Exposition in San Francisco. Some banks supplemented these clubs with savings clubs for small- to medium-sized businesses. After World War I, the Chelsea Savings Bank (Norwich, Connecticut) inaugurated one, calling it the Mercantile Reserve Department. This filled out the bank's club line, which included an Industrial Savings Club, a school savings program, and Christmas and Vacation Clubs.[12]

Special Promotions

By 1930, banks had developed a range of general promotional mechanisms and messages to generate new business. This section documents the development of window advertising, community campaigns, and fear appeal.

Window Displays

During the 1880s, department store window display managers discarded the practice of piling unrelated merchandise and opted for fewer items that were related to one another in some manner. Starting during the 1910s, window display managers began presenting merchandise in realistic settings, and furniture and apparel in entire ensembles (such as ashtrays in a furniture display). There is also some evidence of socioeconomic (or income) segmentation. The window displays used by Bloomingdale's in New York presented merchandise of different price/quality levels for the Park Avenue, Long Island commuter, and Upper-East Side crowds.[13]

But bank managers had no physical products to display, and they were slow to realize the possibilities of the window display as a promotional tool. When they did, during the 1910s, managers of older buildings were unable to take advantage of the new promotional opportunity because of architectural limits (i.e., limited or no windows). An innovator in bank window display advertising was the Guaranty Trust & Savings Bank in Los Angeles (prior to World War I it was the German-American Trust & Savings Bank). Its first display, in December 1916, promoted home safes, and the bank gave away more that month than in any previous month. The bank also advertised cooperatively with local retail merchants. One display, encouraging customers to save for a vacation, presented fishing and hunting gear loaned by a local retailer whose name received prominent display. Other displays featured miniature railroading, automobile operating costs, bees' savings instinct, and Made in Los Angeles Week. While these did not create much new business, they attracted attention and created favorable impressions.

The activities of the Commonwealth Federal Savings Bank (Detroit) in 1922 provide an example of how banks used window displays to forge better relations with commercial customers. The bank's window was a valuable commodity because it was located at a busy downtown intersection (during the 1920s, Detroit was a booming city, the automobile assembly capital of the world, and thousands of pedestrians passed the bank each day). The bank used the window display in two manners. First, the bank promoted itself, one of its more aggressive efforts being directed to the selling of Christmas Clubs just before the holiday season. Second, the bank used its display to reward current commercial customers and to lure potential ones. The assistant cashier stated that thousands of dollars had been offered by manufacturers and retailers for use of the display. The bank refused to accept money, but provided the window free as a goodwill gesture. There was a long waiting list of firms wanting access to the window.[14]

As noted in other cases, Canadian banks lagged their American counterparts in the quickness of adopting new promotional mechanisms. It was only in 1924 that the Canadian Bank of Commerce, for example, began experimenting with poster advertising in bank windows.

> These first posters, which were really an essay in the use of colour in bank advertising, were only moderately successful, but they led the way to a more correct appraisal of the publicity values of such advertising, which has apparently established the coloured poster as a permanent feature of the bank's advertising.[15]

Community Campaigns

By the late 1910s, two types of community campaigns were well established within bank advertising: (1) cooperative campaigns designed with other institutions to increase thrift and (2) community advertising that promoted specific places. In 1915, Edwin Bird Wilson, manager of the Bankers Trust Company's (New York) advertising department, said that the goals of a cooperative community campaign were (1) to increase confidence in banking institutions; (2) to educate the public to the economic usefulness of banking institutions; (3) to increase the stream of small contributions of capital into channels of legitimate business; (4) to educate the public to a higher standard of thrift, and thus increase a community's working capital; (5) to stabilize the finances of a community or of a nation if carried by many towns and cities; and (6) to increase the effectiveness of the individual advertising and other new-business efforts of all the participating banks. These goals demonstrate that bank marketers were attempting to instill within the public a sense of what they *ought* to do.

An example of a cooperative campaign is the one in 1916 by the Chattanooga Association for the Promotion of Thrift. It brought together bank executives, the county judge, the mayor, educators, civic associations, a local union, the local manufacturers' association, and the chamber of commerce. Ministers were asked to discuss thrift in their sermons; educators were asked to lecture on the topic; the association provided speakers; newspaper, billboard, and streetcar advertising was used freely; thrift essay contests were run; handbills were distributed to factories, schools, and civic associations; thrift slides were shown at theaters; and the YMCA designed and displayed posters. New customers maintaining a $20 balance for at least one year were entitled to a 50-cent savings premium. The best thrift essays were published in newspapers, which reported favorably on the campaign. The entire campaign cost $730 (excluding coupon redemption fees), and 760 new accounts were opened during the campaign, an increase of 175 percent over the same month the previous year.

Prior to banks' involvement in community advertising, Canadian and American railroads promoted tourism during the late nineteenth century because they owned both the means of transportation and many of the hotels. Far West states promoted themselves in Europe as suitable destinations for immigrants during the mid-nineteenth century. Early in the twentieth century, nonprofit institutions such as local chambers of commerce, merchant associations, and governments (local ones in particular) entered the field. By 1920, community advertising was an established practice, in part through the 1916 creation of the Community Advertising Department under the umbrella of the Associated Advertising Clubs of the World. Banks became involved in community advertising early in the 1920s. For example, the Manufacturers & Traders National Bank placed a three-quarter page advertisement in *System* (a general business magazine). It called Buffalo "A Comfortable City" and said, "In urging industrial concerns to locate in Buffalo, we have in mind those houses who employ men who are essentially home-makers. They will be happy here."[16]

Fear Appeal

The shift from passive to aggressive *ought to* or *reason why* advertising is evidenced by the banking industry's use of fear appeal early in the twentieth century.   Banks used fear appeal in messages on safekeeping valuables (especially cash), banking hours (having too much or too little money at the wrong hour), and trust services (dying without a will). This shift was anteceded by that in the life insurance industry. During the mid-nineteenth century, American life insurance organizations were artfully blending a man's "distress of his own wife" and the "cry of his own children" into fear-tinged promotional material.   Bankers no doubt learned much from observing the insurance industry's use of fear appeal and crafted messages suitable to their own purposes.[17]

An early account of fear appeal was provided by F. R. Fuller, advertising manager of the Cleveland Trust Company, in 1904.   In 1895, the bank's organizers advertised to cultivate new customers. Given an inferior location (the basement of a downtown building), the first sales booklet in part concentrated on physical amenities: a specially outfitted men's smoking room and a ladies' parlor that provided "all the conveniences of a club free to the poorest patron of the bank." Emulating the upper classes was apparently a strong appeal. Fear appeal also was used: "If a startling burglary occurred in a certain part of the city, this neighborhood was flooded with circulars the following day containing the apt headline 'Burglars Foiled,' and explaining the satisfaction of keeping one's valuables in the safe deposit vaults of the Cleveland Trust Company."

By current standards, some of the advertisements were in poor taste. For example, in 1909 the Second National Bank (Meyersdale, Pennsylvania) depicted a thief pointing a revolver at a sleeping man under the heading "No, Mr. Burglar, I've got my money in the bank, it's safe." Crime victims were given no confidentiality in banks' fear advertisements. A mid-1910s advertisement of the American Trust Company (Jonesboro, Arkansas) said, "Mrs. Annie Zar, tied by wrists to bedposts, kicked in side and $100 in tin box stolen from under mattress." The heading read: "With such risks staring you in the face, can you afford to keep money around the house?" To demonstrate the truthfulness of the claim, the advertisement included a newspaper account of the crime.

Trust services were sometimes couched in terms of inattention to personal finances. During the early 1910s, the Security Trust & Savings Bank (Los Angeles) reprinted a newspaper account of a deathbed confession concerning a $140,000 loss by an elderly man. The bank described its trust services and told how the loss could easily have been averted. Interestingly, a biographer of Security's president, Joseph F. Sartori, at the turn of the century wrote that Sartori himself penned the bank's advertising copy and that "his deep sincerity and love of truth also made him shun an equivocal statement [in advertising] or any form of exaggeration." A 1914 German-American Trust & Savings Bank (Los Angeles) advertisement included a Washington, D.C., newspaper account of how the will of recently deceased Supreme Court Justice Horace H. Lurton was ruled invalid. The major copy boldly pronounced, "Supreme Court Justice Writes an Invalid Will."[18]

Handling New Customers

Because documentation is required before a bank provides service, banks, unlike retailers, are aware of whether the customer is conducting his or her first transaction with the institution. Banks thus made special efforts to create a good first impression. Some banks reserved one or more teller cages to handle new accounts. In 1913 W. R. Morehouse described the new account teller of the German-American Trust & Savings Bank (Los Angeles) and suggested that new account tellers should: (1) adjust their demeanor to that of the new customer; (2) personally introduce every new customer to a senior officer (regardless of the initial account size); (3) be knowledgeable of bank regulations and policy; and (4) be courteous. In some instances, the new account teller was located in the new business department. Morehouse said that physically the teller should be (1) cageless (i.e., without vertical bars), to encourage an open and friendly atmosphere; (2) located as near the bank's main entrance as possible; and (3) located as near senior officers as possible. In addition, a private room should be available for counting new customers' money in privacy and a reserve new account teller should be available to handle unexpected demand for new accounts. A segmentation orientation is even more apparent in the fact that many banks simultaneously operated a specially trained account closeout teller.[19]

CURRENT CUSTOMERS

Early in the twentieth century, bankers formally articulated the difference between potential and new customers, a concern borrowed from manufacturers. In 1912 a banker noted that many manufacturers were asking: "(1) Do we want to sell goods to more customers, or (2) Do we want to sell more goods to our present customers?" Applied to banking, he asked: "Do we want more depositors or do we want our present depositors to transact more business and carry larger balances?" Bankers understood that it was easier and less costly to persuade a current customer to use an additional service than to land an entirely new customer. The number one policy of the Second North Western State Bank (Chicago) during the late 1920s was to "develop the business of existing customers first." The president of the bank said, "We never lose sight of the fact that our most fertile ground is right here in the bank with our present customers." An implication of the strategy was the concentration of efforts on direct mail and solicitation, as opposed to mass media advertising. But the effective use of direct mail and solicitation required an understanding of who current customers were and what services were used. This required the development of a filing system that came to be called the central information file.[20]

Central Information Files

Central information files were the major administrative innovation that banks used to create more business on current customers. For each customer, a card contained demographic information and product usage rates. Central information files were rudimentary, manually maintained databases that speeded credit activities, focused segmented direct mailings, provided advertising guidelines, and generated information on service consumption. A common sentiment of the period was that the files "may rightly be termed one of the most important cogs in the bank's operating machinery." Leroy A. Mershon, secretary of the Trust Company Section of the American Bankers Association said in 1919 that central information files were first introduced in New York City in 1907. He noted that the system at the unnamed bank was a response to the problems created when a customer changed residence. Multiple departments had different addresses on the same customer, and important documents were frequently misdirected.[21]

Growth in the number of services and bank departments created problems in tracking customers. Furthermore, banks required filing systems of some type to facilitate cross-selling efforts. In 1925 W. B. Weisenburger, vice president of the National Bank of Commerce (St. Louis) said:

> In six years time we have added to "Commerce" a savings department, a bond department, and trust and safety deposit departments. These developments have come so rapidly that we did not have the complete interchange of interest between the departments that is so vital. Running a department store of finance, we found it was highly necessary that when a customer came in he be given an opportunity to patronize all departments. In other words, we had to practice the finesse that department stores do in supplying all the wants of a customer. After analyzing the situation carefully, we installed, as a preliminary toward the correction of this situation, a central file by reason of which we were not only able to arrive instantly at those customers who did patronize more than one department, but also secured an immediate cross section of their standing, connections and ability to make use of other financial facilities we had to offer.[22]

Table 7.2 presents a listing of banks adopting central information files. (The bank in New York City that was supposedly the innovator in the area is not included.) Although other banks in New York City probably followed suit, the first central information file identified was that of the German-American Trust & Savings Bank (Los Angeles) in 1914. By 1930, the innovation had been adopted by many major American metropolitan banks.

There was some blurring of central information files with other types of files. For example, smaller banks often blended central information and prospect files, while larger institutions were likely to separate current and prospect files. A 1928 survey of 240 banks with a central information file revealed that 70 percent had distinct current and prospect filing systems. The same study also showed which departments were charged with the expense of operating the files: the banking department was charged 75 percent of the time; the new business department was charged 18 percent of the time; and the advertising department was charged 7 percent of the time. The banking department was normally responsible for operating the banking room (e.g., tellers), while the new business department came closest to what could be called a marketing department: it was

Table 7.2
Central Information Files for Current Customers

Institution	Location	Year
German-American Trust & Savings Bank	Los Angeles, CA	1914
Security Trust & Savings Bank	Los Angeles, CA	1917
Hibernia Bank & Trust Company	New Orleans, LA	1918[a]
Equitable Trust Company of New York	New York City	1918[a]
First National Bank	Cleveland, OH	1918
Bank of New Richmond	New Richmond, WI	1918
St. Joseph Valley Bank	Elkhart, IN	1919[a]
Guaranty Trust Company of New York	New York City	1919
Mercantile Trust Company	St. Louis, MO	1919
Guardian Trust & Savings	Cleveland, OH	1919
Liberty Trust & Savings Bank	Chicago, IL	1920
Old Colony Trust Company	Boston, MA	1920
Atlanta Trust Company	Atlanta, GA	1921
Bank of America	New York City	1921
American Security & Trust Company	Washington, D.C.	1922
Lafayette-South Side Bank	St. Louis, MO	1924
National Bank of Commerce	St. Louis, MO	1925
Chase National Bank	New York City	1926
Scott County Savings Bank	Davenport, IA	1926
American-First National Bank	Oklahoma City, OK	1927
Cleveland Trust Company	Cleveland, OH	1930

[a]Year during which the program was actually begun; otherwise, the year during which the citation appeared.

Sources: W. R. Morehouse, "Bank Letters That Pull and Hold Business," *BMa*, 88 (February 1914): 157–63; T. D. MacGregor, *The New Business Department* (New York: Bankers Publishing Co., 1917), 38; T. D. MacGregor, "How Banks Get New Business," *PI*, 102 (14 March 1918): 106+; Warren M. Avery, "Keeping the Spotlight on New Business," *BMo*, 36 (April 1919): 17–18; H. B. Grimm, "Simple Plan That Won $1,000,000 in Deposits," *BMo*, 36 (October 1919): 10–11; Warren M. Avery, "The Strongest Arm of the New Business Bank," *BMo*, 37 (April 1920): 15–16; E. H. Kittredge, "How a Central File Helps to Pay Dividends," *BMo*, 37 (July 1920): 27–28+; Merrill Anderson, "What One Banker Learned from Big Department Stores," *BMa*, 103 (December 1921): 1071; "Cultivate Old as Well as New Customers," *BMa*, 104 (April 1922): 707+; J. R. Giessenbier, "Building Your Mailing List and Keeping It Up-to-Date," *BMo*, 41 (February 1924): 22–23+; "The Central File," *The Chase*, 8 (February 1926): 440–43 (CM archives).

normally responsible for both advertising and sales, as well as various other activities.[23]

To better understand central information files, the following paragraphs describe their operation by several banks, including the Equitable Trust Company of New York and the Old Colony Trust Company (Boston).

The Equitable Trust Company of New York began a central information file in 1918. It contained data on current customers only. Growth in the number of branches and customers, the limited space for the central file system, and technological innovations in filing systems eventually forced management to seek a new filing method. In 1928 the Findex system was selected to replace its more manual predecessor. Each card in the Findex system contained the regular type of data for the period. The lower portion of each card had a number of holes, each associated with a specific customer characteristic. The cards recorded gender, line of business (52 options), branch, account size (below or above $1,000), one of several New York City locations (e.g., east above 59th West), and services used. If the response for a customer was "yes" on any characteristic, the hole was elongated vertically. If, for example, one wanted a listing of female customers living east above 59th West, rods were inserted into the holes representing east above 59th West and female. Each central information file box, similar to a library card catalog box, was then swiveled upside down and the cards for female customers living east above 59th West would drop down half an inch. Another rod was inserted to lock the cards in place before turning the file right side up. Under the old system, a request for such information might have required more than one week to complete. The Findex system reduced the time to one or two days. Equitable used the central information file for other and perhaps more important purposes: "Without such a file, the officer passing on overdrafts might easily return an item and then discover to his dismay that the maker of the check was a large stockholder or good customer of our Trust Department." Thus the files were an integrative device that coordinated activities across bank functions. Equitable's central information file contained 55,000 entries, and the department received 1,400 inquiries per day, of which about 500 were made over the telephone. Most of these inquiries probably concerned individual customers rather than database requests. The department was operated by six full-time employees.[24]

The Old Colony Trust Company (Boston) operated a central information file as early as 1920. A 1928 study of the bank's central information file revealed that customers used an average of 1.57 services. The bank used its central information file for identifying which consumer and commercial customers were to be solicited personally. The bank's addressing machine (probably an Addressograph) was particularly valuable in segmenting current customers. For each of the 30,000 noncommercial customers, the addressing machine contained a metal plate, and through the insertion of pins, addresses were printed on envelopes only for those customers with desired qualities. Thus the machine could print addresses on envelopes only for female customers with a large savings account but no other bank connection. The machine's capacity was 1,500 letters per hour, but the bank had ordered a new one with a capacity of 4,000 letters per hour.[25]

Parenthetically, in 1896, Joseph F. Duncan had begun the Addressograph Company specifically to sell a machine designed to print addresses. Technological improvements in the replacement of rubber type with metal plates and the replacement of foot power with fractional horsepower motors and, more important, the meeting of a deeply held need, led to the quick penetration of the product in the marketplace. Any organization that engaged repetitively in direct mail was a potential customer. In addition, the machine was designed to print addresses only for specific plates selected through adjusting a set of pins. Banks and other organizations were thus provided with a technology that could cost-effectively select specific target markets from a much larger information file.[26]

Owing to its size (just under half a million customers in 1930), the Cleveland Trust Company operated separate current and prospective customer files. The system contained over 1.5 million cards. Prospective customers' names were checked against the central information file to determine whether any affiliation with the bank currently existed. The bank also developed an affiliation file that allowed solicitors to cross-reference company directorates and business affiliates. Yet another file was the tickler file. An initial commercial solicitation, if not immediately successful, was called a tickle, and the date of the next tickle was added to the file. Tickler files summarized information gleaned from the central information, prospect, and business affiliation files. The new-business manager was sent the tickler files on the date of the expected tickle, which provided one mechanism of monitoring sales leads. The bank also closely watched its better commercial accounts: each was assigned to a bank officer or a branch manager, who was expected to call in person at regular intervals.[27]

Banks also connected central information files with commercial credit analysis. The central information file of the American-First National Bank (Oklahoma City) contained three records per current customer. The first was line of business, length of affiliation with the bank, who initially recommended the customer, probable worth, and line of credit. The second contained loan and business performance and account activity data. The third was reserved for observations on the customer's character. The bank formed a credit committee that jointly determined and periodically adjusted commercial credit lines. Every officer was given responsibility to accept or reject any commercial credit request. Hugh M. Johnson, chairman of the board, said the key benefit of a system that combined credit files and credit committee was that commercial customers were served faster.[28]

House Organs and Related Publications

Banks made available at their sites, or mailed to individuals on special lists, house organs, occasional bulletins, books, booklets, and brochures. Although examples have previously been provided of thrift house organs directed to children and to the general public, the vast majority of the specified audience of house organ-type material were normally commercial customers. In America, large urban banks used house organs and occasional bulletins to attract correspondent banks and commercial customers, and small rural ones used them to attract farm customers. The Bank of Commerce's (St. Louis) *The Commerce Monthly* and the Van Norden Trust Company's (New York) *Van Norden Magazine* are two of many pre-1910 urban bank house organs directed to commercial customers; the *New Era Banker*, published by Bowman's Bank (Kalamazoo, Michigan) and City National Bank's (Kearney, Nebraska) *The Thrifty American* are pre-1910 organs designed for farm customers. Many publications were a special service to current customers, although the actual audience blurred prospective, current, and past customers. As a matter of policy, some banks, but not many, carried outside advertising in their organs. The State Bank (Bancroft, South Dakota) first published *Bancroft Progress* in 1905 and initially accepted advertisements from local retailers. In 1906 the bank decided not to accept outside advertisements; instead, the organ would contain only one back-page advertisement for the bank itself.[29]

The volume of publications by the largest banks is staggering. In 1918, the Guaranty Trust Company of New York distributed 3,843,392 items on 158 subjects to 350,000 individuals. Engaging in hyperbole, a highly placed observer said, "Through proper classification of these [mailing] lists the distribution is so controlled that each publication goes only to those likely to be interested in its subject matter."[30]

Table 7.3 presents the number of irregular publications distributed by the Guaranty Trust Company of New York between 1905 and 1930. They varied in content and length (e.g., *The Argentine Republic*, 1916, 4 pages; *The War Tax Law*, 1917, 132 pages; *The Revenue Act of 1921*, 1921, 220 pages). The table excludes circulars on acquisition of new corporate trustee accounts, legal briefs, annual reports, and reprints of public addresses. Publication volume rose dramatically in 1916, remained high until 1920, and then dropped. A policy of aggressiveness may explain the sharp increase in publication volume, and realization of low returns relative to other promotional mechanisms may explain the subsequent decline.

By the late 1910s, the National City Bank of New York's advertising was heavily reliant on direct mail. The bank distributed some 2.5 million items during 1919, including *The Bulletin*, a monthly report on banking and finance; *The Americas*, a monthly report on international business; *The Foreign Trade Report*, a weekly report; *Blue Sheet*, a weekly report on international trade opportunities; and *Number Eight*, the bank's internally distributed employee magazine. In addition, the bank published more than 15 booklets with such titles as *Cuba, Reconstruction, American Banks in Foreign Trade*, and *Causes Underlying Social Unrest*. Given the relative size of National City Bank of New York and the Guaranty Trust Company of New York, the quantity of their direct mail publications must have been at the upper end of the scale in America.[31]

During the 1910s and 1920s, the Bankers Trust Company (New York) privately published and widely distributed its hardcover, pocketbook-sized Bankers Trust Company series. It included such titles as *Liberty Bonds and Note Values, America's Merchant Marine, The Dominion of Canada, English Public Finance, French Public Finance*, and *Inter-Ally Debts*, ranging from 45 to 369 pages.[32]

Canadian banks did not publish house organs as early as their American counterparts. The Canadian Bank of Commerce's first commercial house organ,

Table 7.3
Irregular Publications of the Guaranty Trust Company of New York, 1905–30

Year	New Publications	Reprints/ Revisions	Total Publications
1905	2	0	2
1906	0	0	0
1907	1	0	1
1908	0	0	0
1909	0	1	1
1910	0	0	0
1911	1	0	1
1912	1	1	2
1913	2	0	2
1914	4	1	5
1915	2	1	3
1916	16	0	16
1917	17	5	22
1918	33	10	43
1919	20	1	21
1920	14	4	18
1921	4	5	9
1922	1	4	5
1923	1	2	3
1924	0	1	1
1925	1	1	2
1926	2	1	3
1927	0	0	0
1928	0	1	1
1929	3	3	6
1930	1	1	1

Note: Does not include circulars announcing acquisition of a new corporate trustee accounts, annual reports to stockholders, legal briefs, and reprints of public addresses.

Source: The National Union Catalog Pre-1956 Imprints, 221 (1972), 45–48.

The Monthly Commercial Letter, initially published in 1915, contained general financial and commercial information on the Canadian economy. In 1923, in response to the popularity of the organ, a French-language version was begun for distribution in Quebec and elsewhere in Canada. Sir Frederick Williams-Taylor, general manager of the Bank of Montreal, brought to the attention of shareholders at the bank's 1926 annual meeting a series of "recently published" organs and occasionals. They included the monthly *Business Summary*, weekly agricultural and crop reports, and several booklets on "scientific farming methods" (of which over 150,000 had been published). By this time, like other Canadian banks, the Bank of Montreal was also distributing booklets for recent non-English-speaking immigrants. At the meeting, Williams-Taylor said:

> Not all of these services perhaps are directly renumerative, but we believe that they have all been of very definite value. They are broadening the facilities available to our clients, creating goodwill, and demonstrating that the Bank is keenly concerned in the public welfare and in furthering the general interest of this country.

By 1928, the bank was advertising in newspapers the availability of its many monthly and occasional reports.[33]

Other Cross-Selling Plans

A relatively common cross-selling exercise was direct mailing general information about bank service to current customers. In 1913 the Mercantile Trust Company (St. Louis) distributed a booklet describing the services and departments of the bank. John Ring, manager of the bank's publicity depart-ment, said of the booklet: "One of the prime purposes for which this booklet will be used will be in soliciting for patrons of one department on behalf of another department." The introduction of the booklet said, "There are many people who are patrons of but one department of our company, and many not as yet patrons of any department. To both these classes this booklet will appeal." The Woodlawn Trust & Savings Bank (Chicago) in 1925 reported that over a one-year period, current customers mailed material on the bank's services deposited on average \$40.96, while those not mailed the material deposited an average of \$12.04.[34]

The World War I Liberty Bond drive brought a large number of banks into contact with small investors having no prior contact with a bank. Banks quickly took advantage of the situation and developed comprehensive cross-selling strategies. The Liberty National Bank (St. Louis) created a Liberty Bond deposit department that safeguarded customers' Liberty Bonds without charge. A passbook, similar to the type used by savings departments, recorded the issue and value of bonds and the dates and amounts of interest payments. The objective was to get customers to roll over the interest payments into an interest-bearing savings account. The service, with variations, continued after the war and was offered by some Canadian banks. In 1921, the Bank of Toronto, for example, advertised that "for a very moderate fee, we will hold stocks and bonds for you in our vaults, collect dividends and coupons promptly when due, and place the proceeds to your credit, or send remittances as directed by you."[35]

Banks also took advantage of workers without savings accounts who were paid by check. For example, in 1919 a Midwest bank located in a factory district commonly cashed pay checks, given adequate identification. Check cashers not having a savings account were given one that would be credited with a 50 cents premium if at least one dollar was deposited. If an account was not opened, the bank explained that the passbook was sufficient identification for check cashing.[36]

Pricing and Customer Profitability

As observed earlier, bank managers were careful to analyze individual demand deposit accounts. The analysis of individual customers was, of course, nothing new to bankers, considering the activities involved in providing credit. Bankers were particularly watchful of demand deposit accounts because their operation was much more labor intensive than that of savings and other nondemand deposit accounts. In 1906, it was estimated that commercial banks specializing in demand deposit accounts and commercial credit employed about two and a half times the number of officers and clerks as comparably sized savings banks (using total deposits as a measure of size).

Around 1900, some of the larger New York City and Chicago banks began employing full-time staff to analyze individual demand deposit account profitability, using standardized mathematical techniques. Managers had known from experience that high-balance, low-volume checking accounts were profitable and that low-balance, high-volume accounts were unprofitable. But there was a whole array of accounts whose profitability could only be guessed at. During the 1900s, *The Bankers' Magazine* recommended that every bank, regardless of size, employ at least one individual capable of analyzing individual demand deposit accounts.

Thus, banks increasingly attempted to manage actual and potential customers in regard to demand deposit accounts. Although analysis of individual accounts was possible, the cost was high, and many banks simply classified demand deposit accounts into two or three groups. It was common to exclude one group from opening a demand deposit account and to require an average minimum monthly balance for the remainder. During the early 1920s, one study of 82 banks reported an average minimum to open an account of $103 and an average monthly balance of $95 (some banks in both instances had minimums of $1,000, and many imposed no requirements). One Chicago bank had lower requirements for women's accounts than for other types. Some banks steered those who failed to meet minimum checking account requirements to their savings department. The same 1920s study reported that 71 percent of the banks in the study made such efforts.

Bankers also were extremely mindful of the attitudes of customers when it came to handling accounts that fell below minimum requirements. Prior to 1910, the norm was for bankers to dicuss account profitability with customers face-to-face. The task was eased by the limited size of the customer base and bankers' general belief that no reasonable customer could expect a bank to carry an account at a loss. Invariably bankers allowed customers to increase their average balance before imposing service fees or, as a final resort, closing the account. But successful efforts to attract new business around the start of the twentieth century led to the opening of so many small accounts that some bankers resorted to direct mail campaigns to inform customers of new demand deposit account requirements. Even in these instances, they provided a grace period before taking more drastic action with the customer's account. For example, during the late 1920s, the evaporation of profit margins, which further accelerated the trend toward demand deposit service fees, led the Farmers Trust Company (Lancaster, Pennsylvania) to impose a service fee on accounts with an average monthly balance below $100. These accounts, which comprised over 60 percent of the bank's 8,800 demand deposit accounts, were a drain on profitability. The Farmers approached other banks in the community to go along with the plan, but they refused out of a fear of alienating a large number of customers. Farmers' unilateral direct mail campaign cost $1,000 and resulted in the closing of 2,597 accounts. Most of the account holders who remained increased their balance to avoid the service fee, and total bank demand deposits increased markedly within three months of the campaign. Owing to the operation of fewer accounts, the bank reduced its workforce. From the beginning, though, bankers were always careful to examine the overall profitability of a customer. They often waived service fees or minimum requirements for customers who purchased multiple services from the bank. And some banks went so far as to exclude all service fees because they found it too difficult to track all the business and family connections of their customers.[37]

PAST CUSTOMERS

The exact point at which a customer becomes a past customer is open to debate. A past customer is one who actually closes an account. But a past customer may also be one who leaves an account inactive for an extended period of time (either by desire or by omission). State statutes dictate the length of time before an inactive account is dormant or dead (between 10 and 25 years during the 1910s in many states), how banks must report dormant accounts, and when banks may cease interest payments.

In 1913 and 1914, W. R. Morehouse of the German-American Trust & Savings Bank (Los Angeles) presented a series of form letters used by the bank's new account department when personal contact was inefficient (as in accounts of medium value and for customers residing at a distance from the bank). Many of the form letters were of the cross-selling variety. There were letters for the new customer who had opened a savings or checking account or had rented a safety deposit box. There were form letters for use six months after a new account had been secured. The bank's new account department maintained a central information file that, in addition to standard customer data, tracked which letters had been mailed when. Inactive accounts were identified by closely monitoring the files. A series of form letters existed for inactive accounts. One asked inactive checking account holders whether they had been offended in any way. Another was for inactive savings account customers cultivated by the home safe campaign. Of the many letters for past customers, one thanked those who had formally closed an account, the goal being to maintain cordial relations.

Morehouse felt that closing an account was as important as opening one, and that banks should operate a department for closing accounts. He said that the department should ascertain why the account was being closed and convince the customer not to sever relations. If the latter was not possible, then the department should convey to the customer that his or her business was appreciated and would be appreciated should he or she decide to return. Morehouse explicitly stated that a goal of the department would be to minimize "knocking" (negative word of mouth).

Morehouse also felt that many accounts should never have been opened. He said that many dormant accounts were opened because of (1) hard selling by solicitors; (2) a fleeting impulse to save that quickly vanished; (3) a determined impulse to save that slowly vanished; or (4) the inability to save resulting from the much stronger impulse to spend. In addition, banks too often failed to properly follow up on new account holders. The "remedy" for the German-American Trust & Savings Bank was to maintain an accurate central information file and to constantly contact customers with direct mail. Inactive commercial account holders were usually subject to personal interviews rather than direct mail appeals. In cases where the bank believed an account would never be profitable, it actively sought to have the customer eliminated from the books.

In 1922 Morehouse, along with F. A. Stearns, advertising manager of the Security Trust & Savings Bank (Los Angeles), revised an earlier book on direct mail letters. *Revised Bank Letters* presented 100 letters and offered suggestions for their use. The first letter was for holders of dormant accounts who had made no transactions for one month. If account activity was observed, then letter seven was suggested; if no response was forthcoming, then letters two through six were suggested at one-month intervals. Other series were for attracting prospective customers, such as parents (one dollar baby premiums), children, factory workers, farmers (bank by mail), and women. Other series addressed closing out accounts; new building or new branch promotions; and the selling of commercial, safety deposit, trust, and bond services. Special letters were included for newlyweds, ministers, teachers, bank employees, and stockholders.

Another bank that operated a department for closing accounts was the Hellman Commercial Trust & Savings Bank (Los Angeles), which called it the close out account department. By 1916, the department was saving 120 to 200 accounts per month from closing entirely. In some cases, depositors would leave a dollar deposit and later build it up, while in other cases the account was retained in its entirety. In either case, through the department many customers had impressed upon them the bank's keen interest in their affairs. The department also stemmed negative word of mouth, and from customers' complaints identified weaknesses in front- and back-office operations.

Banks experimented with reviving inactive or dormant accounts. The Bank of Italy (San Francisco) in 1923 stimulated dormant accounts by direct mail, recorded the response for different account size categories, and found that the likelihood of the holder of a dormant account permanently severing relations with the bank increased with account size. The bank recommended reviving accounts up to the mean bank deposit level and proceeding beyond such with caution. Depositors of large sums were probably aware of their holdings, and the bank's reminder could be offensive. The National Bank of Commerce (St. Louis) in 1925 found that accounts inactive for six months to one year were four times more likely to respond to direct mail appeals with activity or growth than accounts inactive for one to two years. Fourteen percent of accounts inactive two to five years responded to direct mail appeals, compared with one percent of accounts inactive for more than five years. Based on their research, it was clear that it was best to handle an inactive account early on. The bank therefore mailed a series of six personally typed and signed letters to new account customers whose accounts showed no activity or growth after six months. Canadian banks, too, controlled account inactivity and dormancy. The Huron & Erie Mortgage Corporation (London, Ontario), for example, experimented with reviving long-standing dormant savings accounts during the early 1920s.[38]

NOTES

1. Susan P. Benson, *Counter Cultures: Saleswomen, Managers, and Customers in American Department Stores, 1890–1940* (Urbana: University of Illinois Press, 1988), 148–49.

2. Philip Ollerenshaw, *Banking in Nineteenth-Century Ireland: The Belfast Banks, 1825–1914* (Manchester, U.K.: Manchester University Press, 1987), 51.

3. Owen J. Stalson, *Marketing Life Insurance: Its History in America* (Cambridge, MA: Harvard University Press, 1942), 103–214.

4. Vincent P. Carosso, *The Morgans: Private International Bankers, 1854–1913* (Cambridge, MA: Harvard University Press, 1987), 69.

5. Correspondence of H. C. McLeod (Bank of Nova Scotia), Winnipeg sub-section of the Canadian Bankers Association, and the Canadian Bankers Association (BNS archives).

6. Horatio Ford, "Going After Business and Getting It," *BMa*, 85 (July 1912): 9–14.

7. Frederick Kerman and Bryant W. Griffin, *New Business for Banks* (New York: Prentice-Hall, 1926), 162–63.

8. Hosea Mann, "Home Banks Increase Deposits," *BMa*, 77 (September 1908): 405–08; E. St. Elmo Lewis, *Financial Advertising* (1908; repr., New York: Garland, 1985), 853–60; W. R. Morehouse, *Bank Deposit Building* (New York: Bankers Publishing Co., 1918), 64–67.

9. F. B. Kirkbride, "Banking Among the Poor: The Lighthouse Savings Fund Experiment," *Annals of the American Academy of Social and Political Science*, 18 (September 1901): 286–89; "Interesting the Children," *BMa*, 82 (June 1911): 797–99; T. D. MacGregor, *Bank Advertising Plans* (New York: Bankers Publishing Co., 1913), 27–28; Leo D. Woodworth, "Christmas Savings Clubs, 1920," *JABA*, 14 (July 1921): 17–20; "New Magnets for Idle Dollars," *ABAJ*, 16 (May 1924): 751–52; Kerman and Bryant, *New Business for Banks*, 185–86, 193–94; William F. Hass, *A History of Banking in New Haven* (New Haven, CT: privately printed, 1946), 78.

10. "How Banks Are Advertising," *BMa*, 78 (January 1909): 111-12; MacGregor, *Bank Advertising Plans*, 92–94.

11. "A New Savings System," *BMa*, 86 (May 1913): 604–06; "Depositing Employees' Wages," *BMa*, 88 (February 1914): 191; John F. Tinsley, "The Operation of an Industrial Savings Plan During Commercial Depression," *BMa*, 102 (April 1921): 565–67; Elbert H. Crosby, "Reaching for the Savings of the Wage Earners," *BMo*, 39 (October 1922): 13–15; Don Knowlton, "How Much Do Workmen Save," *BMa*, 107 (July 1923): 17–21; G. Prather Knapp, "Plans That Succeed on Industrial Saving," *BMo*, 40 (August

1923): 9–10+; M. G. Farber, "Arguments That Sell Industrial Savings Accounts," *BMo*, 47 (July 1930): 23–24+.

12. MacGregor, *Bank Advertising Plans*, 85–87; James D. Coit, "Thrift and the Mutual Savings Bank," *BMa*, 105 (September 1922): 409–12.

13. Benson, *Counter Cultures*, 18, 102.

14. F. A. Stearns, "Window Displays—The Latest in Bank Advertising," *BMa*, 94 (June 1917): 105+; W. R. Morehouse, "Window Display Advertising," *BMa*, 99 (December 1919): 764–69; W. R. Morehouse, *Bank Window Advertising* (New York: Bankers Publishing Co., 1919); D. G. Baird, "Window Displays in Savings Bank Attract New Accounts and Promote Goodwill," *BMa*, 105 (November 1922): 912–15.

15. A. Trigge, *A History of the Canadian Bank of Commerce*, Vol. 3 (Toronto: Canadian Bank of Commerce, 1934), 160.

16. Edwin B. Wilson, "Some of the Broader Phases of Bank and Trust Company Advertising," *BMa*, 91 (July 1915): 29–35; A. F. Harlow, "How the Banks Taught a City to Save," *BMo*, 30 (July 1916): 28–33; Richard Germain, "The Early Years of Community Advertising," *Journal of Nonprofit & Public Sector Marketing*, 1, 1 (1993): 85–106. Advertisement in *System*, 40 (August 1921): 132.

17. Owen J. Stalson, *Marketing Life Insurance: Its History in America* (Cambridge, MA: Harvard University Press, 1942), 337–39.

18. F. R. Fuller, "What an Advertising Trust Company Has Accomplished in Nine Years," *TC*, 2 (December 1904): 1096–97; MacGregor, *Bank Advertising Plans*, 61–67; "How Banks are Advertising," *BMa*, 89 (November 1914): 537; George M. Wallace, *Joseph Francis Sartori: 1858–1946* (Los Angeles: Ward Ritchie Press, 1948), 65. Advertisements reprinted in *BMa*, 79 (October 1909): 620; *BMa*, 89 (September 1914): 339.

19. W. R. Morehouse, "The New Account Teller and the New Account Department," *BMa*, 86 (March 1913): 334–36.

20. A. M. Ingraham, "Advertising to Present Depositors," *BMa*, 84 (February 1912): 227–28; Fred W. Ellsworth, "Merchandising Ideas of 'Department Store of Finance,'" *PI*, 113 (23 December 1920): 77–78+; J. R. Giessenbier, "Securing More Business from Your Present Customers," *BMo*, 40 (December 1923): 14–15+; Jules C. Smith, "How We Doubled Our Deposits in Three Years," *BMo*, 46 (April 1929): 9–12+.

21. Leroy A. Mershon, "New Accounts Through Old," *JABA*, 12 (September 1919): 151–52; Ellsworth, "Merchandising Ideas of 'Department Store of Finance'"; Vincent J. Corrigan, "Regulating Your Advertising with a Central File," *BMo*, 38 (January 1921): 34+; Bryon F. Heitzman, "Keeping Contact with Customers Through the Central File," *BMo*, 43 (March 1926): 17.

22. W. B. Weisenburger, "Making Salesmen out of Bank Employees," *BMa*, 110 (June 1925): 998.

23. E. V. Newton, "Filing Systems for New Business Use," *BMa*, 121 (October 1930): 453–60.

24. "New Type of Central Information File Adopted by New Business: Findex in Operation," *The Equitable Envoy*, 9 (August 1929): 11 (CM archives).

25. Charles W. Stevens, "The Central File and Its Place in Business Development," *BMa*, 117 (September 1928): 343–47.

26. The Addressograph Company, *Business Office Training Course of Addressograph Company* (Cleveland: Addressograph Company, 1936).

27. Newton, "Filing Systems for New Business Use."

28. Hugh M. Johnson, "Anyone Can Make Loans," *BMo*, 44 (December 1927): 9–10.

29. Lewis, *Financial Advertising*, 394–95, 415.

30. Edward A. Kendrick, "How Direct Advertising Is Helping Banks to Educate the Masses," *PI*, 109 (2 October 1919): 45–48.

31. Ibid.

32. All examples published by Bankers Trust Company, New York: John S. Thompson, *Liberty Bond and Note Values* (1919); Bankers Trust Company, *America's Merchant Marine* (1920); Harvey E. Fisk, *The Dominion of Canada* (1920); Harvey E. Fisk, *English Public Finance* (1920); Harvey E. Fisk, *French Public Finance* (1922); Harvey E. Fisk, *The Inter-Ally Debts* (1924).

33. Trigge, *A History of the Canadian Bank of Commerce*, Vol 3, 46; Merrill Denison, *Canada's First Bank*, Vol. 2 (New York: Dodd, Mead, 1966), 355. Advertisement reprinted in *BMa*, 117 (November 1928): 848.

34. "How Banks Are Advertising," *BMa*, 86 (June 1913): 726; Oscar F. Ecklund, "The Personal Touch in Your Letters to Newcomers," *BMo*, 42 (May 1925): 30–31.

35. Harry E. Gail, "Safe Keeping of Bonds as a Business Getter," *BMo*, 36, (February 1919): 8–9; Gilbert O. Gilbert, "Making Bond Investors Steady Customers," *BMo*, 36 (May 1919): 13; Laurence J. Davis, "Telling the Story of Your Mechanical Aids," *BMo*, 36 (November 1919): 28. Advertisement in *The Globe* (1921) (TD archives).

36. Jackson Heywood, "Free Passbooks to Win Savings Deposits," *BMo*, 36 (July 1919): 7–8.

37. Charles W. Reihl, "Practical Banking: Analysis of Accounts," *BMa*, 73 (August 1906): 280–87; John F. Wilson, "Cost of Handling Checking Accounts," *BMa*, 73 (September 1906): 412–17; T. Thulin, "Scientific Analysis of Accounts," *BMa*, 87 (August 1913): 157–61; W. R. Morehouse, "Eliminating Unprofitable Checking Accounts," *BMa*, 89 (December 1914): 630–37; Harry J. Haas, "Analysis of Bank Accounts," *BMa*, 93 (December 1916): 536–40; Joseph Regan, "Getting the Most for Your Money," *BMo*, 34 (October 1917): 11–13; Joseph Regan, "Analyzing Accounts to Make Them Pay," *BMo*, 34 (November 1917): 14–15+; "Why Banks Should Make a Service Charge," *BMo*, 35 (October 1918): 7–9; "Getting Pay for Services Rendered," *BMa*, 80 (January 1919): 75–76; Franklin J. Lewis, "A $30,000 Account That Lost $468," *BMo*, 36 (March 1919): 12–13; C. Charles Grove, "Statistical Cost Analysis in a Bank," *BMa*, 98 (April 1919): 427–32; C. Charles Grove, "Statistical Cost Analysis in a Bank," *BMa*, 98 (June 1919): 489–98; Thomas C. Jefferies, "Finding out the Value of Each New Account," *BMo*, 36 (June 1919): 16–17; H. B. Grimm, "Depositors Taught That Even a Bank Must Make Money," *PI*, 108 (11 September 1919): 59–60; Thomas C. Jefferies, "How to Determine Banking Costs," *BMa*, 102 (May 1921): 724–29; Alexander Wall, "A Profitable Account," *BMa*, 103 (October 1921): 626–30; M. A. Knight, "The Operation of the Analysis Department," *BMa*, 103 (November 1921): 834–38; S. Reid Warren, "Building up the Unprofitable Account," *BMa*, 104 (May 1922): 820–22; Walter Distelhorst, "Is the Small Checking Account a Liability or an Asset," *BMo*, 39 (July 1922): 22–23+; Clem J. Steigmeyer, "What a Survey Revealed on Small Checking Accounts," *BMo*, 40 (January 1923): 36+; Joseph D. Yerkes, "Are Banks Giving Away Too Much Free Service," *BMa*, 109 (September 1924): 363–66; W. E. Walker, "Introducing Your Customers to the Service Charge," *BMo*, 42 (February 1925): 15+; W. N. King, "What We Found out After a Year of the Service Charge," *BMo*, 42 (October 1925): 21+; Z. D. Bonner, "Account Activity as Basis for the Service Charge," *BMo*, 43 (April 1926): 9–10; "Service Charge Benefits," *BMo*, 45 (March 1928): 38–39; Robert H. Myers, "Analyzing Active Checking Accounts in Moderate-Sized Banks," *BMa*,

117 (December 1928): 983; Earl S. Crawford, "Making Checking Accounts Pay," *BMa*, 119 (September 1929): 509–12; Newton S. North, "Metered Bank Service," *ABAJ*, 23 (November 1930): 405–07+.

38. W. H. Kniffen, "Dormant Accounts," *BMa*, 84 (April 1912): 504–08; W. R. Morehouse, "A Method for Stopping Unnecessary Withdrawals," *BMa*, 87 (December 1913): 633–35; W. R. Morehouse, "Bank Letters That Pull and Hold Business," *BMa*, 88 (February 1914): 157–63; D. R. Branham, "Why Do Your Depositors Close Their Accounts," *BMa*, 92 (April 1916): 535; W. R. Morehouse, "Intensified Cultivation of Old Business," *BMa*, 93 (July 1916): 38–44; D. M'Eachern, "Stimulating the Dormant Account," *BMo*, 37 (July 1920): 37; W. R. Morehouse and F. A. Stearns, *Revised Bank Letters* (Los Angeles: Bankers Service Co., 1922); C. E. Robinson, "Handle Dormant Savings Accounts with Care," *BMo*, 40 (September 1923): 27+; H. H. Reinhard, "The Savings Manager and the Retail End of Banking," *ABAJ*, 17 (April 1925): 612+; Marquis James and Bessie R. James, *Biography of a Bank: The Story of Bank of America, N.T. & S.A.* (New York: Harper & Brothers, 1954), 125, 198.

8

Geographic Segmentation

In this chapter, we focus on geographic segmentation, a major innovation that greatly expanded a bank's trading radius at little cost. Geographic segmentation was implemented primarily through a new product, banking by mail, introduced on a formal basis very late in the nineteenth century. Banks had long used the postal service to conduct business. During the Civil War, soldiers could mail all or part of their pay to savings banks. In the Choctaw Nation (the Indian Territory of what is now a part of Oklahoma) during the 1880s, individuals, including J. D. Lankford (later the state's superintendent of banks), acted as stamp agents and sold "nickel-savings-stamps" that were pasted to sheets in savings books. The agents forwarded collected stamps (when, we assume, a total of at least one dollar was accumulated) by mail, along with signature cards, to the Denison National Bank (Texas), which mailed back passbooks. This system declined considerably, however, with the spread of banks throughout the region during the 1890s. The development of formal banking by mail for distant customers may have been innovative within the banking industry, but there are parallels in other business and nonprofit applications. Certainly, banking by mail (also called "mail order" business) hints that one impetus came from mail order retailers (such as Sears), some of which had been operating successfully in America since the 1880s. Public libraries, too, offered special services to distant customers. Prior to the first bookmobile in America (1906), public libraries established traveling libraries as early as the 1880s. Sets of 100 or so books were shipped by rail (often at no charge to the library or customer) to remote communities, where they remained for three to four months.[1]

BANKING BY MAIL

Banking by mail was differentiated from previous mail-reliant plans by heavy promotion and formal banking by mail departments, standardized forms, and procedure development. The public was quick to accept the new service owing to the large rural population at the end of the nineteenth century (about 70 percent of the nation's population lived in rural areas), the paucity of rural banks, and transportation barriers. Table 8.1 lists banks offering the service prior to 1920. Its quick diffusion by 1910 illustrates the inability of first movers to patent a new service.

The Pittsburgh Bank for Savings was the first to develop a formal banking by mail program (in 1898). Bank deposits grew from $3,350,000 to $12,250,000 in three and a half years, a nominal annual growth rate of 44.8 percent. Clay Herrick said that "a considerable part of the increase [at this specific bank is] being ascribed to advertising for mail business." Other banks also reported either spectacular growth or a significant percent of business derived from the plan. During the 1920s, an assistant treasurer of the Albany City Savings Bank estimated that about half of the bank's 19,551 customers lived out of town and used its banking by mail service.[2]

Banking by mail was frequently advertised in the media, brochures were widely distributed, and direct mail was heavy. During the 1900s the president of the Bowery Savings Bank reported that 27,000 copies of a small booklet titled *Banking by Mail* had been distributed. In general, promotional themes focused on convenience, the ability to deal with a reputable bank from a great distance, the security of the system overall, and local interest rate differentials. Typical were messages such as "Every corner letter-box or smallest cross-roads country post office has thus become a convenient receiving teller" and "This bank is as near to you as the nearest mailbox."[3]

The New York-based Bankers Publishing Company also did its part in promoting the adoption of banking by mail. As early as 1910, it made available a booklet titled *The Reasonableness of Banking by Mail* for distribution by banks to customers (the booklet contained several blank pages for promotional use by the sponsoring institution).[4]

Banking by mail was quickly adopted by Canadian banks. Branches of the Canadian Bank of Commerce, the Royal Bank of Canada, and the Bank of Nova Scotia were offering the service by the mid-1910s. Owing to the severity of Canadian winters, farmers were cultivated by the Canadian Bank of Commerce as mail customers. During the 1920s, branch employees were encouraged to visit each farm customer who banked by mail at least once a year.[5]

During World War I, members of the merchant marine and oversees military personnel were particularly lucrative markets for some banks. The Cleveland Trust Company advertised its banking by mail service in newspapers published near military bases. A major selling point was that Cleveland banks normally offered 4 percent interest on savings accounts, compared with 3 to 3.5 percent offered by banks in other major cities.[6]

Table 8.1
Pre-1920 Banking by Mail

Institution	Location	Year
Pittsburgh Bank for Savings	Pittsburgh, PA	1898[a]
Marquette County Savings Bank	Marquette, MI	1900
Bowery Savings Bank	New York City	1903
Albany City Savings Institution	Albany, NY	1906
Old Colony Trust Company	Boston, MA	1906
Slater Trust Company	Pawtucket, RI	1906
Cleveland Trust Company	Cleveland, OH	1907[a]
First National Bank of Northfork	Northfork, WV	1907
New Netherland Bank of New York	New York City	1908
Franklin Society for Home Building	New York City	1908
Central Bank & Trust Corporation	Atlanta, GA	1908
American National Bank of Nashville	Nashville, TN	1908
Union Trust Company	Rochester, NY	1908
Old National Bank of Battle Creek	Battle Creek, MI	1908
First National Bank of Mount Sterling	Mount Sterling, IL	1908
Citizens Saving & Trust Company	Cleveland, OH	1908
First Trust & Savings Bank	Billings, MT	1908
Salt Lake City Security & Trust Company	Salt Lake City, UT	1908
Equitable Banking & Loan Company	Macon, GA	1908
Planters National Bank of Richmond	Richmond, VA	1908
Scandinavian American Bank	Seattle, WA	1908
Oregon Trust & Savings Bank	Portland, OR	1908
Marquette National Bank	Marquette, MI	1908
Cameron Savings Bank	Johnstown, TN	1908
Commonwealth Trust Company	Pittsburgh, PA	1908
Hibernia Savings & Loan Society	San Francisco, CA	1909
Central Wisconsin Trust Company	Madison, WI	1909
National Bank of Commerce	St. Louis, MO	1909
State Savings Bank of Topeka	Topeka, KS	1909
United States Trust Company	Washington, D.C.	1909
Dominion National Bank of Bristol	Bristol, VA	1909
Fairmont Savings Trust Company	Philadelphia, PA	1910
National Savings Bank of Albany	Albany, NY	1910
First Mortgage Guarantee & Trust Co.	Philadelphia, PA	1910
Superior Savings & Trust Company	Cleveland, OH	1910
Peoples Savings Bank	Pittsburgh, PA	1911
Merchants & Mechanics Savings Bank	Grafton, WV	1911
Wachovia Bank & Trust Company	Winston-Salem, NC	1911
Waterbury Savings Bank & Trust Co.	Waterbury, VT	1912
American National Bank	Richmond, VA	1913
Farmers Deposit Savings Bank	Pittsburgh, PA	1913

Putnam Trust Company	Greenwich, CT	1915
Guardian Savings & Trust Company	Cleveland, OH	1918
Northern Trust Company	Chicago, IL	1919

[a]Year during which the program was actually begun; otherwise, the year of the citation.

Sources: Marquette County Savings Bank, *Banking by Mail* (Marquette, MI: Marquette County Savings Bank, 1900); "Follow up Systems," *BMa*, 77 (August 1908): 243–46; "Bank Booklets," *BMa*, 79 (July 1909): 124; "Some New Booklets," *BMa*, 78 (February 1909): 291; "More Booklets," *BMa*, 80 (February 1910): 329; "Bank Booklets," *BMa*, 80 (April 1910): 686; "Attractive Bank Literature," *BMa*, 82 (January 1911): 119–20; "Banking by Mail," *BMa*, 85 (September 1912): 270–71; "Unique Plan of Banking by Mail," *BMa*, 90 (February 1915): 217. Advertisements reprinted in or brief comment on banking by mail: *BMa*, 72 (January 1906): 133; *BMa*, 73 (September 1906): 474; *BMa*, 73 (December 1906): 1010; *BMa*, 75 (September 1907): 415; *BMa*, 76 (March 1908): 403; *BMa*, 76 (April 1908): 540, 583; *BMa*, (May 1908): 762, 766; *BMa*, 76 (June 1908): 879; *BMa*, 77 (August 1908): 247, 257; *BMa*, 77 (September 1908): 411; *BMa*, 78 (February 1908): 296–97; *BMa*, 78 (January 1909): 112; *BMa*, 82 (June 1911): 118; *BMa*, 86 (February 1913): 185; *BMa*, 87 (November 1913): 544.

There were variants of banking by mail. For example, as early as 1908, the Carnegie Safe Deposit Company (New York) offered safety deposit service by mail. Registered mail was used to send wax-sealed, linen envelopes between the bank and customers. To ensure privacy, the bank promised to return the envelopes with the seal unbroken. Hyperbole characterized the description of the vaults: "No drill could pierce them; the guns of a battleship could scarcely make an impression upon them." By 1911, the Cleveland Trust Company was operating an armored car pickup service for safe deposit customers.[7]

MOTOR VEHICLES

Since motor vehicles were employed to serve distant customers and expand a bank's trading radius, their use may be considered a form of geographic segmentation. One of the earliest examples of a banking motor vehicle comes from Europe: in 1901 a savings bank in Mezieres, France, operated an electric vehicle, an "automobile savings bank," that *Scientific American* called "one of the most brilliant ideas of modern times." The vehicle made scheduled stops at villages and transported two tellers, a bank cashier, a safe, and all documents necessary for the complete transaction of bank business.[8]

The Night & Day Bank (New York) began operating an armored limousine service in 1906. Relatively quickly, more specialized motor vehicles began to appear on the market. By 1910, the Bellamore Company was selling specially designed armored "auto banks." Models were filled with security devices, including an electrified grille separating teller from customer (in many cases, a company's paymaster), sirens and bells, and protective material consisting of multi-layered tempered steel. Customers benefiting the most were those meeting cash payrolls, making large cash deposits, and transferring securities. The adoption of these innovative vehicles, it was written,

> serves a higher function. It brings home to the people a better knowledge of banking, thus educating them to become savers . . . . By making regular trips to manufacturing plants and organizations employing large numbers of people, the Motor Bank Car will turn the attention of the wage-earners toward savings, thus diminishing wasteful expenditures, preventing hoarding, and placing the surplus money of the country where it belongs—in the banks.[9]

A Paterson, New Jersey, trust company in 1911 began an autobanking service for rural customers. The bank on wheels was capable of speeds up to 50 miles per hour and was described in advertising as "fire proof, bullet proof, and burglar proof." When the only bank in Homestead, Florida, closed in 1930, the National City Bank of Miami sent an autobank to the town on an experimental, bi-weekly basis. And the Old National Bank of Spokane in 1924 offered downtown-to-suburbs courier service for suburban merchants.[10]

Motor vehicles were also used during wartime to meet military payrolls. For example, two European offices of the Guaranty Trust Company of New York (London and Paris) became U.S. depositories during World War I. The payment of American forces through the Paris office increased business volume so substantially that within a short period there were more accounts on the books in Paris than in the New York head office. Called a "branch on wheels," an autobank toured behind the lines and cashed soldiers' checks, accepted subscriptions for Liberty Bonds, sold drafts, and disbursed cash to Army payroll officers.[11]

Banks also took their services on board ocean liners. The Farmers & Loan Trust Company (New York) in 1923 operated a branch aboard the transatlantic liner *Leviathan*. Operating hours were geared to landings, and the branch's main business was in foreign exchange and money orders. By 1929, the London-based Midland Bank was operating branches on three English transatlantic liners: *Aquitania*, *Mauretania*, and *Bergenia*.[12]

NOTES

1. Stella Lucas, "Traveling Libraries in Pennsylvania," *Public Libraries*, 2 (February 1897): 1–2; Mrs. Eugene B. Heard, "The Free Travelling Library: An Aid to Education and a Factor in the National Life," *National Education Association: Journal of Proceedings and Addresses* (Thirty-Ninth Annual Meeting, 1900), 648–54; C. L. Chamberlin, "Studies in Bank Advertising," *BMa*, 76 (June 1908): 873–77; William D. Orcutt, *The Miracle of Mutual Savings* (New York: Bowery Savings Bank, 1934), 81; James M. Smallwood, *An Oklahoma Adventure of Banks and Bankers* (Norman: University of Oklahoma Press, 1979), 13.

2. Clay Herrick, "Sundry Topics," *BMa*, 75 (August 1907): 212; Thomas F. Moffett, "Building Deposits by Mail," *BMa*, 104 (April 1922): 656–58.

3. "How Banks Are Advertising," *BMa*, 78 (March 1909): 505; "How Banks Are Advertising," *BMa*, 79 (September 1909): 447; L. L. Hall, "Flashing a Welcome to the New Customer," *BMo*, 36 (August 1919): 16–17; T. D. MacGregor, "If It's Continuous,

It's Cumulative," *Burrough's Clearing House*, 7 (January 1923): 25; Bensen R. Ray, *A Chronology of the Bowery Savings Bank* (New York: Bowery Savings Bank, 1948), 18; Oscar Schisgall, *The Bowery Savings Bank* (New York: American Management Association, 1984), 94.

4. Advertisement appearing in *BMa*, 81 (October 1910): 601.

5. C. L. Chamberlin, "Studies in Bank Advertising," *BMa*, 76 (June 1908): 877; "Advertising Criticism," *BMa*, 79 (September 1909): 442; W. J. Keys, "Developing Mail Order Business," *Caduceus*, 7 (July 1926): 33–34 (CIBC archives). Advertisement reprinted in *BMa*, 79 (October 1909): 624. Memorandum book dated 1915 distributed to customers (BNS archives).

6. "Selling the Savings Habit by Mail to the Boys of Uncle Sam," *PI*, 103 (30 May 1918): 87–88.

7. W. O. McClure, "Getting Safe Deposit Business," *BMa*, 83 (July 1911): 70–74. Advertisement reprinted in *BMa*, 76 (May 1908): 765.

8. "A Bank on Wheels," *Scientific American*, 85 (26 October 1901): 266.

9. "The Bellamore Armored Motor Bank Car," *BMa*, 81 (December 1910): 739–45.

10. "Bank on Wheels," *NYT* (10 February 1911); H. Brunkow, "A Bank-by-Mail Booklet That Won Results," *BMo*, 41 (August 1924): 14–15; "Gleaned from the Month's News," *BMa*, 112 (July 1930): 142.

11. Guaranty Trust Company of New York, *One Hundred Years of Service* (New York: Guaranty Trust Company of New York, 1939), 33–34.

12. "Busy Hours in a Floating Bank," *Literary Digest*, 78 (8 September 1923): 72–73; Luther A. Harr, *Branch Banking in England* (Philadelphia: University of Pennsylvania Press, 1929), 95.

9

Socioeconomic and Credit End-Use Segmentation

Socioeconomic segmentation refers to splitting the market on the basis of income. Many precedents of this type of segmentation exist. During the 1920s, the automotive industry (General Motors in particular) was producing a range of vehicles afffordable to various pocketbooks, Ford's mass market approach notwithstanding. In the insurance business, ordinary life policies that sold in increments of $1,000 were financial instruments designed for the upper classes. These policies were in contrast with industrial insurance, sold in much smaller increments, to the working and lower classes, a product originated by the Prudential Assurance Company of Great Britain in 1848. The Prudential Friendly Society, which was organized in 1875 and later became the Prudential Insurance Company of America, led the way in the United States in industrial insurance, selling it for "three cents a week."

In the department store industry, many examples of socioeconomic segmentation exist. Near the end of the nineteenth century, Macy's and Marshall Field's "were located at opposite ends of an imaginary spectrum of which the poles were price and amenity." Bloomingdale's of New York incorporated socioeconomic segmentation in window display design. Department store bargain basements, which appeared just after 1900, provided merchandise of lower quality and price that was more affordable to the working classes. The most brazen examples in department store retailing center on how these institutions treated upper class-women. Only the most wealthy women were able to secure charge accounts. Floor managers, doormen, and salespeople were encouraged to remember who they were and greet them by name, managers were much more lenient in accepting returns from them, special shopping days and merchandise were reserved for them, and salespeople were apt to serve them before others. Tickets for free afternoon tea were given only to recognized customers and those appearing to be well off. Some stores barred rowdy, disheveled children from their children's lounges or nurseries. During the 1930s, films were distributed on vacationing in Palm Beach and Miami to educate salespeople on how to make more appropriate fashion and accessory suggestions for travelers (no doubt, wealthier resort-patrons).[1]

Similarly, examples of socioeconomic segmentation exist in banking. Women's departments initially targeted wealthy females; while industrial savings plans, Christmas Clubs, and home safe campaigns sought new business from the working classes. Wall Street investment banks traditionally sought out the wealthy as targets for stock and bond sales. It was only after 1900 that a limited number of brokers and banks targeted "small" investors. For example, in 1910, J. Hathaway Pope & Co. advertised that "the moderate or small investor is entitled to as much consideration from an investment broker as a larger one. We are specialists in inactive stocks and bonds and at present have some offerings of particular interest and value to the small investor." In 1920 the Old Second Ward Savings Bank, Wisconsin's largest savings bank, opened a "miniature bond department" at two branches. The main branch was already selling bonds on an informal basis to small investors, mostly bank employees; the department expanded the market to include small investors who were already bank customers. The bank designed special promotional and advertising material for its small investor bond campaign.[2]

Safe deposit service, too, illustrates how financial institutions initially targeted the wealthy for a service. The concept of a "community safe" predated safe deposit service by many years; the distinguishing feature of safe deposit service was the privacy afforded to box renters. In America, the first safe deposit institutions specialized in that line of business alone, and the first of these was the Safe Deposit Company of New York, organized in 1865. This was followed by the Fidelity Trust Company (Philadelphia) in 1866, and the Union Safe Deposit Vaults (Boston) in 1868. One of the earliest national banks to provide safe deposit service was The First National Bank of Chicago in 1879. The service spread west with the organization of the Denver Safe Deposit & Savings Bank during the 1880s, the vaults being hauled from the Missouri River to Denver by oxen.

The upper-class orientation of the first safe deposit vault companies resides in three pieces of evidence. First, the prices charged by early vault suppliers were beyond the means of all but a few. During the 1880s, the Safe Deposit Company of New York charged between $30 and $40 per year, and the Union Safe Deposit Vaults' minimum price was $20 per year. In 1877 the Bank of Nova Scotia, at its head office in Halifax, was one of the first Canadian banks to install safe deposit boxes. One commercial customer paid an annual fee of $25. Second, the first organizers provided the service in part to store federal government bonds, and only a small portion of society could afford such instruments. Third, much of the promotional material shows people of wealth using vault facilities. Whether these promotions depicted average or idealized customers is difficult to say, but when combined with vault pricing and with the objective of storing government bonds, the advertising depiction appears more realistic than idealistic.

Yet like women's departments, safe deposit service outgrew an upper-class orientation and became increasingly available at lower prices to greater numbers of people. Attracted by the apparent "immunity" of safe deposit vault companies from defalcation, thousands of banks had safe deposit vaults by 1900. New entrants drove down costs by installing 50 to 100 boxes inside bank vaults. Because of the lackadaisical manner with which the keys to these vaults were kept, the period of growth around 1900 was called the "cookie jar" period. Boxes were often rented at $2 to $3 per year.[3]

Whether the service was women's departments, the sale of stocks and bonds, or safe deposit boxes, banks and other organizations had little difficulty in identifying wealthy individuals. In smaller cities, just as today, identifying the wealthy was a relatively easy matter. In larger cities, lists of wealthy individuals could be purchased. In 1845 Moses Y. Beach compiled *Wealth and Biography of the Wealthy Citizens of New York City Comprising an Alphabetical Arrangement of Persons Estimated to Be Worth $100,000 and Upwards. With Sums Being Appended to Each Name: Being Useful to Bankers, Merchants, and Others*. By 1847, Brooklyn had its own list of magnates worth upward of $10,000. The lists were both business aids and community boosters demonstrating wealth, growth, and suitability for development.[4]

On the bank asset (loan) side of the equation, the primary segmentation variable is commercial versus consumer—that is, splitting the market on the basis of whether the end use is business or personal consumption. The consumer credit market was long called the "small loan market" because loans were of small value; the term is used interchangeably with "personal consumption credit market." It was not until the late 1920s that commercial banks entered the small loan market, a defining moment in American banking. The almost century-long growth of banking faster than the economy, and the growth of deposits faster than loans, finally overcame capital shortages. During the 1920s, credit availability outstripped commercial credit demand, and as a result banks sought out the small loan market. Not including consumer finance divisions of industrial organizations, such as General Motors Acceptance Corporation, the 1930 market share of the small loan market among various types of lenders on the basis of the dollar value of loans outstanding is presented in Table 9.1. The remainder of this section examines some of the lenders in Table 9.1 and documents their sales efforts.

UNLICENSED LENDERS

Small loans by unlicensed lenders in America appear to have begun just after the end of the Civil War. One of the earliest newspaper advertisements by an unlicensed lender appeared in an 1867 issue of the *Chicago Tribune*. Seven unlicensed lenders advertised in the last November Sunday edition of the

Table 9.1
Market Shares of the "Small Loan" Market, 1930

Institution	Market Share (%)
Unlicensed lenders	28.9
Pawnbrokers	23.2
Personal finance companies	19.3
Industrial banks	13.9
Commercial banks	7.3
Credit unions	2.4
Remedial loan societies	2.3
Axias (private banks, e.g., private immigrant banks)	1.9
Employers' plans	0.8

Source: Evans Clark, *Financing the Consumer* (New York: Harper & Brothers, 1931), 30.

Chicago Tribune in 1872; the number was 13 for the same issue in 1885. Newspaper advertisements are not the best indicator of the number of unlicensed lenders, however, for many preferred to distribute handbills door-to-door or at factory gates. Beginning in 1883, some lenders promoted the confidentiality of their relationship with customers, and by 1890, the small loan business was well established in most American and Canadian cities. Some lenders concentrated on salary assignments (a contract to pay the lender a fixed amount from each pay); others were chattel lenders who used furniture, store fixtures, and so on as collateral; still others loaned on unsecured notes. These unlicensed lenders were the dreaded loan sharks.

The social stigma attached to personal consumption debt, in those days, was unimaginably great. Personal debt was a sign of moral decay and of a hopeless inability to plan and budget. In collecting on loans, unlicensed lenders were astute psychologists who used the stigma as a lever against delinquent borrowers. In the case of salary loans, delinquency resulted in attachment of the borrower's wages. Employers were informed of the employee's debt, a sufficient cause for dismissal in some instances, and were forced to expend legal and accounting resources to handle wage assignment claims. Employees were subject to the ridicule and scorn of coworkers. Part of the reason that employers eventually fought loan sharks was the cost of wage assignment claims. Another tactic involved sending notes to debtors' homes. Initial notes regarding late payment were inconspicuous, but later ones were larger and bore the name of the lending company in bold print. Neighbors could guess at the contents all too easily. Some lenders sent a moving truck to the home of a delinquent borrower. The truck had the name of the lender in big letters or words to the effect of "delinquent borrower repossession." Drivers frequently stood outside the house and loudly threatened to remove furniture. One of the most imaginative psychological levers was the "bawlerout," usually a female, always a person with a loud voice, who visited the debtor at his or her place of employment and bawled out the debtor in front of colleagues. So ingrained were the bawlerouts in popular culture that Forest Halsey wrote a novel titled *The Bawlerout* (published in 1912).[5] Some unlicensed lenders preferred to have branch offices staffed and managed by women because irate male customers were unlikely to assult a female collector.

Unlicensed lenders bitterly defended themselves against public animosity. When the city of Montreal levied a $200 per annum fee on unlicensed lenders, D. H. Tolman, a despised New York loan shark who operated numerous branches, replied in the following manner (in the *Montreal Star*, 1908).

> Dear Sir.—Replying to your letter of the 24th, would say you seem to be under the impression that my office in your city now does a money-lending business, WHICH IT DOES NOT DO. We have done no loaning business in Canada for about two years. We simply buy time. That is if a man wants to sell a week's or a month's future wages we buy the same, just as we would so much of growing crop of wheat or apples on the trees, or any other commodity, for future use. WE TAKE NO NOTES WHATSOEVER, THEREFORE NO INTEREST. Consequently we are not liable for any moneylending license whatsoever. I am, however, perfect willing to pay my business tax, same as anyone else does, any time, in proportion to my rent, and, I don't think that you should try to enforce any license that I an not liable for, or in any way to annoy my employees or to cable at my expense, as I wish to do the proper thing and obey the laws at all times.

The principal manner by which loan sharks could claim that no interest or a legal interest rate was levied was through the practice of note-shaving, which involved not giving the debtor the full value of the loan by deducting exorbitant investigative or commission fees. (Processing fees were legal.) It was the effective interest rate that primarily separated the reputable from the not so reputable lenders.[6]

REMEDIAL LOAN SOCIETIES

While remedial loan societies only accounted for 2.3 percent of outstanding consumer loans in 1930, these semiphilanthropic institutions played a significant role in the battle against loan sharks. Investors recouped part of their capital in the form of dividends, but a major portion of the profits, if any were forthcoming, went toward lowering the effective interest rate charged to customers, in the hope of forcing down loan shark interest rates (but such was hardly ever the case). The first remedial loan society was the Collateral Loan Company of Boston, a pawnbroker business that began in 1857. This was followed by the Workingmen's Loan Association of Boston in 1888, the St. Bartholomew's Loan Association of New York, and the Provident Loan Society of New York in 1894. By 1909, there were 15 remedial loan societies in America. They increased awareness of the loan shark hazard, aided by the National Federation of the Remedial Loan Associations, organized in 1909 partly to raise awareness of that problem.[7]

PERSONAL FINANCE COMPANIES

The two most successful personal finance companies prior to 1930 were Household Finance Corporation and Beneficial Industrial Loan Corporation. Beneficial, started in 1914 by Clarence Hodson in New Jersey, by 1932 operated 303 offices and had just under $40 million in loans.

Household Finance Company was started by Frank J. Mackey. Between 1878 and 1881, he was in the jewelry business and active in Minneapolis society and in commerce as a mining investor and promoter, a seller of safes, and a maker of small personal loans. The latter business proved so successful that in 1881 he secured separate premises for the business, the first of its kind in Minneapolis. In December 1882 he placed the first advertisement for his business in local newspapers: "Money loaned on furniture, pianos, horses, wagons and personal property at low rates without removal and all other articles of value." In 1883 a branch office was opened in St. Paul, followed by expansion into Kansas City and Chicago by 1885. By the end of the decade, the company had expanded to Columbus, Dayton, Cleveland, St. Louis, Baltimore, and Milwaukee. Tight control was maintained over branch operations, each operated under a separate name; there was thus no effort to create a national chain able to take advantage of national advertising. In 1896 a second Pittsburgh branch was opened, and the manager of the office asked for permission to use mail solicitation of past borrowers to gain additional business. The proposal met with skepticism, but approval was given. The result, an increase in business of $10,000 in a few weeks, so impressed senior management that the plan was adopted across the entire chain.

In 1925 the chain was incorporated and adopted the name Household Finance Corporation, in part to generate national advertising economy. A major national advertising campaign was launched in 1928 to announce the chain's intention to reduce lending rates well below the legal maximum allowable. The reduced interest rates, it was hoped, would fuel growth by creating a high-volume, low-margin business. It also required capital infusion, and an issue of 140,000 shares of stock at $50 par value was aggressively promoted. The national campaign simultaneously informed the public of the new interest rate and stock issue. While it made few friends among other small loan firms, the stock very quickly sold out. The interest rate reduction, while successful for Household, led the public to wonder why other firms could not do the same. Household hired Ivy Lee, a well-known publicist who had handled John D. Rockefeller, to improve the firm's image. Lee arranged for magazine and newspaper reporters to interview Household's president, Leslie C. Harbison. In 1930 many favorable newspaper and magazine articles on Household appeared: *American Magazine* published "Harbison Lends Millions on the Best Security in the World—the American Family"; *The American Legion Monthly* published "The Power Behind the Loan"; and *Forbes* published "Little Bits About Big Men." Harbison and Household were portrayed as a modern savior of the American family that loaned on a fair basis and asked for a fair rate in return.

The success of the personal finance companies during the 1930s was attributed to (1) the ability to shift capital and trained employees from office to office as the need arose, (2) lack of dependence on any one geographic region, (3) the ability to spread the cost of skilled management among many offices, (4) national advertising opportunities, and (5) minimized risk through the spread of statutory reductions in allowable interest rates across states. Many of these benefits stemmed from the fact that personal finance companies, despite performing bank credit functions, were not treated by regulators as banks, and thus were free from the restrictive location and branch limitations confronting state, private, and national banks.[8]

INDUSTRIAL BANKS

In 1910 banker and lawyer Arthur J. Morris was granted a state charter to operate the Fidelity Savings & Trust Company (Norfolk, Virginia). The bank was the forerunner of what were called "industrial banks," the term "industrial" being borrowed from the insurance industry. Morris sought to fill the consumer credit void, combat loan sharks, and provide credit to the working and lower classes, not through a public or philanthropic institution, but through a chartered bank run on a for-profit basis. His bank was considered a hybrid institution by the Virginia State Corporation Commissioner: "It isn't a savings bank; it is isn't a state or national bank; it isn't a charity." Morris based his bank in part on European "people's banks" (e.g., Scotland's cash-credit banks, Germany's Raiffeisen Bank and Schulze-Delitzsch Bank, and Italy's Luzzatti Bank) and the Caisse-Populaire credit union started by Alphonse Desjardins at Levis, Quebec, in 1900. The lending policy of the bank centered on borrower character plus earning power, repayment matched to earning capacity, and a rational use for the loan. The bank did not loan on salary assignment, chattel mortgage, or any other tangibles. Two cosigners of the same character and income as the borrower were required. Within one year of operation, the bank had changed its name to Morris Plan Bank of Norfolk and had loaned out about $45,000 to over 300 borrowers.

To avoid usury laws, the bank technically did not provide loans. Borrowers invested in the bank's Class C certificate notes, each worth $50 at maturity. Each certificate required an investment of one dollar per week for 50 weeks. When the loan was due in 52 weeks, the borrower cashed the investment note and paid the proceeds to the bank. The margin earned by the bank was on an up-front investigation fee dependent on the size of the loan and on an interest rate at or near the allowable maximum.

Morris began to canvass the nation and plant the seed for the growth of banks organized in a similar fashion. In 1911 the Atlanta Loan & Savings Company and the Mutual Loan Company (Baltimore) were chartered, and in 1912 others were organized in Washington, D.C., and Richmond (Virginia). These first Morris Plan banks were organized under the aegis of Morris' law firm. Morris took stock in these companies, but soon sought outside help as the project overwhelmed his capabilities. The Fidelity Corporation, organized in

1912 with Morris as president, was superseded by the creation of the Industrial Finance Corporation in 1914. The Fidelity Corporation and its successor owned the Morris Plan of Industrial Bank, Morris Plan of Industrial Banking, and Morris Plan tradenames. The board of directors of the Industrial Finance Corporation read like a who's who and included Charles H. Sabin, vice president of the Guaranty Trust Company of New York; Newcomb Carlton, president of Western Union Telegraph Company; and Herbert L. Satterlee, who later became a justice of the U.S. Supreme Court. The Industrial Finance Corporation established Morris Plan banks throughout the nation, purchasing between 10 and 25 percent of each bank; trained employees in Morris methods of lending; performed audits; and influenced state regulations. By 1927, there were 106 Morris Plan banks in America.

Corporations similar to the Industrial Finance Corporation include (1) the Chicago-based Wimsett system, which was organized in 1921 and by 1927 had 123 franchises; (2) the Citizens Finance Company, organized in St. Louis during the early 1920s, with 44 outlets by 1931; (3) the Industrial Banking Corporation of America, begun in 1928 and having stock in four industrial banks by 1931; and (4) the National Bankers Industrial, started in 1915 by Beneficial, with ties to six offices by 1931. The comaker loans made by the Morris Plan and similar banks placed them in the same category as credit unions and, later, personal loan departments of commercial and savings banks.[9]

COMMERCIAL BANKS

During the mid-1920s, a few chartered banks began exploring the small loan market. A study published by the American Bankers Association reported that just three banks provided small loans in 1925. The number approximately doubled every year through 1930: eight in 1926, 16 in 1927, 22 in 1928, 65 in 1929; and 141 in 1930. Early entrants into the market limited promotion to classified advertising and some poster and display material. In the 1920s, promoting personal credit was still frowned upon. Although banks generally "let the business naturally come to us," some did seek out factory workers as potential credit customers. Some employers cooperated by providing names and addresses to banks, in the belief that financially distressed employees were better off dealing with reputable banks than with loan sharks.[10]

It was the entry of the National City Bank of New York into the small loan market in 1929 that signaled a major shift in the source of personal consumption credit. It was the first reputable (i.e., large) bank to enter the small loan business in America, and its first personal credit department made unsecured loans similar to those offered by Morris Plan banks. While the concern of social critics and government officials about the loan shark problem may have had an influence, the entry of National City Bank was not born out of altruistic ideals. First, the bank possessed capital. An aggressive search for deposit customers during the 1920s resulted in their number growing from 6,300 in 1922 to 232,000 in 1929. Total deposits grew from about $2 million to over $62 million during the same period. Second, the bank received a great deal of favorable publicity for helping out the "distressed little person." The 12 percent interest rate and tight cost and screening controls enabled the department to turn a profit within a year.[11]

One additional point deserves mention. In the first year of operation, the average borrower was 34 years old, earned $2,755 per year, and had been employed steadily for five years. Most borrowers were clerks (22 percent), salesmen (13 percent), or public employees (10 percent). The borrower profile suggests that the average National City Bank personal debtor was firmly ensconced in the nascent middle class. National City Bank apparently skimmed the cream of the small loan market and thus probably had little or no impact on the loan shark problem.[12]

Canadian Banks

The formal entry of Canadian Banks into the small loan business did not occur until the passage of the 1954 Bank Act, which allowed chartered banks to issue home mortgages for new housing construction and to make loans against personal or movable property (chattel mortgages). Merrill Denison, author of a history on the Bank of Montreal, observed:

> The granting of small personal loans, of course, was not a new field for the chartered banks, but such operations had always been hampered by the relatively greater risk involved and the heavy per unit cost of managing loans of this type. The right to take mortgage security went a long way toward overcoming one of these problems and the other was solved by discounting the loans or by implementing a service charge. In this way the banks were able to earn a return in line with their risks and costs. Loans under special programs such as the Bank of Montreal Family Finance Plan have become increasingly important and now [in 1966] account for nearly twenty five percent of total chartered-bank loans in contrast with some seven percent in 1953.[13]

NOTES

1. William Carr, *From Three Cents a Week . . . The Story of the Prudential Insurance Company of America* (Englewood Cliffs, NJ: Prentice-Hall, 1975), 1–9; Susan P. Benson, *Counter Cultures: Saleswomen, Managers, and Customers in American Department Stores, 1890–1940* (Urbana: University of Illinois Press, 1988), 21, 89–91, 148.

2. Willis Pollock, "Rounding up the Small Bond Buyer," *BMo*, 38 (February 1921): 20+. Advertisement reprinted in *BMa*, 81 (November 1910): 734.

3. T. D. MacGregor, *Bank Advertising Plans* (New York: Bankers Publishing Co., 1913), 6–7; Bank of Nova Scotia, *The Bank of Nova Scotia: 1832–1932* (Halifax: Bank of Nova Scotia, 1932), 75.

4. Henry Lanier, *A Century of Banking in New York: 1822–1922* (New York: Gilles Press, 1922), 142–50.

5. Briefly, in the story, a bawlerout falls in love with the bank teller she is supposed to bawl out. She mistakenly bawls out the bank president, who is the actual owner of the loan shark business. Both she and the teller are fired, but they find alternative employment and live happily ever after.

6. Clarence W. Wassam, *Salary Loan Business in New York* (New York: Charities Publication Committee, 1908), 74–75; Louis N. Robinson and Rolf Nugent, *Regulation of the Small Loan Business* (New York: Russell Sage Foundation, 1935), 38–42, 70–71.

7. Robinson and Nugent, *Regulation of the Small Loan Business*, 79–84.

8. Ibid., 143–44; Herman Kogan, *Lending Is Our Business: The Story of Household Finance Corporation* (Chicago: Household Finance Corporation, 1965).

9. Peter W. Herzog, *The Morris Plan of Industrial Banking* (New York: McGraw-Hill, 1928); Evans Clark, *Financing the Consumer* (New York: Harper & Brothers, 1931), 62–70.

10. Howard W. Haines, *The Small Loan Department* (New York: Bankers Publishing Co., 1931), 18, 34.

11. Harold van B. Cleveland and Thomas F. Huertas, *Citibank: 1812–1970* (Cambridge, MA: Harvard University Press, 1985), 120–21.

12. "National City's Small Loan Service to More Than 50,000 Families," *BMa*, 118 (June 1929): 969+.

13. Merrill Denison, *Canada's First Bank*, Vol. 2 (New York: Dodd, Mead, 1966), 395–96.

III

Staff

10

Welfare Work

As noted by Susan Porter Benson in her history of the department store industry, employee welfare work and formal training, both begun early in the twentieth century, were eventually blended into the personnel movement of the 1920s. Benson observes that a triad of competing forces made difficult the implementation of welfare work in department stores: (1) customers, mostly female and many upper-class, whose expectations of service had been elevated by coddling managers and staff; (2) the sales force, mostly working-class women, who formed their own culture, work rules, and indoctrination methods, and who differed substantively from customers on the basis of class; and (3) managers, mostly men. Welfare work in the department store industry, as in manufacturing industries, was critical because of both direct and indirect effects on productivity and because of the impact these programs had on an organization's public image. Around 1905, to facilitate welfare work implementation, some department stores began employing special secretaries to coordinate activities that included, but were not limited to, gymnasiums, lunchrooms, and libraries. Welfare work, despite paternalistic overtones, was viewed by retail managers, by the end of the 1920s, as a necessary component of operations. Formal training of direct workers, begun by department stores during the 1900s and firmly established by the 1920s, sought to transfer selling skills through "general education, merchandise training, and salesmanship training."[1]

This contrasts with the insurance industry, where the "drummer" nature of the sales force implied many hours on the road or in isolated agency (or branch) offices. From the start of the life insurance industry in America through the very early twentieth century, formal training was unheard-of. Some salesmen were tutored by experienced agents, and others were given booklets on overcoming customer resistance, but many were sent out cold. In 1902, Equitable offered the first formal training for newly hired life insurance agents, a summer course that lasted from 30 to 60 days. This was followed by a 1904 program offered by Travelers Insurance.[2]

Bankers, too, understood the criticalness of contact between teller and customer. Common were sentiments such as "The individual concerned [a customer-contact person] does not merely represent the bank; he is the bank" (James Clarke, second vice president, National Bank of Commerce in New York, 1920) and "A teller must remember that to the customer in his line, *he is the bank*" (Harry Baldwin, assistant secretary, Washington Mutual Savings Bank, Seattle, 1925). The key, according to bankers, was to build an esprit de corps among the staff, resulting in more satisfied and productive employees and hence in more satisfied customers: "The chief value of this spirit of goodwill [built through welfare work] in a bank organization is the fact that it gets across the counter to the customer."[3]

But in banking there were few significant conflicts of interest between managers and staff. There was much self-selection in the banking industry; those seeking entry were already of a conservative mind, and such attitudes were quickly reinforced by both informal and formal socialization forces within the bank. Men dominated the tellers' cages, upper management, and the queues; and where demand was sufficient, women were employed to staff and operate women's departments. In banking, a relatively homogeneous workforce (regarding a conservative attitude) and a relatively homogeneous customer base (regarding the desire for conservative management) existed. Welfare work in banking, unlike that in the department store industry, was not characterized by a web of competing interests, and unlike some manufacturing industries (such as steel or automotive assembly), there was no great push for direct labor unionization.

This chapter discusses spirit-building activities and programs undertaken by banks. These include employee magazines, training and communication of roles, employee clubs, and financial welfare programs.

EMPLOYEE MAGAZINES

Early in the twentieth century, some banks began publishing employee magazines. These were not unique to banking, for by 1920 at least 500 American organizations were publishing them (including the majority of the nations's largest industrial concerns). Table 10.1 presents a list of banks publishing an employee magazine prior to 1930.

The philosophy and content of bank employee magazines were not unlike those in other industries. The 1904 premiere issue of *The Review*, published by The First National Bank of Chicago, said:

> With the immense size and business of the bank, it is well nigh impossible for the clerks in one department to hear the interesting news and humorous incidents in the other departments. How many bookkeepers, for instance, have time or opportunity to meet tellers for a social chat, even for only a few minutes, and

Table 10.1
Employee Magazines

Institution	Location	Magazine Name	Year
The First National Bank of Chicago	Chicago, IL	The Review	1904[a]
National City Bank of New York	New York City	Number Eight	1905[a]
New York National Exchange Bank	New York City	Our Neighborhood	1905
Cleveland Trust Company	Cleveland, OH	The Eagle Eye	1906
Hibernia Bank & Trust Company	New Orleans, LA	The Hibernia Rabbit	1908
Guaranty Trust Company of New York	New York City	Guaranty News	1912[a]
Fidelity National Bank & Trust Co.	Kansas City, MO	Fidelity Spirit	1914[a]
Metropolitan Trust Company	New York City	Metco Meteor	1916[a]
Old Colony Trust Company	New York City	Old Colony NewsLetter	1917[a]
Chase National Bank	Boston, MA	The Chase	1918[a]
First National Bank	New York City	Live Wireless	1918[a]
National Bank of Commerce in New York	Northboro, IA	Commerce Comment	1920
Northern Trust Company	New York City	TNT	1920
Bank of Italy	Chicago, IL	Bankitaly Life	1920
Bank of Buffalo	San Francisco, CA	The Teller	1920
First National Bank of Tulsa	Buffalo, NY	After Three O'Clock	1920
Fourth National Bank	Tulsa, OK	The Big Fourth	1920
Chemical National Bank	Wichita, KS	Chemical Bulletin	1920
Northwestern National Bank of Minnesota	New York City	The Big Drum	1920
	Minneapolis, MN		

Table 10.1 Continued

Institution	Location	Magazine Name	Year
Continental & Commercial National Bank of Chicago	Chicago, IL	The Four Cs	1920
The Equitable Trust Company of New York	New York City	The Equitable Envoy	1921[a]
American Bank of Commerce & Trust Co.	Little Rock, AR	American	1921[a]
American National Bank	Oklahoma City, OK	American Eagle	1922
Bank of California	San Francisco, CA	Californian	1922
Bank of Pittsburgh	Pittsburgh, PA	Bankofpitt Monthly	1922
Bankers Trust Company	New York City	Pyramid	1922
Central National Bank of Tulsa	Tulsa, OK	In the Eye	1922
Exchange National Bank of Tulsa	Tulsa, OK	Exchange Spark	1922
Dollar Savings & Trust Company	Youngstown, OH	Dollars and Sense	1922
First National Bank	Portland, OR	Pep	1922
First National Bank	Bartlesville, OK	Better Service	1922
First National Bank	Minneapolis, MN	Periscope	1922
Bowery Savings Bank	New York City	The Chest	1925[a]

[a]First year of publication.

Source: Bank archival material; "Employees' Magazines as Distinguished from House-Organs," *PI*, 110 (19 February 1920): 42; "Another Installment List of Employees' Magazines," *PI*, 111 (1 April 1920): 99; "Employees' Magazines Listed Passes Five Hundred Mark," *PI*, 111 (8 April 1920): 60.

vice versa? Through the medium of our little monthly newspaper, however, all of us will be enabled to spend a half hour occasionally in laughing with our fellow clerks in their jovial moods, and sympathizing with them in their sorrows, and thus promote, and cement, stronger than ever, the bond of fraternal feeling of good fellowship.[4]

Employee magazines contained articles and notes on current affairs, economic conditions, government regulation, bank operations, technology, training programs, social events, bank club activities, retirements, promotions, marriages, births, and deaths. Although employee magazines invariably were sanctioned by management, not all were published by employees. Magazines published by employees differed from those published by management. First, employee-published magazines were less formal and stiff than management organs. Mundane technology tips (such as saying "Good-bye" or "Thank you" when concluding a telephone conversation), and office gossip ("A very sweet voice has been calling lately at one minute past five and asking for Charles Stiefel") were more likely to be found in magazines published by employees.[5]

Second, management-published magazines occasionally blurred the distinction between house organ and employee magazine. For example, when the First National Bank (Northboro, Iowa) began its employees magazine in 1918, there was no local newspaper. Managers published local interest articles, accepted paid advertising from local merchants, and distributed the magazine outside the bank. More important, management-published employee magazines were often viewed by employees as mechanisms for whipping them into shape. For example, *Inside Service*, published monthly by the Mississippi Valley Trust Company (St. Louis), disseminated the ideas of the bank's president. Such magazines were criticized by some bankers who felt that an employee magazine "should be a magazine by employees, for employees." [6]

Canadian banks also published employee magazines: *The Nova Scotian* (Bank of Nova Scotia, begun in 1907); *The Royal Bank Magazine* (begun in 1920); *Caduceus* (Canadian Bank of Commerce, begun in 1920); *Home Bank Monthly* (Home Bank of Canada, published by 1920); *Bank Notes* (Dominion Bank, begun in 1921); and *Manitoba Union Bank Monthly* (Union Bank of Canada, published by 1922). These publications differed from those published by American banks mainly because of geographic dispersion. For example, *The Royal Bank Magazine* was "a medium whereby the officers of the various branches can be brought into closer personal touch with each other, and with the Executive." The bank at that time had 6,000 employees who were spread over more than 700 domestic and foreign branches.[7]

FORMALIZATION OF TRAINING AND ROLE COMMUNICATION

Formalization refers to the presence of written rules, procedures, and communications. It has long been observed that larger organizations are more formalized in order to counter compartmentalization, hierarchical layers, and, if applicable, geographic dispersion. Because of their size and geographic spread, the large Canadian banks of the late nineteenth century were more formalized than American banks. The Merchants' Bank of Halifax—now Royal Bank—in 1885 assembled *Rules and Regulations,* documenting branch operating procedures. In addition to many technical items, the manual covered business hours, employee attendance rules, legal holidays, and expected employee behavior. An example of the latter is that male employees were not allowed to marry without the consent of the bank until they were earning $1,000 per year. Dismissal was automatic for violators. Marriage on a lesser salary created undue absence from the bank during periods of maximum training, and, because of the economic hardship associated with child rearing, ensured a lifestyle not befitting the employee's social position. This rule was still in effect in the bank's updated 1901 manual. The Bank of Nova Scotia published several versions of its *Rules and Regulations* before the turn of the century. The 1917 manual stated that male employees were to shave daily, dress neatly, and behave politely when in contact with the public. "Any officer who is indifferent to these considerations, or who fails to give prompt, courteous, and careful attention to the public must be relegated to some position where his want of regard will not offend." Managers discouraged smoking by employees under twenty-one years of age because it was thought to stunt growth. Tobacco consumption was forbidden during business hours because it was "so unbusinesslike that even habitual smokers regard such a practice with disfavor." The branch manager manuals of the large Canadian banks were comprehensive. The Bank of Nova Scotia's 1917 *Rules and Regulations* was 350 pages long, and its 1927 edition was over 500 pages.[8]

Consistent with relationships between size and formalization, the Crown Bank of Canada's (Toronto) *Rules and Regulations* (1908) was much smaller than those of its larger competitors. Women were expected to live with their parents, and if that was infeasible, they were to clear their place of residence with the bank. Expected attire for women was a dark or neutral color with plain cuffs and collars. Perfumes and scented soaps were not tolerated. Female employees were not allowed to work after 6 P.M. on weekdays or 3 P.M. on Saturdays unless accompanied by the women's department manager. Female employees had to resign when they married.[9]

American banks, because of their size, published less onerous rules and regulations. The Cleveland Trust Company's 1923 *Manual of General Directions* for Employees contained material on the bank's history, trial employment terms, handling personal problems, courtesy to the public, the bank's subsidized cafeteria, and welfare services (including health, insurance and pension plans). It was not a branch manager's operating manual of the kind distributed by the larger Canadian banks. The Cleveland Trust Company also closely monitored branch operations. In 1928, when the bank had 58 branches, a representative from the department of branches visited each bank twice a year to evaluate physical properties. Whereas the bank monitored financial operations through audits, the property inspections rated branches on maintenance, janitorial standards, neatness, and cleanliness. The bank handed out small cash awards to the best janitors.[10]

When an American bank was able to operate distant branches, an extensive branch manager manual similar to Canadian ones was created. A. P. Giannini, president of the Bank of Italy, visited western Canada in 1910 to view firsthand how the Canadian banks managed remote, distant branches. Acquisition and natural growth added a large number of branches to the bank's California network between 1920 and 1925, necessitating a second foray into western Canada by Giannini during the late 1920s. An assistant secretary and auditor who collected information on accounting procedures and formats learned to appreciate branch manager manuals. One was created for the Bank of Italy, and during the 1930s it became known as the *Standard Practice Manual*. Giannini revised it at least once, and by the 1950s it was a foot thick.[11]

American banks adopted formal, in-house training programs during the 1910s. In 1917 the National City Bank of New York institutionalized a banking apprenticeship class. Initially, the bank selected three high school students who were hired as apprentices (e.g., pages, file clerks, messengers) and were trained for from two to four years. Aside from normal work duties, they attended lectures twice a week on topics that included courtesy, geography, telephone usage, bank rules, and pneumatic tube operation. Exams were given every month. The bank published training manuals for pages, messengers, and file clerks. During the mid-1910s the bank began a college training class for university graduates, who typically entered the bank in the foreign service department. The classes were operated by the City Bank Club. The National City Bank of New York also operated a interview bureau that formally tracked employee performance, health, character, continuing education, confidence, cooperativeness, courtesy, accuracy, aptitude, enthusiasm, and punctuality. It was also a mechanism for employees to informally discuss methods of improving operations with the managers. Feedback was provided to employees, and this was thought to foster a more competent workforce.[12]

Many other banks formalized their training procedures. The Harris Trust & Savings Bank (Chicago) bond sales training program lasted up to two years. In 1928, the two-month training course of the Guardian National Bank (Chicago) taught bond sellers, among other things, "the nomenclenture of securities, to avoid a patronizing attitude, to approach prospects with boldness tempered by courtesy, to picture securities so that they gradually evolve into moving machinery, to obtain an appointment for a future call," and "to record facts about each prospect." Interpreting securities as "moving machinery" is difficult, but Guardian may have wanted the sales force to conceive of financial instruments as tangibles that could be handled physically. By 1919, the Northern Trust Company (Chicago) offered courses for pages and junior clerks in english, arithmetic, spelling, bookkeeping, and athletics. One evening a month was "group meeting night," when senior officers lectured employees on bank operations and put assistant cashiers and tellers through "real-life" service simulations.[13]

Of course, not all programs were formalized, and not all bankers viewed the workforce affectionately. President Frank A. Drury of the Merchants National Bank (Worcester, Massachusetts) insisted that only officers be allowed to use the bank's front door. Employees were required to crank a telephone in a quiet, dignified manner, and in "complete silence." Drury threatened to fire employees who spat on walls, floors, or radiators. Every morning rules were read aloud to employees, and later in the day each employee signed a sheet containing the rules.[14]

The spread of internal rules was fostered by a trade press containing an incredible amount of material on employee training, especially after 1910. For example, a chapter W. R. Morehouse's *Bank Deposit Building* (1918) covered employees. He provided 35 rules that employees should know before serving the public. Most of the rules, which were probably enforced by the Guaranty Trust & Savings Bank (Los Angeles), concerned operations (e.g., tellers' cages, transactions) directly addressing faster, more accurate service provided by more knowledgeable employees. Other rules banned tobacco consumption during operating hours, lending or borrowing by or from employees on the premises, and frequenting saloons or bucket shops. Morehouse said women should be given 60 minutes for lunch (versus 45 minutes for men).[15]

DINING FACILITIES

As a part of attracting and retaining a quality workforce, banks operated on-site dining facilities or provided lunch stipends. This was especially the practice among New York City banks. The Bowery Savings Bank offered a 35 cent lunch stipend for all employees as early as 1880. The National Bank of Commerce in New York began providing lunches in 1886 (by the early 1920s the bank was also providing free on-site medical service from a physician and a nurse, a recreation room, a pension and disability plan, partial reimbursement of banking courses completed outside the bank, and thrift and employee clubs). The bank also promoted its welfare work with employees to persuade customers that it was operating in their best interest. A lunch club was operated by the National City Bank for some time, but operations were suspended in 1919. (Whether it was because employees preferred to eat at establishments of their own choice, as described in 1930, or a cost-cutting measure is debatable.) Due to space constraints, the Bank of Manhattan Trust Company replaced on-site lunches with an allowance after moving to a new facility during the 1920s. The Chase National Bank continued to provide lunch at various premises during the 1920s, despite the costs associated with absorbing the Equitable Trust Company of New York and the Park National Bank. At the bank's main office, three floors were devoted to dining facilities where the 3,000 employees were fed in shifts of 1,500. During the 1920s, the luncheon club of the Chemical Bank & Trust Company halted operations after the bank moved to a new building, because of space and cost constraints. The dining club and cooperative store of the Guaranty Trust Company of New York had 49 full-time employees and served approximately 35,000 lunches per month in 1918. Waiters had three minutes to set a table and serve lunch, water, and dessert. Employees paid for the meals, but the luncheon club and cooperative were operated on nonprofit bases. The cooperative sold groceries, meats, candy, and tobacco at wholesale prices. *The Bankers' Magazine* said, "The spirit of this [Guaranty's] enlightened idea of co-operating with the employee can be exhibited in a greater or lesser degree in any bank."[16]

Banks outside New York City offered dining facilities. The First National Bank of Chicago provided lunches as early as 1873, and by 1883 had installed its own kitchen facilities. In 1912 the cafeteria's capacity was 200. Officers and department heads ate in a private room. Christmas and Thanksgiving were celebrated with special meals. During the mid-1910s, the Fidelity National Bank & Trust Company (Kansas City) began operating a nonprofit cafeteria. Salaries and utilities were covered by the bank, making food there about half of restaurant prices. Egalitarianism was promoted by barring private rooms or tables for officers. The National Bank of Commerce of Detroit devoted a portion of the fourth floor of a new 1918 structure to employee needs. Bank president Richard P. Joy said:

> On the basis that nothing is too good for our own, the cuisine and service of the dining rooms and the appointments of recreation smoking rooms are the best we can obtain for our employees. Good food and congenial associations work wonders in keeping people fit. With this arrangement in operation, members of the bank staff do not have to step outside in inclement weather; they are able to return to work promptly, and the spirit of their service is of that grateful kind which automatically breeds courtesy to the customer.[17]

COUNTRY PROPERTIES

During the 1910–1930 period, some organizations purchased summer estates for their employee's benefit. In the department store industry, San Francisco's Emporium in 1916 purchased a 32-acre resort for employees, but this was a rare event in that industry. During the late 1910s, the Hibernia Bank & Trust Company (New Orleans) purchased a summer house on the Gulf Coast with direct access to swimming and tennis and indirect access to golf. "A large number of the Hibernia 'family' spend their vacations at Resthaven, and the home is usually filled to its capacity from the opening of its season in the spring until its close in the fall." Sometime during the early 1920s the Guaranty Trust Company of New York purchased a country residence on 60 acres in the Berkshires, a two-hour train ride from New York City. It accommodated 20 and was "an ideal haven for a period of care-free rest from the routine of business, or convalescence from illness." N. H. Latimer, president of the Dexter Horton National Bank, donated his summer home, Norvall Hall, to the bank during the 1920s. Twelve miles from downtown Seattle on Puget Sound, it was refurnished and accommodated 75 overnight guests. Employees paid 25 cents a day to visit, 35 cents for an overnight stay, and 40, 50, and 60 cents for breakfast, lunch, and dinner, respectively. Two full-time employees maintained the house and cooked meals. In late 1919 or early 1920, Benjamin Gratz, a director of the First National Bank (St. Louis), gave his summer estate to the bank's employees. On 120 acres astride the Meremee River in the foothills of the Ozarks, it gave employees a place to swim, canoe, hike, and play tennis. The Metropolitan Trust Company (New York) also operated a summer property for employees.[18]

EMPLOYEE CLUBS

Although employee clubs were staff-organized, their functions and activities were subject to senior management influence. The clubs operated country homes, published employee magazines, and organized social activities and training programs. The sections that follow describe the clubs of two large American banks: the National City Bank of New York and Chase National Bank. Material is also presented on Canadian bank clubs.

City Bank Club

One of the earliest and best-regarded employee clubs was the City Bank Club, operated by the National City Bank of New York. It began in 1904 after employees approached senior management with the idea of forming a fraternal association. James Stillman, president of the bank, approved wholeheartedly. He donated $10,000 to the club, "to be used in any way you consider most advisable." The constitution of the club stated that its purpose was "The advancement of its members along educational lines, the mutual benefit to be derived from the social intercourse of the clerks with one another, and the promotion of a spirit of cordiality and fraternity among men who are associated in business each day." Interest earned from Stillman's donation financed club activities. Initially, meetings were held once a month and guests such as Joseph French, dean of the New York City University School of Commerce, and George Marlor, assistant U.S. treasurer, spoke on banking matters. The club financed publication of *Number Eight*, the employee magazine (first published in 1905). In 1908 Stillman donated an additional $10,000 to the club as a Christmas gift. In 1912 he gave $100,000 to the club to commemorate the centennial of the bank. Stillman convinced the board of directors to donate a like amount. This backing allowed the club to increase its services, especially educational ones. In 1912 classes were offered in english, composition, mathematics, penmanship, French, German, and Spanish. In the following year, classes were begun in stenography, foreign exchange, and economics, and in 1914 in commercial law. University professors taught some classes (e.g., commercial law was taught by a Yale professor). The club operated a library containing fiction, biographies, and banking texts.

The club was not all work and no play, however; Mr. Vanderlip, president of the bank between 1909 and 1913, lent his "magnificent" estate to the club for a one-day June outing from 1908 until at least 1914 for athletic contests, dancing, Shakespearean comedies, and vaudeville performances. In 1911, the club rented a summer home on Long Island Sound. But its distance from the bank led to disappointing usage. In 1913, the club rented a summer home nearer the bank, at Belle Harbor, Long Island. During the summer of 1915, dances, dinner parties, and clambakes were held. The house had a player piano and offered reasonably priced meals. A separate summer house at Sea Gate, New Jersey, was obtained for female employees in 1915. The club sponsored athletic activities. In 1929, Y.M.C.A. classes for females were available in dancing, basketball, and swimming. The club sponsored an annual ski outing and St. Patrick's dinner dance. Essay contests were held, and the best entries appeared in *Number Eight*. During the 1920s, the club operated a boardinghouse on Monatgue Street, Brooklyn, for single, young, male employees; the rate was $55 per month. It operated a buy-direct store prior to Christmas that provided discounts to employees on silk hosiery, jewelry, silverware, cameras, cigars, cigarettes, men's shirts and socks, ties, dolls, games, and toys.[19]

Chase Bank Club

The Chase Bank Club was formed in 1909 by 70 of the bank's 200 employees. At first, the club concentrated on athletics. Unlike the bankers hockey leagues organized in Canada, which took on a following beyond that of employees and evolved into a promotional tool, the appeal of New York City intramural bank athletics never extended beyond bank employees. The Chase Bank Club entered the Bank Clerks' Bowling League in 1909, and leagues for basketball, baseball, tennis, and golf by 1919. The employment of women resulted in the organization of women's basketball and swimming during the 1920s. In 1923, at the American Institute of Banking convention in Cleveland, Chase played baseball against the Merchants Trust Company of Chicago. In 1925 a long-distance telegraph bowling match was played between Chase and the National Bank of Tucson (Arizona).

The club's focus expanded in 1914 to include educational activities. In that year, a ten-dollar first prize and a five-dollar second prize were offered to club members submitting the best bank essays. During the late 1910s, a club library was formed, and courses were offered in elementary banking, economics, and advanced business correspondence. Employees were required to forward written job descriptions that were added to departmental manuals; prizes were awarded to the best. In 1925 the prestigious Cannon Prize Examination was first held. By the age of 21, Henry W. Cannon operated his own bank, the Lumberman's National (Stillwater, Minnesota), and in 1884, at age 34, he served for two years as comptroller of the currency. He was president of Chase between 1886 and 1904, chairman until 1911, and a director until his death in 1934. The $8,000 that Cannon donated financed two prizes of $100 for the highest-scoring male and female. Cannon donated another $5,000 in 1926, but by the 1950s the fund no longer provided adequate prize money to attract the most qualified. Chase added to the pot. The Cannon Prize Examination was continued through the 1960s with annual awards amounting to $5,000, and was halted in 1978.

Social activities were an important component of the Chase Bank Club. During the late 1910s, dances were held in the main corridor of one of the bank's largest branches. In 1920 several rooms were donated to the club to house dances, movies, and the bank's annual dinner. Music at the dances was provided by the Chase Bank Club orchestra. The 1930 merger of the Equitable Trust Company of New York with Chase so swelled club membership that the club rooms became too small.[20]

Canadian Bank Staff Associations

Canadian banks operated staff associations similar in intent to American bank clubs, but were organized consistent with geographic dispersion. During the 1920s, branches individually organized social clubs. Other clubs (or staff associations) spanned multiple branches of a single bank. In 1920 the Staff Association was formed at Vancouver by employees of the Canadian Bank of Commerce, and the first meeting was attended by staff from across British Columbia. Other clubs were open across banks. The Association of Fort William Bankers, Ontario, was organized in 1922 to promote education, recreation, and social activities. Association officers were from the Royal Bank of Canada, the Dominion Bank, the Canadian Bank of Commerce, and the Bank of Nova Scotia. A similar association existed in Toronto (the Toronto Bankers' Educational Association).[21]

An athletic activity sponsored by Canadian banks was ice hockey. In 1891 representatives of the Bank of Montreal, the Imperial Bank, the Bank of British North America, and the Dominion Bank organized the Bank Hockey League of Toronto. The 1891 champion was the Dominion Bank, and the Bank Managers Challenge Cup was awarded in the Canadian Bank of Commerce's boardroom by B. Edmond Walker, the bank's general manager. To encourage smaller banks lacking the workforce to field competitive teams, an intermediate league was formed in 1894. The premiere Toronto bank hockey league played continually until 1904; between 1905 and 1920, several seasons passed with no league play, most notably during World War I. By the start of the twentieth century, there were leagues in Winnipeg, Montreal, Halifax, and Vancouver. In 1921 in the Toronto league, the Dominion Bank defeated the Canadian Bank of Commerce in a best-of-seven championship series. The Dominion Bank's employee magazine described the play as "militant," and said that "the teams followed Queensbury rules pretty closely." No doubt a few fights broke out and at one point in the first game, only five players were on the ice. About 1,500 fans attended the first game of the series. The Toronto Bank team then played a two-game, total-point series against the Royal Bank team, which had won the senior Montreal league championship for the newly offered Bogert Cup. The total points were even after two games, and a tiebreaker was played in Toronto before a crowd of 5,000.

The leagues symbolized much more than corporate pride: they evolved into a sophisticated promotional tool. The *Toronto Star* and the *Montreal Star*, as well as other local dailies, reported on league play as early as the 1920s. On

March 10, 1925, the *Winnipeg Free Press* nostalgically published a photograph of the winning team of the 1899–1900 Winnipeg league. Some players went on to professional hockey careers. Lionell P. Conacher—not to be confused with his all-star, Hall of Fame brother, Charlie "Chuck" Conacher—was a member of the Dominion Bank's 1921 championship team. He played defense for the New York Americans and the Montreal Maroons between 1925 and 1937. Punch Imlach played on the Dominion Bank 1937–1938 Toronto championship team. Imlach later coached the Toronto Maple Leafs to four Stanley Cup victories, including three consecutive victories during the 1961–1964 seasons. Other players became senior executives. The Bogert Cup was named after C. A. Bogert, a player on the original 1891 Dominion Bank team who eventually became the bank's president. And E. W. Hamber, who played during the early 1900s, was a director of the Dominion Bank during the 1920s. Standard histories of ice hockey make no mention of bank hockey leagues.[22]

Canadian banks, like their American counterparts, ran essay contests. The Canadian Bank of Commerce, for instance, in a 1930 issue of *Caduceus* announced first and second prize awards of $25 and $15, respectively, for the best essays on "the determining factors in the choice of a bank by the prospective depositor" and "should Canada erect a retaliatory tariff against the United States?" Ten- and five-dollar prizes also were offered for the best personal anecdote related to banking and the best finish to a limerick.[23]

At the beginning of the twentieth century, the Canadian Bank of Commerce maintained a library at its head office that contained material on finance, economics, and Canadian history. The bank paid all shipping costs for books sent to employees at remote locations. Shortly thereafter, it provided its remotest branches with their own libraries. By 1909, over 80 branches were stocked, and by 1922 almost 250 branches had libraries. Also in 1909 the bank provided Toronto employees with leisure rooms at one of its offices. A piano, billiards tables, and other gaming amenities were available.[24]

ATHLETICS

The devotion to athletics apparent within the American and Canadian employee clubs was not isolated from the broader popularization of physical exercise. The emergence of athletic and gymnastic clubs and societies during the latter half of the nineteenth century was an outgrowth of physical well-being elevated to a moral duty. Among the many clubs organized—including the New Jersey Athletic Club, the Caledonian Club, and the St. Timothy's Working Men's Club—was the Bank Clerks' Athletic Association of Philadelphia (1887). Open to employees of Philadelphia banks, insurance, and railroad companies and "any man of good moral standing," the association by 1891 rented tennis, baseball, cricket, football, lacrosse, and track and field facilities. To commemorate an 1891 track meet in Philadelphia against 23 other clubs, the association published an 80-page souvenir program that contained over 100 advertisements from more than 90 institutions. The majority of advertisers were Philadelphia bank and trust companies, but suppliers of bicycles, guns, sewing machines, grocery products, organs, tobacco, beer, and general merchandise (e.g., Wanamaker) also advertised.[25]

Banks without formal employee clubs encouraged participation in physical activity. In 1904 The First National Bank of Chicago formed a baseball team that played in Chicago's Commercial League. To spur consumption of its products, A. G. Spaulding & Brothers provided a cup valued at $150. The umpires in the league were paid, and the bank covered the team's expenses. Bank teams participated in bowling leagues, and inhouse baseball games were played on an occasional basis: in 1905 a game was played at the American League Park between the Currency Pen and the Tellers. The bank never formed an employee club, but did formally adopt a physical activity orientation through the 1912 organization of an athletic department. The department operated a gymnasium and handball court and was open six days a week. Supervised calisthenics and track were offered four times a week.[26]

Not to be overlooked is that a connection between banks and athletics did not exist in America and Canada exclusively. The National Provincial Bank, the Union Bank of London, and the London Joint-Stock Bank formed the Three Banks Club during the 1890s. In 1898, the club purchased 26 acres of land and a pavilion at Lower Sydenham (near London). Employees played tennis, cricket, field hockey, and rugby. After the wave of mergers in English banking that followed World War I, National Provincial came into sole ownership of the facilities. Rowing and swimming facilities were eventually made available, and by 1933 when the club had over 2,000 members.[27]

FINANCIAL WELFARE PROGRAMS

Financial welfare programs include pension plans and special savings plans. They are the focus of this section.

Pension Plans

In his definitive *Industrial Pension Systems in the United States and Canada* (1932), Murray Latimer said that three factors propelled the growth of private pension plans during the nineteenth century. First, the railroad industry in particular wanted to eliminate the elderly from the workforce for both safety and cost purposes. Second, a pension cultivated continuous service and discouraged strikes. Third, a pension enhanced the reputation of the firm and allowed it to hire more capable employees.[28]

According to Latimer, formal private pension plans first arose during the 1860s in the British railroad industry, but many firms on both sides of the Atlantic had long informally cared for the superannuated and disabled. In North America, the first company to implement a pension was the Grand Trunk Railway of Canada, by provision of an act of the Canadian Parliament (1874). The plan was contributory (i.e., the employer contributed a portion of profits to the plan), and by 1910, 74.3 percent of all Canadian railway workers were covered. The next two plans were established by American railroads: the American Express Company in 1875 and the Baltimore and Ohio Railroad Company in 1880.

In adopting pensions, railroads were followed by nonrail public utilities, bank and insurance firms, manufacturers, and retailers. The first public utility to establish a pension plan was the Consolidated Gas Company of New York in 1892; the first bank was the Bank of Nova Scotia in 1886; and the first manufacturer was Alfred Dolge & Son (Dolgeville, New York), a maker of felt products, in 1882. The only retailer to offer a pension plan before 1900 was Wanamaker, the Philadelphia-based department store. Of only 12 pension plans established prior to 1900, five were instituted by banks. Some manufacturers adopted pension plans before banks did, but the overall adoption by manufactures lagged that of banks well into the twentieth century. By 1930, most major banks had pension plans, but most major manufacturers (including General Motors and Ford) and most retailers did not. The late adoption of pension plans in the department store industry was due primarily to the minimal education and formal training required of salespeople, which was reflected by high employee turnover rates in the industry. In contrast, banks required highly skilled individuals, and pension plans produced a more loyal workforce.

Table 10.2 presents a list of banks and the year in which each began a pension plan. The Bank of Nova Scotia was the first bank in North America to operate a pension plan. Five of the earliest eight banks to adopt pension plans were Canadian, in part explainable by the size of these banks. The First National Bank of Chicago was the first American bank to adopt a pension plan (in 1899). James B. Forgan—a senior officer made president in 1900—strongly influenced the adoption decision. Forgan's receptivity stemmed from previous employment with the Bank of Nova Scotia, which had adopted a pension plan in 1886. As the twentieth century progressed, the more prominent and larger American banks offered pension plans: National City Bank of New York in 1912; Shawmut National Bank (Boston) in 1912; National Bank of Commerce in New York in 1913; and the Northern Trust Company (Chicago) in 1913.

Table 10.2 also shows which banks contributed profits or payroll costs to their pension plan. Of all the industries studied by Latimer, the banking industry had the largest proportion of contributory plans. Pension plans were axiomatic in the largest American and Canadian banks by 1930, much as nonfinancial welfare work was in the department store industry by the same year.

The Equitable Trust Company of New York's pension plan, begun in 1925, provides a good example of the purposes and conditions of a typical bank pension plan. Prior to its implementation, the bank had no formal method of caring for the superannuated or the disabled, but it had for some time informally cared for employee financial needs on an individual basis. The plan that was settled on had the following features: (1) retirement was optional at age 60, with continued employment at the discretion of the employee; (2) retirement was mandatory at age 70 except by a special request of the board; (3) employees paid an average of 5.5 percent of their salary into the plan; (4) the company paid 4

Table 10.2
Pension Plans

Institution	Location	Corporate Contribution	Year Begun
Bank of Nova Scotia	Toronto, Ontario	yes	1886
Dominion Bank	Toronto, Ontario	yes	1887
Canadian Bank of Commerce	Toronto, Ontario	yes	1894
The First National Bank of Chicago	Chicago, IL	yes	1899
National Bank of Commerce	St. Louis, MO	no	1900
Royal Bank of Canada	Montreal, Quebec	yes	1904
Bank of Toronto	Toronto, Ontario	no	1904
Western Savings Fund Society	Philadelphia, PA	no	1904
Union Savings Bank & Trust Co.	Cincinnati, OH	yes	1911
Speyer & Company	New York City	no	1911
First National Bank of the City of New York	New York City	yes	1911
Illinois Merchants Trust Company	Chicago, IL	yes	1911
National City Bank of New York	New York City	no	1912
First National Bank	Minneapolis, MN	yes	1912
Farmers & Mechanics Savings Bank of Minneapolis	Minneapolis, MN	yes	1912
Shawmut National Bank	Boston, MA	no	1912
Union Trust Company	Chicago, IL	no	1912
National Bank of Commerce in New York	New York City	no	1913
First National Bank of Detroit	Detroit, MI	no	1913
Guardian Savings & Trust of Cleveland	Cleveland, OH	yes	1913
Northern Trust Company	Chicago, IL	yes	1913
Bankers Trust Company	New York City	yes	1913
Security Trust Company	Wilmington, DE	no	1913
Chicago Trust Company	Chicago, IL	no	1913
Rhode Island Hospital Trust Co.	Providence, RI	no	1914
Manhattan Banking Company	New York City	no	1914
Columbia Trust Company	New York City	no	1915
Commercial Trust Company of New Jersey	Jersey City, NJ	no	1916
Washington Loan & Trust Company	Washington, D.C.	no	1916
Fidelity-Philadelphia Trust Company	Philadelphia, PA	no	1916
Security Trust & Savings Bank	Los Angeles, CA	yes	1916
Central Savings Bank in the City of New York	New York City	no	1916
Livestock National Bank	Omaha, NE	yes	1917
Cleveland Trust Co.	Cleveland, OH	no	1917
Fidelity National Bank & Trust Co.	Kansas City, MO	no	1917

Table 10.2 Continued

Continental & Commercial National Bank of Chicago	Chicago, IL	yes	1918
Central Trust Company of Illinois	Chicago, IL	yes	1918
Boston Safe Deposit & Trust Co.	Boston, MA	no	1918
National Newark & Essex Banking Company	Newark, NJ	no	1919
Bank of Italy	San Francisco, CA	no	1919
Midland National Bank of Minn.	Minneapolis, MN	yes	1920
First National Trust & Savings Bank	Los Angeles, CA	yes	1920
American Express Company	New York City	no	1921
Fidelity & Deposit Company of Maryland	Baltimore, MD	no	1921
Marine Trust Company	Buffalo, NY	no	1923
Equitable Trust Company of New York	New York City	yes	1925
Commerce Trust Company	Kansas City, MO	no	1925
Granite Trust Company	Quincy, MA	no	1925
Farmers & Mechanics Savings Bank of Minneapolis	Minneapolis,MN	yes	1925
Market Street Title & Trust Co.	Philadelphia, PA	yes	1927
Union Trust Company of Detroit	Detroit, MI	yes	1928
Union Joint Stock Land Bank of Detroit	Detroit,	yes	1928
Union State Bank of Fordson	Fordson, MI	yes	1928
Bowery Savings Bank	New York City	yes	1930
Mercantile Commerce Bank & Trust Company	St. Louis, MO	yes	1930
Suffolk Savings Bank for Seamen and Others	Boston, MA	yes	1930

Sources: Murray W. Latimer, *Industrial Pension Systems in the United States and Canada*, 2 vols. (New York: Industrial Relations Counselors, 1932), 1022–25, 1057–60, 1090, 1105–07; Manhattan Banking Company, resolution adopted its board of directors (15 January 1914) (CB archives).

percent of the employee's salary into the plan; and (5) the annual pension payment equaled 1.5 percent of the average salary over the previous ten years of service, multiplied by the number of years of service. There were a number of others details covering disability, discontinuance of service prior to retirement, and death. By the end of 1925, 95 percent of Equitable employees had enrolled in the pension plan.[29]

Employee Savings Plans

Employee savings plans were less frequent than pensions. Latimer identified five savings plans within the banking industry: Harris Trust Company & Savings

Bank (Chicago) in 1916; Straus & Co. (New York) in 1917; Empire Trust Company (New York) in 1920; American Trust Company (Boston) in 1921; and National Bank of the Republic (Chicago) in 1924.

Participation in Harris Trust & Savings Bank's "profit sharing plan," begun in 1916, was mandatory for employees with three or more years of service. They paid between two and five percent of their salary, and the bank contributed 150 percent of the amount. When retiring, employees selected a lump-sum payment, an annuity, or reinvestment.

An employee savings plan was begun in 1916 by the Guardian Trust & Savings Bank of Toledo (Ohio). Employees voluntarily contributed a maximum of five percent of their salary to the plan, the bank contributing a like amount. After ten years, or five years for a women if she married (they were expected to end their employment in such a case), employees could withdraw their funds, including the bank's contribution and earned interest. It was thought that this plan would foster more continuous service.[30]

Savings and Loan Associations

By 1919, in addition to a pension, the Northern Trust Company (Chicago) had operated an employee savings and loan association for several years. The association provided loans and a $500 death benefit to members. At the end of the year, profits were distributed to the members (i.e., employee shareholders). The eight– to twelve– percent return attracted a vast majority of the firm's 352 employees as shareholders. The purpose of the association, from management's perspective, was not altogether altruistic. Other Chicago employers began to offer savings and loan associations to their employees, and some entrusted plan management to the Northern Trust Company. This suggests that some banks may have adopted savings and loan associations and pension plans as promotional tools (i.e., illustrative working models) to create trust department business.

Another savings and loan association was the Equitable Trust Company (of New York) Employees' Association, which began operating during the early 1920s. It combined aspects of a financial association and a club. Employees were allowed to purchase up to 25 shares at a dollar each. Income was earned by providing credit to employees, and profits were disbursed to shareholders. The association operated a discount store and publicized its stock in the bank's employee magazine and on cards posted throughout the bank. Clothing, tires, hardware, printing services, eyeglasses, furniture, and electrical goods were available.[31]

Other Financial Plans

By the time that banks such as the Guaranty Trust & Savings Bank (Los Angeles) instituted profit-sharing plans during the 1910s and 1920s, the precedent had long been established in American business. In 1884, C. A. Pillsbury & Company, the Minneapolis flour milling concern, began sharing profits; in 1889, $40,000 was distributed. Wanamaker, the retailer, distributed $213,785.36 in profit shares in 1889 and 1890. The practice was supported by the bank trade press: "The idea is becoming deeply grounded in the minds of both classes all over the country, and experiments of the above-mentioned nature, adapted to the different kinds of business, are undergoing trial."[32]

A second financial plan, more long-term in nature, was a merit-based promotion policy. An early instance in banking occurred during the 1890s, when *The Bankers' Magazine* recognized the efforts of The First National Bank of Chicago. The bank was "perhaps the first to establish a system of promotion among its employees, whereby the official occupying the lowest place may hope for possible advancement to the highest." Bank president Lyman Gage, who later served as President McKinley's secretary of the Treasury, said:

> But the opportunity is there for all. It is a free, fair competition, is purely a test, not only of the youngest boy's ability, but also of every man in the employ of the firm. I believe our bank was the first to inaugurate the idea among financial institutions, but there are others, I think, who have adopted it in the later years. I can say that we have found it to produce the most satisfactory results."

A third financial incentive was based on exactness of work. The First National Bank of Chicago was also an innovator in this field. It instituted a "daily marking" system—a method of recording who made errors and who found them—to formally track the performance of the bank's clerks. The program was begun in 1889, and in that year $600 was awarded.[33]

INSIDE ADVERTISING

"Inside advertising" refers to promoting activities or services internally throughout an institution. Financial welfare plans, club activities, and educational opportunities required inside advertising. For example, bank libraries, created during the 1910s by large banks as central repositories for bond and stock prices, economic data and trends, training and departmental manuals, and reference works on banking, finance, and international trade, quickly adopted the marketing analogy. Bank librarians discussed their special advertising problems with the bank advertising department (if one existed), and aggressively promoted their services to bank employees. Bank librarians engaging in internal promotion included those at the Central Trust Company of Illinois (Chicago), the Bank of Italy (San Francisco), the Union Trust Company (Cleveland), and the First Wisconsin National Bank (Milwaukee). The most common methods were publishing articles in employee magazines, distributing monthly or occasional bulletins, and posting notices on employee bulletin boards. A more involved promotion was undertaken by Ruth Nichols, a Federal Reserve Bank librarian, at the 1924 American Bankers Association Chicago meeting. One exhibit was a working model of a library that included new furniture (later installed in a Chicago public library), desks, tables, and other fixtures, a card catalog, posters, and banking books and periodicals. A financial librarian attended the exhibit to educate bankers in library functions and services, the association allowed promotional inserts on the exhibit to be included in convention material, and the

Chicago Daily News radio station (WMAQ) interviewed one of the librarians on the show entitled "Financial Libraries."[34]

AN INCENTIVES AUDIT

In 1919 Glenn C. Munn was hired by the Chase National Bank (New York) as an assistant manager of the personnel department. Possessing degrees from the University of Michigan, he had taught economics and accounting at New York University and at the University of Chicago prior to World War I. Although an accountant by trade, his main contribution to banking lay in the area of personnel management. In 1920 he proposed an "incentives audit" encompassing: (1) immediate incentives, which addressed monetary concerns, working conditions, education and training, institutional prestige and soundness, merit recognition, peer relations, and fairness of relations with supervisors; (2) prospective incentives, which concerned monetary, prestige, and encouragement dimensions; and (3) remote incentives, which included the belief that "top positions" are worth working for, that direct labor can advance a person who is qualified. Many of the audit details were concerned with welfare work, including recreation and reading facilities, corporate-provided or -sponsored lunches, internal publicity for individual meritorious achievement, employee clubs, and financial programs such as pensions or death benefits. The audit—and the material presented in this chapter—demonstrates that the 1920s integration of welfare work, formal training, and miscellaneous work condition issues into personnel management within American industry was paralleled by developments within the banking industry.[35]

NOTES

1. Susan P. Benson, *Counter Cultures: Saleswomen, Managers and Customers in American Department Stores, 1890–1940* (Urbana: University of Illinois Press, 1988), 142–53.

2. Owen J. Stalson, *Marketing Life Insurance: Its History in America* (Cambridge, MA: Harvard University Press, 1942), 576–604.

3. James I. Clarke, "The Spirit of Service," *JABA*, 13 (September 1920): 137; Harry G. Baldwin, "Tellers as Salesmen of Your Service," *BMo*, 42 (January 1925): 36; W. R. Snodgrass, "Building a Family Spirit," *BMo*, 45 (January 1928): 34.

4. "Salutary," *The Review*, 1 (May 1904): 1 (FNBC archives); see also Edward H. Kittredge, "House Organs for Banks," *The Printing Art*, 41 (July 1923): 456.

5. "How to Use the Bank's Telephone," *The Chase* (1923), repr. *BMa*, 106 (January 1923): 92; "Notes," *Number Eight*, 6 (7 December 1929): 5 (CB archives); "Telephone Do's and Don'ts," *Number Eight* (1930), repr. *BMa*, 121 (August 1930): 180.

6. Osgood Baley, "A Bank Newspaper That Pays for Itself," *BMo*, 35 (November 1918): 11; "Group Meetings for Employees," *BMo*, 36 (April 1919): 30–31; Kittredge, "House Organs for Banks."

7. Publication starting dates provided by RB, CIBC, and BNS archives.

8. Merchants' Bank of Halifax, *Rules and Regulations* (Halifax, Nova Scotia, 1885); Royal Bank of Canada, *Rules and Regulations* (Montreal, 1901) (RB archives); Bank of Nova Scotia, *Rules and Regulations* (Toronto, 1917) (BNS archives).

9. E. E. B. Reesor, "Women in Banking," *BMa*, 76 (January 1908): 59–66.

10. F. H. Houghton, "Problems of Branch Management," *BMa*, 121 (July 1928): 29–30.

11. Marquis James and Bessie R. James, *Biography of a Bank: The Story of Bank of America N.T. & S.A.* (New York: Harper & Brothers, 1954), 206.

12. "Giving the Boy His Chance," *BMo*, 34 (September 1917): 55; J. Franklin Lewis, "The Man Problem—How One Bank Handles It," *BMo*, 34 (December 1917): 14–15.

13. J. Franklin Lewis, "Gingery Messages from a Bank President," *BMo*, 36 (January 1919): 7; Ralph C. Kent, "We Train Our Bond Salesmen to Polish Doorknobs," *BMo*, 45 (May 1928): 62–63.

14. Mildred M. Tymeson, *Worcester Bankbook* (Worcester, MA: Worcester County Trust Company, 1955), 80–81.

15. W. R. Morehouse, *Bank Deposit Building* (New York: Bankers Publishing Co., 1918), 17–28. A "bucket shop" is a "low ginmill where alcoholic beverages were dispensed in small amounts in buckets" (*Webster's Third New International Dictionary*).

16. "Winning the Loyalty of Workers," *BMo*, 35 (November 1918): 34; National Bank of Commerce in New York, *National Bank of Commerce in New York: A Great American Bank* (New York: National Bank of Commerce in New York, 1921), 27–30; John W. Harrington, "The Bank as an Employer," *BMa*, 121 (October 1930): 439–46; R. Benson Ray, *A Chronology of the Bowery Savings Bank* (New York: Bowery Savings Bank, 1947), 18.

17. "Superb Lunch Service," *The Review*, 9 (October 1912): 92–93 (FNBC archives); J. M. Winston, "Improving Your Methods Through Welfare Methods," *BMo*, 35 (April 1918): 21; W. R. Snodgrass, "Building a Family Spirit," *BMo*, 45 (January 1928): 34.

18. "Making Good on Service," *BMa*, 93 (December 1916): 556–58; "Country Homes for Bank Employees," *BMa*, 105 (July 1922): 26–29; Benson, *Counter Cultures*, 143.

19. "Sea Gate," *Number Eight*, 9 (July 1914): 35; "Belle Harbor," *Number Eight*, 9 (July 1914): 36; "The City Bank Club," *Number Eight*, 9 (October 1914): 16; Arthur Titus, "The Start of the City Bank Club," *Number Eight*, 14 (September 1919): 5; "Gym and Dancing Classes for Girls to be Formed," *Number Eight*, 6 (9 February 1929): 3; "No Snow Needed to Make Bear Mountain Outing Jolly," *Number Eight*, 6 (2 March 1929): 3; "St. Patrick's Eve Dinner and Dance for N.Y. Branches," *Number Eight*, 6 (2 March 1929): 3; "Club's Buy-Direct Store Offers Large Discount List," *Number Eight*, 6 (7 December 1929): 5 (CB archives); John W. Harrington, "The Bank as an Employer," *BMa*, 121 (October 1930): 436–39.

20. "In Retrospect: The Chase Bank Club," *The Chase*, 15 (July–August 1932) 165–66; "In Retrospect: The Chase Bank Club: Part II," *The Chase*, 15 (October 1932): 253–54; "In Retrospect: The Chase Bank Club: Part III," *The Chase*, 15 (December 1932): 331–32 (CM archives); undated document, "42 Years Later—Prize Winners Tell of First Cannon Examination"; personal correspondence from Ann Gibson, assistant archivist, Chase Manhattan National Bank, to Richard Germain (30 December 1991).

21. "Bankers' Tutorial Classes," *Caduceus*, 1 (October 1920): 12–3; "Vancouver Staff Association," *Caduceus*, 1 (December 1920): 25; "Bank Notes: Fort William," *Caduceus*, 3 (April 1922): 33 (CIBC archives).

22. "Sports," *Bank Notes*, 1 (January 1921): 29–32; "Sports," *Bank Notes*, 1 (May 1921): 21–25 (TD archives); photographs reprinted in "Hockey," *Caduceus*, 6 (April 1925): 45 (CIBC archives); Zander Hollander and Hal Bock, *The Complete Encyclopedia of Ice Hockey* (Englewood Cliffs, NJ: Prentice-Hall, 1974).

23. "Prize Competition," *Caduceus*, 10 (January 1930): 13 (CIBC archives).

24. Victor Ross, *A History of the Canadian Bank of Commerce*, 2 vols. (Toronto: Oxford University Press, 1922), 244–45.

25. Bank Clerks' Athletic Association of Philadelphia, *Spring Sports of Bank Clerks' Athletic Association* (Philadelphia, 1891).

26. Note in *The Review*, 1 (May 1904): 6; "Base Ball," *The Review*, 2 (June 1905): 24; "Athletic Department," *The Review*, 9 (April 1912): 190 (FNBC archives).

27. Robert S. Rait, *The History of the Union Bank of Scotland* (Glasgow: John Smith & Son, 1930), 332–38; Hartly Withers, *National Provincial Bank: 1833–1933* (London: National Provincial Bank, 1933), 54–56, 89.

28. Murray W. Latimer, *Industrial Pension Systems in the United States and Canada*, 2 vols. (New York: Industrial Relations Counselors, 1932).

29. Mr. Loasby, "Mr. Loasby Explains New Pension Plan to Employees," *The Equitable Envoy*, 4 (January 1925): 3–4 (CM archives).

30. Gilbert O. Gilbert, "Giving Your Workers a Share of the Profits," *BMo*, 34 (November 1917): 28; "Guardian's Profit Sharing Fund," *BMo*, 35 (March 1918): 17–18; Latimer, *Industrial Pension Systems*, 1006.

31. Philip J. Syms, "Making the Job Appeal to the Workers," *BMo*, 36 (February 1919): 16–17; "Facts About the Equitable Trust Company Employees' Association," *The Equitable Envoy*, 3 (March 1922): 41 (CM archives).

32. "Profit Sharing with Employees," *BMa*, 43 (October 1889): 246; "Profit Sharing," *BMa*, 45 (July 1890): 40–41; W. R. Morehouse, "Helping Bank Employees to Help Themselves Through Profit-Sharing," *BMa*, 100 (April 1920): 553–56.

33. "Civil Service in Banks," *BMa*, 45 (May 1890): 850–51.

34. "Inside Publicity," *Special Libraries*, 18 (January 1927): 12–21.

35. "New Assistant Manager: Personnel Department," *The Chase*, 2 (October–December 1919): 242 (CM archives); Glenn G. Munn, "The Human Equation in Banking," *BMa*, 101 (December 1920): 921–23.

11

Organization

Thus far, scant attention has been paid to how banks were organized regarding promotional activities. The transition from passive to aggressive organizations required concomitant changes in organizational design. The chapter begins with a discussion of advertising and advertising agencies. This preliminary material is important because only around 1900 did banks internalize some of the functions previously performed by advertising agencies. Simple advertising or publicity departments evolved, especially in larger banks, into what were called "new-business departments," the focus of the second part of the chapter.

ADVERTISING AGENCIES

Albert Frank-Guenther Law (AFGL) is a New York-based advertising agency specializing in financial advertising and publicity. With roots that go back to 1872, AFGL is the oldest advertising agency in America specializing in financial services. Older agencies exist. One of the earliest agents in America was Volney Palmer, who founded his agency in 1843. Other agencies prior to AFGL—such as John Hooper & Co., City and Country Advertising Agents—promoted their services in 1860s newspaper advertisements to bankers, merchants, steamship and railroad agents, and other businessmen. AFGL was born out of the efforts of Albert Frank, Rudolph Guenther, and Russell Law. Albert Frank was a major force in the early years of financial advertising. He was a cofounder of Mandel & Frank (1872). In 1881 he gained control of the firm and took in John J. Kiernan, a New York state senator and owner of the Kiernan News Agency. In 1893 the company changed its name to Albert Frank & Co. Very little is known about the early years of the firm. It specialized in financial advertising, mostly stock and bond sale announcements, and did some travel and resort promotion. The agency expanded its services to include artwork, text preparation, and verification. In 1916 the agency began publishing *The Frank Fidelity*, an internally distributed employee magazine. By 1924 Albert Frank & Co. had branches in Boston, Chicago, and London.[1]

Rudolph Guenther was born in Vienna in 1872. In 1890, he and his father formed the Guenther-Bradford advertising agency in Chicago. After working as a sales representative and copywriter, Rudolph become the agency's New York City representative in 1895. In 1907 he formed his own general advertising agency, and by 1911 promotions spoke of specialization in "financial advertising." Guenther's interest in financial advertising was furthered by the success of the World War I Liberty Bond drive, in which he played a role. Russell Law and Rudolph Guenther joined forces in 1919 and created Rudolph Guenther-Russell Law, an agency that increasingly concentrated on financial advertising. Russell Law, previously an advertising manager for the *Wall Street Journal*, had formed his own advertising agency in 1914.[2]

Rudolph Guenther-Russell Law was the pre-eminent financial advertising agency in America during the 1920s. In 1921 the company completed construction of a five-floor building in the Wall Street area. The agency regularly studied national financial advertising volume during the 1920s, and the *New York Times* frequently quoted Guenther on the results and on related financial developments. For instance, in 1927, under the headline "Guenther Predicts Record Advertising," he was quoted as saying:

> It is reasonable to believe that 1927 will witness the use of newspaper and magazine advertising space on a scale never before attained in the history of American finance. This is supported by the fact that thus far in 1927 more money has been appropriated, generally speaking, for investment and so called institutional advertising than in the same period of 1926, which was a record year for all time.

Guenther was adept at getting his and his company's name into the *New York Times*. This no doubt served the interests of the newspaper, since generic promotion of financial advertising may have increased demand. In 1927 and 1928, Chicago and San Francisco branches, respectively, were established, and representation was made available in London and Berlin. In 1929 the firm was the first advertising agency to make a public offering of common stock.[3]

In 1932 Albert Frank and Company and Rudolph Guenther-Russell Law merged to form Albert Frank-Guenther Law. Guenther lived into his nineties and was active in the business until his death in 1961. The company has often been among the top 50 American advertising agencies since the 1950s. Whereas Guenther actively publicized his name during the 1920s, the post-1950 policy of AFGL is low-key. Unlike agencies specializing in consumer goods, AFGL does not hold press conferences announcing acquisition of large accounts. It is also characterized by having rather long agency–client relationships. Currently, the longest continuous agency–client relationship in America exists between AFGL and J. P. Morgan & Company, over 75 years.[4]

The case of Philadelphia-based N. W. Ayer & Son illustrates that financial advertising never amounted to much within a general advertising agency. For select years, Table 11.1 presents the percentage of billings from financial (e.g., banks, insurance firms) and service organizations and total agency billings. Financial advertising as a percentage of total agency billings rose from 0.50 in 1877 to 3.19 in 1925. The Depression had a pronounced effect: financial advertising fell to 0.58 percent of the agency total in 1930. Also presented are total service firm billings, which peaked in 1921 at 16.18 percent of the agency total and fell to 6.93 percent in 1930.

A 1927 study revealed that financial advertising never approximated the volume of tangible goods advertising. In New York City newspapers over a ten-month period, the distribution by number of advertising lines among several product types was dry goods, 62.4 percent; women's specialty shops, 14.2 percent; automotive goods, 11.1 percent; food, 7.3 percent; and banks, 5.0 percent.[5]

The low volume of financial advertising in newspapers and the small percentage of agency billings from financial institutions does not detract from the fact that prior to 1930, financial advertising in America was of sufficient volume for niche firms like AFGL to flourish. These niches existed despite anti-branching legislation, which crippled the industry's ability to mount national campaigns. A national campaign such as that in 1918 by the Equitable Trust Company of New York, which promoted bonds, were rare and commented upon as such in the trade press.[6]

BANK ADVERTISING POSITIONS AND DEPARTMENTS

During the nineteenth century, advertising by banks was of insufficient volume to warrant the employment of an in-house advertising staff; a supervisor of another function was made responsible for advertising in addition to his normal duties. In the insurance industry—for instance, the Pennsylvania Company for Insurances on Lives and Granting Annuities in 1813—it may have been the actuary who developed and purchased advertising space. In banking, it may have been the cashier or vice president. At The First National Bank of Chicago prior to 1903, advertising was the responsibility of one of the two vice presidents.[7]

Around 1900, banks began establishing in-house advertising or publicity departments. Table 11.2 provides a pre-1915 listing of banks, the title of the person in charge of advertising, and the year that the title was identified. Through the 1930s, in most small banks the cashier remained responsible for overseeing advertising activities. Even within large banks, some nonadvertising managers were keenly interested in advertising and promotion. Joseph F. Sartori, president of the Security Trust & Savings Bank in 1900, and president of the much larger Security-First National Bank of Los Angeles during the late 1920s, took a personal interest in bank advertising: "For many years he wrote the

Table 11.1
Bank and Service Advertising Volume, N. W. Ayer & Son

Year	Financial Institution Agency Billings (%)	Service Firm Agency Billings (%)	Total Agency Billings ($)
1877	0.50	6.80	131,628
1878	0.60	8.30	185,519
1900	0.34	9.58	1,440,827
1901	0.27	10.76	1,925,972
1921	0.70	16.18	11,066,467
1925	3.19	13.14	16,701,149
1930	0.58	6.93	38,068,616

Notes: Financial institution agency billings are the sum of bank, insurance, and related financial advertising. Service firm agency billings are the sum of financial institution billings plus communication, transportation, school, college, correspondence school, hotel, restaurant, and travel billings.

Source: Ralph M. Hower, *The History of an Advertising Agency: N. W. Ayer & Son at Work, 1869–1939* (Cambridge, MA: Harvard University Press, 1939), 638–42.

advertising copy himself and carefully trained himself to find precisely the right words to express his meaning."[8]

The Royal Bank of Canada

The relationship between size and the internalization of promotional functions is illustrated well by the fact that one of the earliest, if not the earliest, bank in North America to do so was the Royal Bank of Canada. In 1900 the bank established an advertising department under A. G. Tait (his title was advertising manager, a position he held until his death in 1921). A 1945 document from the bank provided the following list of responsibilities:

1. Publication of *The Royal Bank Magazine* (the bank's internally distributed employee magazine)
2. In 1924, and probably earlier, the design and distribution of calendars
3. Distribution through schools of book covers for students
4. Beginning in 1930, distribution of posters to branches
5. Dissemination of the report of the annual meeting
6. Distribution and design of budget books
7. Distribution of instructional banking forms to schools
8. Production and distribution of books on livestock and poultry farming methods
9. Distribution of blotters
10. Publication and distribution, on a quarterly basis, of a list of branches and bank officers

Table 11.2
Pre-1915 Advertising Positions

Title/Institution	Location	Year
Publicity manager		
Northern Trust Company	Chicago, IL	1905
American National Bank of Nashville	Nashville, TN	1908
International Trust Company Bank	Denver, CO	1909
Seattle National Bank	Seattle, WA	1912
St. Louis Union Trust Company	St. Louis, MO	1912
Mercantile Trust Company	St. Louis, MO	1913
Advertising manager		
Real Estate Trust Company	Pittsburgh, PA	1903
Cleveland Trust Company	Cleveland, OH	1904
Harris Trust & Savings Bank	Chicago, IL	1907
Colonial Trust Company	Pittsburgh, PA	1908
Mellon National Bank	Pittsburgh, PA	1908
Citizens Savings & Trust Company	Cleveland, OH	1908
Commerce Trust Company	Kansas City, MO	1908
Union Trust Company	Chicago, IL	1908
American Security & Trust Company	Washington, D.C.	1908
Bankers Trust Company	New York City	1909
Safe Deposit & Trust Company	Pittsburgh, PA	1911
Wachovia Bank & Trust Company	Winston-Salem, NC	1911
New Netherland Bank of New York	New York City	1912
Sacramento Bank	Sacramento, CA	1912
Northwestern National Bank of Minneapolis	Minneapolis, MN	1912
First National Bank	Montgomery, AL	1912
American National Bank	Richmond, VA	1912
Cashier		
Old National Bank of Spokane	Spokane, WA	1908
Quincy National Bank	Quincy, IL	1908
First National Bank	Napa, CA	1908
DeKalb Exchange Bank	DeKalb, TX	1909
First National Bank	Berkeley, CA	1914

Sources: F. R. Fuller, "What an Advertising Trust Company Has Accomplished in Nine Years," *TC,* 1 (December 1904): 1096–97; Geo E. Robertson, "Bank Publicity," *TC,* 2 (February 1905): 102–04; "Harris Trust Savings System," *BMa,* 75 (October 1907): 596; "Bank Ad Men," *BMa,* 76 (April 1908): 573; "How Banks Are Advertising," *BMa,* 77 (July 1908): 95; Francis R. Morison, "The Intellectual Side of Advertising," *BMa,* 77 (July 1908): 79; "Advertising Criticism," *BMa,* 77 (August 1908) 247; "How Banks Are Advertising," *BMa,* 78 (May 1909): 858; G. P. Blackiston, "Serial Bank Advertising," *BMa,* 82 (March 1911): 399–400; "Who's Who in Bank Advertising," *BMa,* 101 (September 1921): 405.

11.   Production and distribution of *Canada the Land of Opportunity*, a book first issued in 1923 and by 1945 revised five times; it was illustrated and contained "information likely to be of use to prospective settlers."

This list of functions is in fact incomplete. C. E. Bourne, who succeeded Tait as the bank's advertising manager and held that post until 1935, described the mass media advertising operations of the bank in 1928. The annual advertising cycle began with branch managers completing a standardized form on which they listed the newspapers they wanted to advertise in, desired advertising frequency, newspaper circulation estimates, advertising rates, and estimated advertising expenditures. The requisition was compared with head office standards and adjusted, if necessary. Upon approval, branch managers signed contracts with newspapers in their area. The advertising department prepared about 40 advertisements (i.e., proof sheets) and mailed them to branch managers who had received permission to advertise. Branch managers selected the 8 to 12 that they thought best suited to their locale. In this manner, the advertising department kept tabs on which advertisements were popular among branch managers. Orders were placed, and electrotypes were shipped directly to branch managers from the foundry. Control over advertising in national media was centralized in the head office.

Advertising by foreign branch managers in Cuba, Europe, and South America followed the same process. They selected from among the same advertisements that Canadian branch managers did, but they made suggestions concerning translations and changes in illustrations. Regarding advertising in Cuba, Bourne said, "We have to turn them into Spanish first and, incidentally, change any winter clothes the happy depositor may be wearing in our illustrations into tropical costumes." Bourne stressed that great care was taken in translations: "Anyone who has had anything to do with changing advertising from one language to another will realize that it is not sufficient for the advertisements to be a literal translation."

The advertising department also constructed a direct mail manual for branch managers. Branch managers requisitioned direct mail material on standardized forms that were analyzed by the head office for anomalies. Unusual orders from branch managers for direct mail material were probably the result of inexperience (they were not promotion specialists). Bourne ascribed to zealotry an order for 3,000 children's blotters titled "Learn to Swim," placed by a branch manager in a small western town of 1,000. He felt the same about a manager who ordered thousands of booklets on forest fire prevention. The branch was located on the prairie, and the nearest forest was about 200 miles distant (prairie wildfires may have been the branch manager's concern). Another major promotional item designed and distributed by the advertising department was the annual calendar, produced in English, French, Chinese, and Spanish. It was ordered during the summer, when printers offered a discount.[9]

NEW-BUSINESS DEPARTMENTS

As advertising expertise developed in banks and as their scale increased, the realization dawned that advertising was much more than promotion and that an advertising department limited to promotion failed to fully coordinate the multitude of marketing effects on organizational sales and growth. The response was the creation of the new-business department, which resembles current conceptions of a marketing department.

The responsibilities of new-business departments included (1) soliciting new accounts and investigating prospects (e.g., references); (2) investigating closed accounts; (3) operating account opening and account closing departments; (4) media advertising and direct mail promotions; (5) building an esprit de corps (i.e., welfare work); (6) operating printing machinery; (7) operating and administering employee new-business contests; (8) operating and administering central information files and related cross-selling efforts; and (9) publishing daily bulletins. A major purpose frequently concerned coordination. The new-business department was described as (1) a "'clearing house' for the work of all departments in the work of trying to obtain new customers for the Company"; (2) a "centralization point for new business information, and to form a connecting link between the various departments and branches of the bank and the public"; and (3) a department that "must not monopolize all efforts toward new business but must cooperate with other departments in increasing their efficiency, by offering friendly suggestions and by acting as a 'clearing house' for them."[10]

The responsibilities of an actual, but unidentified, new-business department in a large bank are presented in Table 11.3. The department handled bank advertising and related promotions, as well as the central information and prospect files. It integrated functions by coordinating, across departments, the solicitation training of clerical, teller, and new-business staff; by publishing an officers' daily bulletin to promote the "interchange of ideas"; and by publishing a weekly employees' magazine. The daily bulletin was a one- or two-page summary of the previous day's business. It may have shown deposits at the end of the day, deposits at the end of the day one year previous, account openings (with amounts and referrals) and closings, and a summary of major bank news, such as an expansion of business by a commercial customer. An ideal department would have combined responsibility for publicity, personal selling, employee welfare (e.g., pension plan, employee education), central information files, mailing lists, and tracking competitors: "It is a good policy to be posted on the best methods of progressive banks in other parts of the country." [11]

Table 11.4 lists banks that operated a new-business department. The majority of them are large institutions, which is consistent with a relationship between size and workforce specialization. But size alone is an insufficient explanation. Some small banks had a new-business department consisting of a single individual (e.g., Tri-State Loan & Trust Company, Fort Wayne, Indiana). The

Table 11.3
New-Business Department Functions (1925)

1.	To make recommendations to the president on all new-business questions and carry out orders of the president on such matters
2.	To advise and work in concert with heads of profit-making departments as to selection of men for new-business work, training of these men, and control of their activities outside the bank
3.	To act in concert with the personnel department in connection with new-business activities in training employees engaged in clerical/counter work
4.	To collect from profit-making departments all information about prospective customers needed in connection with the new-business effort, to collate this information at a central point, and to distribute it throughout the bank
5.	To produce all advertising for all departments and attend to its publication in newspapers, through mails, or otherwise
6.	To prepare prospects lists for solicitation, securing names from the directors of the bank, the files of the profit-making departments, the affiliations of customers, and all other sources; to see that the data on these names are full and complete, not only from the standpoint of helping the solicitor to make a successful contact but also from the standpoint of knowing in advance that business secured from solicitation will be acceptable and profitable. Also to prepare and maintain mailing lists for use in distributing printed matter issued for profit-making departments
7.	To prepare and maintain an accurate central information file showing all necessary data regarding customers of all profit-making departments and to operate this file with a view to having each customer deal with as many departments as possible and increase relations with each department to the limit of his or her particular case
8.	To publish an officers' daily bulletin for disseminating information as above and for the interchange of ideas on new business and public relations generally
9.	To publish, in concert with the personnel department, a weekly bulletin for the entire personnel of the bank, the purpose of this bulletin being to raise morale, to give specialized employees a broader view of the whole situation, and to stimulate new-business efforts by the personnel
10.	To record the results of new-business efforts by officers, solicitors, and operating employees, and to be prepared at all times to furnish data on which judgments as to ability in this connection may be based
11.	To control necessary mechanical operations in connection with advertising, such as illustrations, engraving, printing, mimeographing, multigraphing
12.	To control information service throughout the bank, with special reference to information for the new savings depositor, the woman customer, and all other customers who need or desire it

Source: G. Prather Knapp, "Controlling the Bank's New Business Department," *BMo*, 42 (April 1925): 12–13+.

remainder of the chapter is devoted to discussing in more detail some of the banks listed in Table 11.4.

The First National Bank of Chicago

One of the earliest banks to establish a new-business department apparently was The First National Bank of Chicago. Events during the five years prior to the establishment of the new-business department put tremendous pressure on the bank's organizational design. In 1900 the bank purchased the Union National Bank. However, the addition of $17 million to the bank's $50 million deposit base did not materially affect the marketing structure of the bank. The 1902 structure had two vice presidents whose responsibilities were "City discounts A–K" and "City discounts L–Z." One of them was also responsible for the bank's advertising. Later in 1902 the bank purchased the Metropolitan National Bank. Deposits now totaled about $100 million, and strains soon appeared in the bank's structure that were even more apparent when the bank began a savings division for consumers in 1903. In this context, James B. Forgan formally proposed a new structure that the board accepted: "To specialize and divide the work by assigning to individual officers the care and management of the accounts of customers in specific lines of business. A senior and junior officer will work together in the management of all accounts in a particular line of business."

Six divisions were created, each eventually headed by a vice president aided by an assistant vice president. The six divisions were the following:

Division A — Collateral stocks and bonds; grain, flour, and feed; meat products, livestock commissions; coal; doctors and lawyers

Division B — Dry goods, millinery; woolens, clothing, cloaks; furnishing goods, hats, caps; jewelry and merchandising sundries; ladies' accounts

Division C — Agricultural implements, buggies, automobiles, and other vehicles; iron and steel products; lumber, furniture, etc.; manufacturing sundries

Division D — Stone, brick, and cement contractors; wallpaper, paints, oils, glass, etc.; boots, shoes, leather, hides, and wool; real estate and insurance; publishing, printing, engraving, and paper; miscellaneous

Division E — Wholesale and retail liquors, brewers and brewers' supplies; tobacco; produce commissions and cold storage; grocers, drugstores, restaurants; bakers and hotels

Division F — Banks and bankers

Forgan expected the vice presidents "to use their best endeavor to work up new business in the special lines assigned to them" and required them to forward an annual report "showing how the business of the bank has been developed during the year in the special lines of business." The reorganization was linked not only to "better controlling credits" but also to organizing a senior-level solicitation staff. The reorganization resulted in a firm that combined elements of divisionalization and functionalism. Responsibility for commercial customers was

Table 11.4
New-Business Departments

Institution	Location	Year
The First National Bank of Chicago	Chicago, IL	1905
Bankers Trust Company	New York City	1917
National City Bank of New York	New York City	1917
Guaranty Trust Company of New York	New York City	1918
Irving National Bank	New York City	1918
First National Bank/First Trust & Savings Company	Cleveland, OH	1918
Hibernia Bank & Trust Company	New Orleans, LA	1918
Guaranty Trust & Savings Bank (formerly German-American Trust & Savings Bank)	Los Angeles, CA	1918
Shawmut National Bank	Boston, MA	1918
Metropolitan Trust Company	New York City	1919
St. Joseph Valley Bank	Elkhart, IN	1919
Marine Trust Company	Buffalo, NY	1920
Chicago Trust Company	Chicago, IL	1921
American Security & Trust Company	Washington, D.C.	1922
Lake Shore Trust & Savings Bank	Chicago, IL	1922
First National Bank	New Haven, CT	1926
Reliance State Bank	Chicago, IL	1926
Pacific Southwest Trust & Savings Bank	Los Angeles, CA	1928
Union Trust Company	Chicago, IL	1928
Fidelity Union Trust Company	Newark, NJ	1928
Tri-State Loan & Trust Company	Fort Wayne, IN	1928

Sources: "Banking and Financial Notes," *BMa*, 90 (May 1915): 690–91; "Women Temporarily Having Luncheon Outside of the Bank," *Number Eight*, 12 (February 1917): 50–51 (CB archives); T. D. MacGregor, "How Banks Get 'New Business,'" *PI*, 102 (14 March 1918): 106+; Irwin G. Jennings, "What 'New Business' Bureau Really Is," *BMo*, 36 (February 1919): 10–11; William J. Kelly, "How to Conduct an Employees' Savings Contest," *BMa*, 103 (November 1921): 850–52; Mahlon D. Miller, "Some Reasons Why Banks Lose Business," *BMo*, 39 (April 1922): 22+; Heylinger Church, "Speeding up the Tellers' Routine Work," *BMo*, 43 (July 1926): 23+; F. O. Birney, "To Analyze Territory for New Business Work," *BMo*, 43 (September 1926): 12–14; Fred W. Loco, "To Get Profitable Accounts," *BMo*, 45 (January 1928): 23–25; Leopold A. Chambliss, "A Two-Way Plan for Building Trust Business," *PI*, 145 (4 October 1928): 104+; Asa A. Knowles, *Shawmut, 150 Years of Banking: 1836–1986* (Boston: Houghton Mifflin, 1986), 156.

divided according to line of business, but the remaining departments of the bank reflected a functional structure. There were still a bond department, a safe deposit department, and a soon-to-be-organized new-business department.[12]

The new-business department of The First National Bank of Chicago apparently was organized in 1905, and it hardly seems a coincidence that it appeared just after the bank's growth by acquisition and establishment of a savings division. Fred W. Ellsworth was the first manager of the new-business department. The department operated the bank's printing machinery and produced the bank's stationery, direct mail, advertising literature, daily reports, and employee magazine (*The Review*). Advertisements were designed by the department, and electrotypes were manufactured. By 1909, Ellsworth's new-business department was given responsibility for personal solicitation. He noted that the entire bank, from the president to the bellboy, served the public: "Each one has his particular function to perform, his own share in serving and satisfying present customers."[13]

Hibernia National Bank & Trust Company (New Orleans)

Fred W. Ellsworth left The First National Bank of Chicago and joined the Guaranty Trust Company of New York in 1910. He organized its first advertising department and was the bank's secretary at his departure in 1916 for the Hibernia National Bank & Trust Company to serve as vice president and director. By 1918, Hibernia's first new-business department was fully operational. The bank's business-building activities centered on the new-business department and the publicity department. The new-business department operated and maintained a central information file and organized lists of current commercial customers by line of business, lists of potential customers by geographic region, and lists of "active" and "reserve" prospects. A research staff provided information "advantageous to new-business solicitors in their daily work." The publicity department advertised consumer services, and commercial and out-of-town bank business was cultivated in the financial trade press, supplemented with sales force efforts. The publicity department worked a cooperative program with other banks to promote school savings banking in the city. Between 1918 and 1920, deposits doubled from $24 million to over $50 million, and total resources jumped from $30 million to over $70 million. Ellsworth observed:

> Some of this gain can be attributed to the natural development of business which has occurred everywhere during the past two years, but the fact that our gain is considerably more than the average would seem to indicate that our policy of continuous, concentrated effort along advertising and new business pays—and pays well.[14]

Ellsworth completed a term as president of the Financial Advertisers Association during the 1910s, and in 1920 *The Bankers' Magazine* bestowed upon him the title "the father of bank advertising."[15]

Guaranty Trust & Savings Bank (Los Angeles)

This bank—formerly the German-American Savings Bank—was one of the earliest to adopt employee new-business campaigns (1912) and central information files (as early as 1914). Its new-business department, established as early

Figure 11.1
Organizational Chart, Guaranty Trust Company of New York, 1917

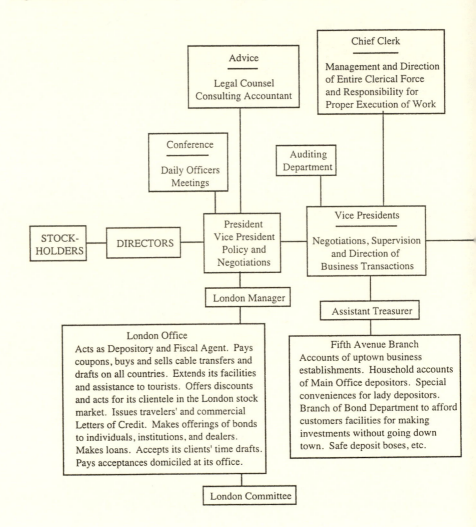

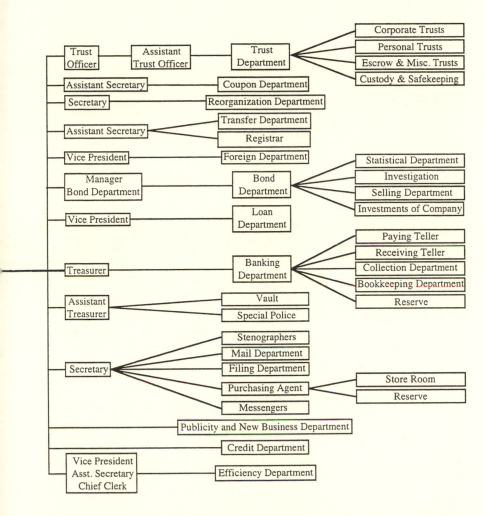

Source: William H. Kniffen, *Practical Work of a Bank* (New York: Bankers' Publishing Co., 1919), insert between pp. 44–45.

as 1918, awarded monthly prizes of up to five dollars for the best employee suggestion on eliminating waste. The department, by acting as a clearinghouse for suggestions, created direct lines of informal communication between the head of the new-business department and supervisors and staff of other departments. These lines bypassed vertical chains of command and fostered horizontal, collaborative communication. The new-business department was located in the center of the main banking room, making it accessible to customers and making customers visible to the department manager. If long queues formed before tellers' cages at any point during the day, new-business department staff were instructed to operate idle teller cages in order to speed service. A reserve teller to open new accounts was also available when the number of new customers was large. Both systems were flexible and handled transaction bulges. Furthermore, the new-business department, responsible for all bank advertising, involved senior staff in the creative advertising process by passing around planned promotions and seeking input. The department designed and administered monthly employee exams that covered transaction processing, accounting methods, answering common customer questions, and dealing with fellow employees.[16]

Guaranty Trust Company of New York

The examples discussed thus far have not described how new-business departments fit into a bank's overall organizational structure. Figure 11.1 presents the 1917 structure of the Guaranty Trust Company of New York. The relative complexity of the chart reflects the scale of the organization. By 1927, it was the eighth largest bank in the world and third largest in America (see the Appendix). The structure contains a publicity and new-business department. It was responsible for the "custody of mailing lists for advertising purposes, preparation of advertisements, arranging for publication of advertisements. Preparation of officers bulletins, etc. Interviewing individuals and companies to place before them the facilities and service offered by the company." The trust department retained its own sales force, and there may have been a good deal of cross-training in personal selling in this area. There is also an efficiency department, which was "to promote the efficiency of the Company and give customers best possible service. Prepares standing of each department monthly from reports and criticisms made by all officers and departments." The horizontal communication inherent in the performance of such functions suggests lateral integration. The addition of a central information file to the bank as early as 1918 must have further enhanced lateral communication. The notion that vertical communication channels dominated large American organizations prior to 1950 may require revision in light of these findings.

NOTES

1. Stephen Fox, *The Mirror Makers: A History of American Advertising and its Creators* (New York: Vintage Books, 1985), 14; advertisement in *NYT*, 5 April 1862; one-page internal document, "Albert Frank & Company" (1924); Albert Frank-Guenther Law Celebrates Centennial (1972) (AFGL archives).

2. Advertisement in *BMa*, 83 (July 1911): 129; page proofs of 1966 biographical material on Rudolph Guenther for inclusion in *National Cyclopedia of American Biography* (AFGL archives).

3. Examples of articles published by the *New York Times* based on statements made by Rudolph Guenther include "Investment Bankers Back," 26 September 1924; "Finds Advertising Helps," 29 September 1926; "Newspapers in Four Years Gain 60% in Financial Advertising," 8 October 1929. See also "Guenther-Law Opens Chicago Office," *NYT*, 7 April 1927; "Guenther Predicts Record Advertising," *NYT*, 19 May 1927; "Guenther-Law in San Francisco," *NYT*, 21 June 1928; "Guenther-Law Service in Europe," *NYT*, 15 February 1928.

4. Albert Frank-Guenther Law Celebrates Centennial (1972) (AFGL archives); personal conversation with Robert Becton, senior vice president and director of public relations, Albert Frank-Guenther Law (November 1991).

5. H. C. North, "Bank Advertising Outgrows the Financial Pages," *Sales Management*, 14 (2 June 1928): 922+.

6. "Equitable Trust Co. to Advertise Bonds Nationally," *PI*, 102 (24 January 1918): 31–32.

7. Owen J. Stalson, *Marketing Life Insurance: Its History in America* (Cambridge, MA: Harvard University Press, 1942), 51.

8. George M. Wallace, *Joseph Francis Sartori: 1858–1946* (Los Angeles: Ward Ritchie Press, 1948), 65.

9. C. E. Bourne, "Advertising a Bank with 900 Branches," *BMa*, 117 (December 1928): 1031–36; H. A. Mortimer, "Advertising Department" (1945), an internal Royal Bank document providing starting date of department, departmental managers, and executive tenure (RB archives).

10. T. D. MacGregor, *The New Business Department* (New York: Bankers Publishing Co., 1917), 10; "The New Business Department," *BMa*, 100 (March 1920): 394–95; "Cultivate Old as Well as New Customers," *BMa*, 104 (April 1922): 707+; Motley H. Flint, "Solicitation Management," *BMo*, 44 (August 1927): 25.

11. H. B. Grimm, "The New Business Department," *BMa*, 102 (February 1921): 213.

12. Henry C. Morris, *The History of The First National Bank of Chicago* (Chicago: R. R. Donnelly & Sons, 1904), organizational chart, rear folio; The First National Bank of Chicago, *The First National Bank of Chicago* (Chicago: M. A. Donahue, 1913), 62–64; James B. Forgan, *Recollections of a Busy Life* (New York: Bankers Publishing Co., 1920), 130–50, quotation at 146.

13. F. W. Ellsworth, "A Bank Printing Plant," *BMa*, 77 (October 1908): 579–80; F. W. Ellsworth, "The New Business Department," *BMa*, 78 (April 1909): 708–10.

14. F. W. Ellsworth, "Merchandising Ideas of 'Department Store of Finance,'" *PI*, 113 (23 December 1920): 77–78+.

15. "Who's Who in Bank Advertising," *BMa*, 101 (August 1920): 243; "Banking and Financial Notes," *BMa*, 90 (May 1915): 690–91.

16. A. W. Shaw Company, *Advertising and Service* (Chicago: A. W. Shaw Company, 1918), 247–50.

12

Conclusion

The evidence presented clearly supports the thesis laid out at the beginning of the book—that the transformation of American banks from passive responders to aggressive seekers of business—a transition characterized by service, segmentation, and staff—was complete by 1930. First, bankers were highly responsive to elements of service quality. They inspired confidence in banking institutions through impressive bank structures that tapped into longevity symbolism, heavily promoted tangibles, and used confidence-building themes such as growth and management quality. Some were astute psychologists at handling runs. Bankers kept well informed and sought varied means of improving transaction velocity, accuracy, and security. Increasing accessibility to palaces of finance through hours of operation and personal accessibility did much to increase public acceptance of banking service. Not only did bankers address these and other service quality determinants in practice, but they understood that confidence, velocity, and so on, determined customers' perceptions of service quality. An understanding of gap theory, service properties, and a potential difference between product and service marketing, all complete by 1930, rounded out the bankers' service repertoire.

The second component of the transformation of banking was segmentation. As a whole, the industry crafted marketing mixes for (1) demographic segments, including children, women, members of various nationality groups, and African-Americans (racism was observable in the latter); (2) new or potential, current, and past customers; (3) geographic segments (distant customers in particular through banking by mail); and (4) socioeconomic and credit end-use segments. Segmentation efforts invariably were experimental, and some, such as miniature banking rooms for children, were never widely adopted due to insufficient return. Others became widespread and were profitable in both the short and the long run, but the long run does not mean indefinitely. For instance, women's departments were widely available by 1930, but slowly faded due to changes in customs, habits, and labor markets.

Moreover, as one would expect in a service industry where patents are unobtainable, the time between the development of a profitable marketing mix for a specific segment and its widespread adoption was quite short. The diffusion of banking by mail, Christmas Clubs, and industrial savings plans was relatively quick. Another factor explaining the spread of ideas was the professionalization of bank promotion. *The Bankers' Magazine* and *The Bankers' Monthly* disseminated ideas. Particularly important was the 1906 appearance of "Bank Publicity," a regular feature in *The Bankers' Magazine* under the aegis of T. D. MacGregor, that contained a wealth of information on the latest in bank promotion. Professional organizations also played a part in the quick spread of ideas—the Banking Publicity Association of the United States was organized in 1905 and the Financial Advertisers Association in 1915.

Unlike segmentation, which is customer-based, differentiation is product- or supplier-based; banks engaged in both. There were many service augmentations used in the process. Some banks promoted themselves as a combination of more accurate, reliable, long-lived, professional, accessible, personable, modern, and humane. They also sought an advantage over the competition by claiming to be safer, bigger, stronger, friendlier, and smarter. Not all such claims were puffery. As demonstrated throughout the book, some banks did have extended operating hours; some banks were larger, faster, more accurate, and so on, than others.

The evidence suggests that the banking industry did not follow the production economy periodization of the development of segmentation. U.S. banks were using phase three segmentation variables well before 1920 (proposed as the onset of phase three segmentation among manufacturers). In banking, gender was used by 1840, nationality/race by 1860, age by 1890, and geography by 1900. The development of segmentation by user status came in phases, with new-business efforts (before 1900) preceding current and past customer marketing mixes (by 1920). Furthermore, in insurance, special plans were developed for Germans and women (during the 1860s), and in the department store industry special plans were created for wealthy versus and low-income customers (by the 1900s). The banking industry—and, indeed, other service industries—may be an anomaly that progressed through the production economy segmentation phases much earlier than manufacturing industries. On the other hand, a more cogent explanation is that the banking industry did not require scale economies or the dissolution of communication and transportation barriers in order to segment markets. The banking industry appears to have effectively engaged in phase three segmentation between 1840 and 1900 despite infrastructure deficiencies and the onerous legal barriers to intrastate and interstate banking. Thus, the production economy periodization may be limited in its applicability to manufacturing firms, and manufacturing organizations may have been imitators, not innovators, in the development of segmentation bases.

The final component in the transformation of the banking industry required a new orientation toward employees and appropriate organizational structures (staff). During the late nineteenth and early twentieth centuries, the banking industry assiduously cultivated an esprit de corps among staff for both direct (i.e., productivity) and indirect (i.e., better customer relations) purposes. Banks encouraged employees to create athletic and social clubs and publish employee magazines. They provided country estates for recreational and recuperative purposes and enacted financial fringe benefits. Around 1900, banks first created advertising and publicity departments. As banks grew in scale, these departments were given additional responsibilities and some, especially those within larger banks, were transformed into new-business departments. The integration of businesswide promotional activities engendered by these departments completes the triad of interests formally articulated in the marketing concept. The marketing concept is a formal statement, first proposed during the 1950s, that the goal of marketing is to meet consumer needs and wants in an integrated manner while meeting the need for corporate profits. Obviously profit, and in many cases simple survival, was a crucial concern for bankers. Meeting needs and wants is evidenced by attention to service quality determinants and by crafting marketing mixes for specific market segments. Finally, integration is observed in the way new-business departments coordinated the promotional and related activities of banking institutions.

This does not mean that all banks were customer-driven all of the time. Indeed, product proliferation may be symptomatic of something other than a customer concern. During the late 1920s, the complaint was heard that services were "installed on the theory that they make for good-will which by some diplomatic legerdemain can be translated into dollars and cents on the credit side of the ledger." By 1930, in addition to safe deposit service, time deposits, savings accounts, demand deposit accounts, trust services, stock and bond sales, credit of various sorts, insurance, and travelers' checks, services offered included those listed below.

Distribution of seeds	Foreign language service
Delivery of payrolls	Providing weather reports
Theater & amusement reservations	Reading & writing rooms
Hotel reservations	Amored car service
Distribution of Christmas baskets	Payroll insurance service
Deposits for newborn babies	Keeping reserved seats in amusement houses
Distribution of bats and balls to athletic clubs	Collection of school savings
Paying customers' household bills	Keeping ticker tape in lobby
Purchasing commutation tickets	Providing scales
Cold storage for furs	Open extra hours
	Collecting subscriptions for charities
	Employing a veterinarian

Operating financial news radio station	Carrying unprofitable accounts
Collecting money due on land contracts	Children's accounts
	Free public telephone service
	Providing real estate atlas[1]

Promotional proliferation existed in addition to product proliferation. The service-segmentation-staff trichotomy does not exhaust all promotional activities. By 1915 banks were giving away an incredible number of items containing the name of the distributing bank: soap dishes, key rings, ash trays, notebooks, ink wells that looked like bank buildings, drinking cups (described as sanitary), tobacco and money pouches, pen knives, rulers, flower seeds, and bookmarks. They distributed residential architectural plans, calendars, maps, address books, transatlantic mail schedules, newspapers, documents on domestic and foreign parcel post rules and rates, and newspapers. They offered books and booklets on cooking, gardening, preserving, the national mint, travel, baseball, and, in response to regulatory changes, tax laws. They entered floats in parades, erected street signs containing bank advertisements, installed advertisements on rooftops for aviators, and hosted rare coin exhibits. In rural communities, banks displayed local produce and sponsored agricultural essay and crop-growing contests.[2]

The "department store of finance," a phrase introduced between 1900 and 1910 and widely used by 1930, described a range of products much wider than credit and deposit. Product and message proliferation and an axiomatic customer orientation mediate our understanding of the service-segmentation-staff trichotomy in providing a clear-cut response as to whether bankers were engaged in publicity, marketing, or a combination of both. This parallels events in the department store industry, where an excessive customer orientation between 1880 and 1910 unreasonably elevated customer expectations and greatly frustrated store managers and staff. This orientation was combined with constantly escalating promotion (e.g., by 1900, department stores ran full-page newspaper advertisements, and by the 1920s some were sponsoring in-store bicycles races and live orchestra concerts). The combination of service at any cost for any return and heavy promotion led to publicity rather than marketing characterizations of pre-1930 department store activities. But it is not comforting to label all bankers as publicity seekers because some were ill-advised, ill-trained, or mindless of cost versus return. If a profitability orientation is the key—not of the firm but of specific promotional efforts or of specific customers—then we need look no further than the 1910s, when articles appeared in *The Bankers' Magazine* discussing the cost versus return of specific advertising campaigns and the profitability of individual demand deposit customers.[3]

To all this we must add one additional observation. The contention that service marketing lags product marketing in sophistication, made during the 1960s and 1970s to illustrate the exclusionary bias of marketing, is nothing new. In 1908 Dr. Channing Rudd, an employee of the *Wall Street Journal*, said to the New York Chapter of the American Institute of Banking, "Financial advertising is today practically where commercial [product] advertising was twenty years ago. I predict that the style, methods and policies of financial advertising will be completely transformed within the next few years." Messages of sudden, revolutionary change were, and remain, a dominant theme of an American society marked by a progress ethos, and service organizations lagging product organizations in the modernity of their methods is thus not an entirely modern observation.[4]

The years since 1930 can be divided into the Depression through the end of World War II and the post-World War II period. Three developments mark these periods. The first is the appearance of deposit insurance for federally chartered banks with the passage of the Banking Act of 1933. The act reduced the salience of the confidence theme and the competitive advantage gained by sound, conservative management. But old habits die hard, and the confidence theme has not been totally eliminated from banking and related financial service industries. Anniversaries are still occasions for celebrating longevity, Prudential continues to use "the Rock," and Dean Witter television advertisements show a respectable, middle-aged man, on grainy film in a 1930s scene, discussing the firm's policy of "measuring success one investor at a time."

Second, there has been the gradual erosion of anti-banking laws during the post-World War II period, although deregulation has in no way led to national banking on the scale observed in Canada, England, or elsewhere. National marketing campaigns exist in the credit card industry, financial and brokerage services, and insurance, but not in banking.

Third, and particularly noticeable in consumer markets, is the shift in focus from thrift to credit. A bank promoting thrift today is as common as a bank promoting personal consumption credit a century ago. Banks entered the consumption fray later than other industries. The leader in many regards in fostering consumption prior to 1900 was the department store industry, which engaged in extensive promotion and offered a combination of generally low prices, little in the way of high-pressure sales tactics and bargaining, and liberal returns. During the 1920s, the financial arms of major industrial concerns, such as General Motors Acceptance Corporation (GMAC), helped legitimize personal consumption credit. Banks trailed industrial financial subsidiaries in providing such credit, not because of a lack of wherewithal but because there was sufficient demand for credit from less risky sources. In some instances, banks financed the financial subsidiaries of industrial organizations. GMAC regularly advertised its obligations to bankers during the mid-1920s in *The Bankers' Magazine* as "appropriate and sound for short term investment."[5]

The shift of locus in banking from thrift to credit, even if the industry was imitating rather than innovating, is important in explaining the current prevalence of consumption and the dearth of savings in the United States, but its implication that bank marketing has undergone tremendous change is negligible. The shift in banking from thrift to credit is similar to the shift in the automobile industry from selling manual- to automatic-transmission vehicles. The product pushed changes, but the orientation remains constant. This position is in agreement with a statement made by Stanley C. Hollander, who concluded that a negligible shift in marketing orientation, but not in methods, occurred before (1850–1950) and after (post 1950) the introduction of the marketing concept. An aggressive orientation to business was firmly established in the banking industry by 1930. External events since 1930, however, have had a major impact on banking. The Depression led to demarketing in banking, and World War II led to industrial shortages and government rationing. In a sense, a marketing hiatus appears to have existed between 1930 and 1950 due to prolonged, back-to-back external shocks. Marketing may not, as the big bang theory of the universe would have us believe, be a continually expanding practice.[6]

NOTES

1. W.O. McClure, "Getting Safe Deposit Vault Business," *BMa*, 83 (July 1911): 70–74; E. Bird Wilson, "How American Bankers Association Travelers' Cheques Are Being Popularized," *BMa*, 84 (April 1912): 550–55; "How Banks Are Advertising," *BMa*, 84 (May 1912): 708; T. D. MacGregor, *Bank Advertising Plans* (New York: Bankers Publishing Co., 1913), 18; "Union Trust Opens Radio Station," *BMa*, 105 (October 1916): 677–78; "Modern Bank Offers You Everything but Parking Place for Your Chariot," *Daily Oklahoman*, 7 December 1924; Alfred C. Bosson and A. W. W. Marshal, "Fur Storage as a Bank Service," *BMa*, 111 (September 1925): 419–20; "Plenty of Service but Not Much Profit," *BMa*, 118 (May 1929): 719.

2. Leon F. Titus, "Boosting the Community," *BMa*, 80 (March 1910): 507; Eleanor Montgomery, "A Rare Coin Exhibit," *BMa*, 84 (May 1912): 701–02; "How Banks Are Advertising," *BMa*, 84 (May 1912): 709; MacGregor, *Bank Advertising Plans*, 1–40, 115–24, 134–40; "How Banks Are Advertising," *BMa*, 86 (January 1913): 62; "How Banks Are Advertising," *BMa*, 86 (June 1913): 724–26; "How Banks Are Advertising," *BMa*, 87 (December 1913): 673–74.

3. On the profitability of individual bank advertising campaigns, see, for example, "Commercial Bank Advertising," *BMa*, 85 (October 1912): 390–94. On retailing, see Ronald A. Fullerton, "Art of Public Relations: U.S. Dept. Stores, 1876–1923," *Public Relations Review*, 26 (Fall 1990): 68–79.

4. Dr. Channing Rudd, "Kinds of Financial Advertising," *BMa*, 76 (February 1908): 230.

5. Advertisement in *BMa*, 111 (November 1925): 798.

6. Stanley C. Hollander, "The Marketing Concept—A Deja View," in George Fisk, ed., *Marketing: Management Technology as a Social Process* (New York: Praeger, 1986), 3–29; personal conversation with Stanley C. Hollander on the "big bang" theory of marketing expansion.

Appendix: The 100 Largest Banks in the World, 1927

Bank	Deposits ($ in millions)
1. Midland Bank, London	1,782
2. Lloyds Bank, London	1,770
3. Barclays Bank, London	1,543
4. Westminster Bank, London	1,429
5. National Provincial Bank, London	1,296
6. National City Bank, New York City	1,275
7. Chase National Bank, New York City	792
8. Guaranty Trust Company, New York City	720
9. Bank of Montreal, Montreal	700
10. Bank of Italy N.T. & S.A., San Francisco	645
11. American Exchange-Irving Trust Company, New York City	622
12. Royal Bank of Canada, Montreal	621
13. Bankers Trust Company, New York City	562
14. Continental National Bank & Trust Company, Chicago	541
15. National Bank of Commerce, New York City	537
16. Equitable Trust Company, New York City	479
17. Banca Commerciale Milano, Milan	404
18. Canadian Bank of Commerce, Toronto	403
19. Illinois Merchants Trust Company, Chicago	383
20. Deutsche Bank, Berlin	362
21. First National Bank, Boston	360
22. First National Bank, New York City	350
23. Dresdner Bank, Dresden	325
24. Darmstädter und Nationalbank, Berlin	318
25. Central Union Trust Company, New York City	311
26. Bank of New South Wales, Sydney	308
27. Bank of Liverpool & Martins, London	294
28. Union Trust Company, Cleveland	294
29. Yasuda Bank, Tokyo	292
30. Hongkong & Shanghai Bank, Shanghai	286
31. First National Trust & Savings Bank, Los Angeles	286
32. Yokohama Specie Bank, Yokohama	285

33.	The First National Bank of Chicago, Chicago	274
34.	District Bank, Manchester	269
35.	Union Discount Company, London	260
36.	Credito Italiano, Milan	257
37.	American Trust Company, San Francisco	257
38.	Commercial Banking Company, Sydney	256
39.	New York Trust Company, New York City	256
40.	Société Générale, Paris	253
41.	Chartered Bank of India, Australia & China, London	250
42.	Chatham Phenix National Bank & Trust Company, New York City	250
43.	Security Trust & Savings Bank, Los Angeles	248
44.	Peoples Wayne County Bank, Detroit	247
45.	Sumitomo Bank, Tokyo	246
46.	Manufacturers Trust Company, New York City	244
47.	Dai Ichi Ginko, Tokyo	240
48.	Standard Bank of South Africa, London	238
49.	Comptoir National d'Escompte, Paris	236
50.	Corn Exchange Bank, New York City	232
51.	Cleveland Trust Company, Cleveland	218
52.	Co-operative Wholesale Society, Manchester	216
53.	Bank of Manhattan Company, New York City	216
54.	Mitsubishi Bank, Tokyo	214
55.	Marine Trust Company, Buffalo	212
56.	Royal Bank of Scotland, Edinburgh	202
57.	Bank of London & South America, London	202
58.	Philadelphia-Girard National Bank, Philadelphia	200
59.	Anglo-South American Bank, London	195
60.	Bank of Nova Scotia, Halifax	190
61.	Old Colony Trust Company, Boston	190
62.	Commerz-und Privatebank, Hamburg	189
63.	National Shawmut Bank, Boston	189
64.	National Park Bank, New York City	186
65.	National Bank, London	183
66.	Bank of China, Peking	173
67.	National Bank of Australia, Melbourne	171
68.	Direction der Disconto-Gesellschaft, Berlin	169
69.	Crédit Lyonnais, Lyons	169
70.	Chemical National Bank, New York City	167
71.	Bank of America, New York City	167
72.	Nederlandsche Handel-Maatschappij, Amsterdam	167
73.	Commercial Bank of Scotland, Edinburg	166
74.	Mellon National Bank, Pittsburgh	166
75.	Seaboard National Bank, New York City	166
76.	English, Scottish & Australian Bank, London	165

77.	Williams Deacons' Bank, Manchester	163
78.	Union Bank of Australia, London	163
79.	National Bank of India, London	160
80.	Bank of Scotland, Edinburgh	160
81.	Glyn Mills and Co., London	159
82.	Hanover National Bank, New York City	159
83.	Banco de la Provincia de Buenos Aires, Buenos Aires	159
84.	Farmers Loan & Trust Company, New York City	154
85.	Skandinaviska Kreditaktiebolaget, Gothenburg	152
86.	Clydesdale Bank, Glasgow	149
87.	Bank of New Zealand, Wellington	148
88.	Svenska Handelsbanken, Stockholm	148
89.	Industrial Trust Company, Providence	147
90.	Bank of Australia, London	147
91.	Bank of Dublin, Dublin	145
92.	First National Bank, Detroit	145
93.	Banque National de Crédit, Paris	144
94.	First National Bank, St. Louis	142
95.	Yerkshire Penny Bank, Leeds	138
96.	Fidelity Union Trust Company, Newark	137
97.	Banco Español del Río de la Plata, Buenos Aires	136
98.	Guardian Trust Company, Cleveland	135
99.	British Linen Bank, Edinburgh	135
100.	Union Bank of Scotland, Glasgow	128

Source: "The World's 100 Largest Banks," *BMa*, 116 (February 1928): 379. The majority of the figures are from 31 December 1927 statements.

Selected Bibliography

Albany Savings Bank. *Albany Savings Bank: 1820–1899*. Albany, NY: Albany Savings Bank, 1899.

American Bankers Association. *School Savings Banking*. New York: Ronald Press, 1923.

Ann Arbor Savings Bank. *The First Fifty Years of the Ann Arbor Savings Bank: 1869–1919*. Ann Arbor, MI: Ann Arbor Savings Bank, 1919.

A. W. Shaw Company. *Advertising and Service*. Chicago: A. W. Shaw Company, 1918.

Bank of North America. *The Bank of North America, Philadelphia*. New York: Robert Grier Press, 1906.

Bank of Nova Scotia. *The Bank of Nova Scotia: 1822–1932*. Halifax: Bank of Nova Scotia, 1933.

Bankers Trust Company. *Twenty-five Years of Bankers Trust Company*. New York: Bankers Trust Company, 1928.

Barrett, Albert R. *Modern Banking Methods and Practical Bank Bookkeeping*. 5th ed. New York: Bankers Publishing Co., 1907.

Benson, Susan P. *Counter Cultures: Saleswomen, Managers and Customers in American Department Stores, 1890–1940*. Urbana: University of Illinois Press, 1988.

Boston Five Cents Savings Bank. *The Boston Five Cents Savings Bank: Fiftieth Anniversary of Incorporation, May 2, 1904*. Boston: Boston Five Cents Savings Bank, 1904.

Burrell, O. K. *Gold in the Woodpile: An Informal History of Banking in Oregon*. Eugene: University of Oregon Press, 1967.

Chemical National Bank. *The Chemical National Bank*. New York: Chemical National Bank, 1913.

Cleland, Robert G., and Frank B. Putnam. *Isaiis W. Hellman and the Farmers and Merchants Bank*. San Marino, CA: Huntington Library, 1965.

Clemes, Lorne. *A Century of Leadership: The Story of the Bank of Lenawee County*. Adrian, MI: Bank of Lenawee County, 1969.

Cleveland, Harold van B., and Thomas F. Huertas. *Citibank: 1812–1970*. Cambridge, MA: Harvard University Press, 1985.

Cole, David M. *The Development of Banking in the District of Columbia*. New York: William Frederick Press, 1959.

Cross, Ira B. *Financing an Empire: History of Banking in California*. Chicago: S. J. Clarke Publishing Company, 1927.

Diffenderfer, Frank R. *A History of the Farmers Bank of Lancaster, the Farmers National Bank and the Farmers Trust Company of Lancaster: 1810–1910.* Lancaster, PA: Farmers Trust Company of Lancaster, 1910.

Dommett, Henry. *A History of the Bank of New York: 1784–1884.* New York: G. P. Putnam and Sons, 1884.

Donavan, Frank P., and Cushing F. Wright. *The First Through a Century, 1853–1953: A History of the First National Bank of Saint Paul.* St. Paul, MN: First National Bank of St. Paul, 1954.

Erie County Savings Bank. *An Historical Sketch of the Erie County Savings Bank: 1854–1909.* Buffalo, NY: Erie County Savings Bank, 1909.

Ernest, Fletcher. *Some Mile-stones in the History of the National Park Bank of New York.* New York: National Park Bank of New York, 1917.

Erving, Henry W. *The Connecticut River Banking Company: One Hundred Years of Service.* Hartford, CT: Connecticut River Banking Co., 1925.

Evans, Clark. *Financing the Consumer.* New York: Harper & Brothers, 1931.

Farmers & Mechanics National Bank of Georgetown. *A Century Old.* Washington, D.C.: First National Bank of Georgetown, 1914.

First National Bank of Fort Smith. *The Story of the First National Bank of Fort Smith, Arkansas, Founded February 29th 1872, the Oldest and Largest National Bank in the State.* Fort Smith, AR: First National Bank of Fort Smith, 1922.

First National Bank of Syracuse. *The First National Bank of Syracuse: The Story of Fifty Years.* Syracuse, NY: First National Bank of Syracuse, 1913.

Fleming, Walter L. *The Freedmen's Savings Bank.* Chapel Hill: University of North Carolina Press, 1927.

Haas, William F. *A History of Banking in New Haven.* New Haven: Privately printed, 1946.

Hagerstown Bank. *The Hagerstown Bank at Hagerstown Maryland: Annals of One Hundred Years, 1807–1907.* New York: Knickerbocker Press, 1910.

Haines, Howard W. *The Small Loan Department.* New York: Bankers Publishing Co., 1931.

Harper, William H., and Charles H. Rawell. *Fifty Years of Banking: 1857–1907.* Chicago: Merchants Loan & Trust Company, 1907.

Harris Trust & Savings Bank. *Forty Years of Investment Banking: 1882–1922.* Chicago: Harris Trust & Savings Bank, 1922.

Henschen, Henry S. *A History of the State Bank of Chicago from 1879 to 1904.* Chicago: Lakeside Press, 1905.

Herzog, Peter W. *The Morris Plan of Industrial Banking.* New York: McGraw-Hill, 1928.

Holdsworth, John T. *Financing an Empire: History of Banking in Pennsylvania.* Chicago: S. J. Clarke, 1928.

Home Savings Bank of the City of Albany. *Home Savings Bank of the City of Albany, Its History and Achievements: 1872–1922.* Albany, NY: Home Savings Bank of the City of Albany, 1922.

Hubbard, Timothy W., and Louis E. Davis. *Banking in Mid-America: A History of Missouri's Banks*. Washington, D.C.: Public Affairs Press, 1969.

Hubert, Philip G. *The Merchants National Bank of the City of New York: A History of Its First Century Compiled from Official Records at the Request of the Directors*. New York: Merchants National Bank of the City of New York, 1903.

James, Cyril F. *The Growth of Chicago Banks*. New York: Harper & Brothers, 1938.

James, Marquis, and Bessie R. James. *Biography of a Bank: The Story of Bank of America N.T & S.A.* New York: Harper & Brothers, 1954.

Jenk, W. L. *First National Exchange Bank, Fifty Years of Banking: 1871–1921*. Port Huron, MI: First National Exchange Bank, 1921.

Kerman, Frederick, and Bryant W. Griffin. *New Business for Banks*. New York: Prentice-Hall, 1926.

Kniffen, William H. *The Practical Work of a Bank*. New York: Bankers Publishing Co., 1919.

Knowles, Charles E. *A History of the Bank for Savings in the City of New York: 1829–1929*. New York: Bank for Savings, 1929.

Lanier, Henry C. *A Century of Banking in New York: 1822–1922*. New York: Gilles Press, 1922.

Leach, Josiah G. *The History of the Girard National Bank of Philadelphia*. New York: J. B. Lippincott, 1902.

Lewis, E. St. Elmo. *Financial Advertising*. 1908. Repr. New York: Garland, 1985.

MacGregor, T. D. *Bank Advertising Plans*. New York: Bankers Publishing Co., 1913.

——— *MacGregor's Book of Bank Advertising*. New York: Bankers Publishing Co., 1921.

McSherry, William. *History of the Bank of Gettysburg 1814–1864; The Gettysburg National Bank 1864–1914*. Gettysburg: Gettysburg National Bank, 1914.

Mechanics Trust Company of New Jersey. *The Mechanics Trust Company of New Jersey*. Bayonne, NJ: Mechanics Trust Company of New Jersey, 1911.

Mills, G. E., and D. W. Holdsworth. "The B. C. Mills Prefabricated System: The Emergence of Ready-Made Buildings in Western Canada." In *Canadian Historic Sites*. Occasional Papers in Archaeology and History, No. 14. Ottawa: Indian and Northern Affairs, 1975.

Morehouse, W. R. *Bank Deposit Building*. New York: Bankers Publishing Co., 1918.

———. *Bank Window Advertising*. New York: Bankers Publishing Co., 1919.

Morehouse, W. R., and F. A. Stearns. *Revised Bank Letters*. Los Angeles: Bankers Service Co., 1922.

Morris, Henry C. *The History of The First National Bank of Chicago*. Chicago: R. R. Donnelly & Sons, 1904.

Noel, Thomas J. *Growing Through History with Colorado: The Colorado National Banks, the First 125 Years, 1862–1987.* Denver, CO: Colorado National Banks, 1987.

Orange National Bank. *The 100th Anniversary of the Orange National Bank.* Orange, NJ: Orange National Bank, 1928.

Pease, Zephaniah W. *The Centenary of the Merchants National Bank.* New Bedford, MA: Merchants National Bank, 1925.

Philadelphia National Bank. *The Philadelphia National Bank.* Philadelphia: Philadelphia National Bank, 1903.

Ravell, Charles H. *Sixty Years of Banking.* Battle Creek, MI: Old National Bank, 1910.

Robinson, Louis N., and Rolf Nugent. *Regulation of the Small Loan Business.* New York: Russell Sage Foundation, 1935.

Rockwood, Charles G. *One Hundred Years: A Record of the Work of the Oldest Bank in the State of New Jersey.* Newark, NJ: National Banking Co., 1904.

Ross, Victor. *A History of the Canadian Bank of Commerce.* 2 vols. Toronto: Oxford University Press, 1922.

Rule, W. G. *The Story of the Oldest Bank West of the Mississippi.* St. Louis, MO: Boatmen's National Bank of St. Louis, 1947.

Scott, Charles E. *A Century's Record: 1814–1914.* Bristol, PA: Farmers National Bank of Bucks County, 1914.

Seward, Anne. *The Women's Department.* New York: Bankers Publishing Co., 1924.

Shoyer, William T. *A Century of Saving Dollars: 1855–1955.* Pittsburgh: Dollar Savings Bank, 1955.

Smallwood, James. *An Oklahoma Adventure of Banks and Bankers.* Norman: University of Oklahoma Press, 1979.

Stalson, Owen J. *Marketing Life Insurance: Its History in America.* Cambridge, MA: Harvard University Press, 1942.

State Street Trust Company. *The Log of the State Street Trust Company.* Boston: State Street Trust Company, 1926.

Sussex National Bank of Newton. *First Hundred Years of Sussex National Bank of Newton New Jersey: 1818–1918.* Newton, NJ: Sussex National Bank of Newton, 1918.

The First National Bank of Chicago. *The First National Bank of Chicago.* Chicago: M. A. Donohue & Co., 1913.

Tomlinson, Paul G. *A History of the Trenton Banking Company: 1804–1929.* Princeton: Princeton University Press, 1929.

Trenton Banking Company. *The Trenton Banking Company: A History of the First Century of Its Existence.* Trenton, NJ: Trenton Banking Company, 1907.

Trigge, A. *A History of the Canadian Imperial Bank of Commerce.* 3 vols. Cambridge, MA: Harvard University Press, 1942.

Wallace, Helen B. *A Century of Banking*. Harrisburg, PA: Harrisburg National Bank, 1914.

Wassam, Clarence W. *Salary Loan Business in New York*. New York: Charities Publication Committee, 1908.

Welton, Arthur. *The Making of a Modern Bank*. Chicago: Continental and Commercial Bank of Chicago, 1923.

Index

About the Author

RICHARD N. GERMAIN is an Associate Professor of Marketing at Oklahoma State University. He has research and publishing interests in marketing history and physical distribution management.

ISBN 0-313-29921-8

EAN

9 780313 299216

90000>

HARDCOVER BAR CODE